COOKING AT THE MONASTERY:
Hommous To Tabouleh in the Garden of Allah

Written by George Lewis

Tony—
Happy 90th.
This should let you
know all my little
secrets on cooking.
Good wishes
George

Edited by Karen Lewis Jackson

Cooking At The Monastery:
Hommous To Tabouleh In The Garden of Allah

ISBN: 1442155523

EAN-13: 9781442155527

Dedication

About some ten odd years ago, my good friend Bill Craine said to me, "George, you ought to write a cookbook." I told him he'd imbibed too many Old Fashioneds, but he persisted. "You would only have to write a recipe a week." Well, I took his advice and here we are. After doing the first fifty recipes in two weeks, his advice proved to be true. Too true, for many a week I would labor over a recipe and keep plodding to the tune of a recipe a week. Sometimes I would get two or three. But anyway, that's how this book got to be written.

June Lewis Scheiffer

Bill[1] was instrumental in moving me off my butt to write this book. My sister June also played a key role, providing a lot of the ethnic stories that set the backdrop for the recipes. These stories provide a snapshot of an era we were all a part of, which can never be rekindled, only brought back by tales of a culture, the memory of which will fade with the passing of my generation.

Also, thanks to my colleagues and assorted friends, who insisted I blow the dust off the cover and get the damn book out of my desk drawer, where it has not rested in peace for the last five years. In particular, I can't thank enough Fr. Mike and all of the wonderful staff at the Christ The King Retreat House and Conference Center for their support and friendship during the years I worked there.

Lastly, a special thanks to my niece Karen who faces felony charges for hacking into my computer and getting it to publisher's row. As for the felony – all charges were dropped!

Many of these stories are old family folk lore and are told with the best of remembrances and recollections. As there is no member of that era alive today to dispute or substantiate their authenticity, one has to rely on the word of the writer. And so, with great pleasure, I dedicate this book to Bill Craine and my sister June Lewis Schieffer, two people well worth knowing.
- George Lewis

---

[1] I got to know Bill Craine some 50 years ago or so. Bill was a Dapper Dan. He would come into our restaurant impeccably dressed, wearing a suit or sports coat. He was your classic "man's man", with a good word for everything, an easy going way with people and always a good word of advice. He was more "family" than customer. In fact, Bill taught me to tend bar, literally, from the other side of the mahogany ridge (back then, bars were made of mahogany.) He taught me the proper way to make a drink, something I adhere to and instruct anyone working with me to follow. Bill's technique: put your ice in the glass and pour the booze over the ice. For some reason, that rule holds true for making a better drink, something about the booze marrying well if it's poured over the ice, creating a far smoother drink. Try it. You will agree. He also knew his wines. Back then, this was a knowledge limited to an elitist few, considering that Chianti and Concord Grape were about the only wines any bar/restaurant would carry. Bill was a connoisseur of proper etiquette, another trait I hold firmly to when dealing with the public. Sadly, it is sorely lacking today.

Editor's Note:

In the winter of 2008, I called my uncle and asked for his help with a Middle Eastern dinner I had to prepare. He suggested I come up to Syracuse New York, to the Catholic retreat house where he worked, and we could use the professional kitchen there and prepare most of the food for the dinner. Being no dummy, I took him up on his offer and we had a wonderful day cooking, with him teaching me and a cousin how to make various dishes. That evening, I asked him for written copies of the recipes for the dishes we'd prepared, and he directed me to a file on his computer where all his recipes were stored. There I found this, the legendary cookbook that the family had heard rumors about for years. I think he expected me to grab a few recipes out of the file; instead, I emailed myself the entire file. Perusing it at my leisure at home, I discovered not just the recipes but a wonderful treasury of stories about small town life in the early to mid-twentieth century, in the strongly ethnic community in Upstate New York, featuring some relatives and townspeople I knew well, some I vaguely remembered, and some I'd only heard about. I set about putting the document into a publishable form.

Once Uncle George heard about my intentions and finished cursing me for stealing the file, he and I started collaborating. He sent me a number of pictures he'd collected over the years, and we worked on adding them to the book. I read the recipes over as best I could and asked for clarification and elaboration at times when steps or ingredients were unclear. I've made a number of other changes to clarify what I would call my uncle's 'unorthodox' grammar, but tried very hard to preserve the unique voice he used in writing this book, so that as you read it, you'll feel as I did, like you are in a kitchen with George, up to your elbows in kibbee, and he is relating to you stories of a world long past (while correcting your cooking techniques).
Enjoy!

-Karen Lewis Jackson

Editor and Author at a family wedding

Table Of Contents

Preface:

The reason I decided to write this book is that it is the complete opposite of everything that I stand for. I am the perfect candidate for a forum on "are you a former non-church-goer?" and why? My cooking usually attracts a full table of close family friends who love to criticize everything but the $2.00 bottle of wine they bring to dinner. But they come, and do they eat, and we all enjoy each other's company. Occasionally they get treated to a couple of old century family favorites our Christian forbearers brought with them from "Ya Jubail" -- The Mountains of Lebanon, "yummy-yum". That's where the real criticism comes to light, especially when a rude cousin with a long history of ignorance claims my "Warek Ahr-reesh" (stuffed grape leaves) are not as good as his mother's. For the sake of argument and Aunt Rosie's good reputation I succinctly told him that his mother was peacefully resting up on the hill and these were the best he was going to get. If they didn't meet up to his taste-buds he should not eat them so there would be more for the rest of us. After that tirade the other relatives had nothing but praise, fearing I might banish them from the grape leaves they were dipping into the hommous dip.

In the course of conversation we were discussing the recipes and the nature of the cooking I was doing at my job, which was as the chef/kitchen manager at the Christ The King Retreat House and Conference Center in Syracuse, New York. At first sight, when I started the job, the kitchen and facilities were impressive, and on second sight the pantry and company reminded me of those memorable days in the high school cafeteria and its Chef Boyardee™ Raviolis and Del Monte™ String Beans. I lied to the priest (my first one in a house of God), telling him, "Everything was great." Like "H" it was. There was nothing but canned, packaged, bottled, and frozen. No fresh garlic, onion, parsley, potatoes, or celery. "Ya Allah, Ya Allah," "Oh My God, Oh My God!" What was I to do, boasting, as I did, the dubious distinction of never using a canned vegetable, with a sheer disdain for those that use frozen? But alas, here I was assigned to the kitchen at "The Monastery", or better known to those who drop by the kitchen as "Th' Monastry."

The Monastery - Let me tell you a little about it. It's a magnificent sprawling estate sitting atop a mile-long hill, looking down upon and reigning over some of the city's 'hoitier toitier' neighborhoods. It's a jewel of a-turn-of-the-century mansion with five peaceful acres of hills, gullies and impeccable gardens, adorned by hand-crafted marble statues of just about every saint you can think of. The grounds are overseen by flocks of wild turkeys, squirrels, and macho-looking rose-eating deer, who just love to devour those fragrant petals of

Party at the Retreat House

American Beauties, much to the dismay of Father Michael Carmola. Better known as "Father Mike", he is the good and pious "Hooly Ki-Beer," or in non-Lebanese terms, "Big Priest." He is the head jibben (Big Cheese) who leads the flocks of faithful who come here to be dined with a bit of wine and saturated with peace, love, spiritualism, and of course, prayer! After all, the main ingredient up here is prayer; that's why most of the people come and I guess that is why we call it a retreat. You can roam through our gardens (and think you're in heaven), find solitude in our chapel, reflect in many of our rooms, refresh your soul with a swim, and fill yourself with the good Lord's bounty in our picturesque and comfortable dining room. We put out breakfast, lunch, and/or dinner, serving anywhere from 5 to 100 people daily depending the group. We do a lot of pasta, especially for the younger people, chicken and beef, salads, desserts, and cookies, which are always a favorite. Fish is not a big favorite, nor are potatoes. "Hooly Ki-Beer" isn't fond of them and we sneak them in on occasions when we have to balance out the menu. He would have had a hell of a time getting fed by Christ that day in Galilee with the loaves and fishes. Imagine asking for something like lasagna.

Hopefully most of these recipes, thoughts and collections will serve to help those of you in the kitchen who like to dab around but don't want to spend the entire day putting dinner together. It will also help you to turn frozen, boxed, prepared or canned foodstuffs into something edible when such a need occurs. And for all you millions of institutional cooks here are a few new ideas on an old twist of the can opener.

Why the canned-frozen-prepared and packaged? The pantry and freezers were filled with these, and both not wanting to be wasteful and knowing how to cook, it was simple enough to take food from its lowest form and bring it to its highest elegance. Furthermore, I'm totally convinced that only one out of every two hundred people is discerning enough to really be able to tell whether or not the dishes are made from scratch. I would garner to say if you were afraid or intimidated by these gastronomic unknowns, don't be, for it is laid out here for you in simple enough lessons to enable any of you to cook if you're not afraid to try.

Author tending bar at a party at the Retreat House

Basics for your Pantry

A couple of things you are going to need in order to make your cooking life easier: garlic, olive oil, your choice of vinegar, green onions (scallions), oregano, basil, parsley, mint and sage. Fresh lemons, mushrooms and tomatoes are good to have on hand too. Add carrots, celery and peppers, and you have the basics to go along with the recipes in this book. Dried herbs can be used, which I prefer in some of the recipes, but otherwise fresh is best. When I was a kid I would go with my mother to the riverbanks and fields and pick bundles of fresh spearmint and take them home to dry for the winter. We would pick the leaves from the stems, lay them out on newspaper and let them dry for 2 weeks, put them in air-tight gallon glass jars and store them on a kitchen shelf.

I still follow this practice and back in the late 70's I had five generations of family for an Easter brunch. Being an early spring we had fresh mint growing profusely. I picked the mint and was drying it the way we always did, and amidst the party I overheard a teen-aged nephew whisper to his teen-aged cousin "don't believe a thing they tell you, it's really marijuana."

I dry other herbs in the same fashion: basil, oregano, thyme, sage, etc. Sometimes I make bundles and hang them upside down to dry and rub the leaves together when I need them. That can get messy, especially if you have had dried flower arrangement experiences. But it saves you the time of picking the leaves from the stems.

Garlic Paste

A staple of my cooking and kitchen is garlic paste. I will refer back to this many times, so I'm including the recipe for it here. Try it and use it often!

4 or 5 garlic cloves, peeled and sliced thin
1 to 2 teaspoons salt

Take garlic and put into a bowl (wood preferred)
Sprinkle 1/3 of salt on top of garlic
With a flat surfaced wooden handle, start pounding garlic and mash it to a paste.
You will have to continue to sprinkle on the salt atop the garlic and pound until paste takes a dry form, like brown sugar. Don't be afraid to pound it, for it has to lose its wetness and become dry. If it remains sticky, add more salt and keep pounding and mixing together.

The whole process should take 3 to 4 minutes.

Cover mixture tightly when not using or it will dry out and be extremely difficult to use.

Roast Loin Of Pork

Tonight we are going to do a roast loin of pork. The weather outside is sunny, and the temperatures are going to drop to about 15 degrees so we'll turn it into comfort food with church supper flair. Cranberry chutney in orange cups, mushrooms reduced to fine wine gravy, using the remains of last night's Merlot. Roasted potatoes and Harvard Beets. "Heysoos-a-christi," Father isn't going to like that. In the old days, before the monastery had television, that could get you a couple dozen Hail Mary's at the chapel. Employee or not! The beets add a certain kind of sweetness and when you give them that Harvard touch it gives you a tart/sweet vinegar/sugar taste. It works perfectly. Another nice addition would be apples in a green salad and corn relish, if we get time. For dessert, chocolate pudding with sliced bananas and whipped cream. Sound good?

To begin we have to roast the loin of pork. I use a 10 lb. loin that will feed 20 people. For 2 to 6 people or so a 3 to 5 lb. roast will do. Rinse roast in cold water and pat dry. Set on a roasting pan and rub with rosemary, sage, parsley, thyme, garlic and onion powder, black pepper and Worcestershire sauce. Bake at 350° for 1 1/2 hours or until your thermometer reaches desired doneness for your taste. My experience has been 1 1/4 to 1 1/2 hours and it should be fine.

Remove the roast from the pan, set on your carving board, and save the pan juices. Let it sit at least 10 minutes before carving.

Before starting the gravy, make a roux to thicken the sauce. Start with 2 tablespoons cornstarch, and mix with ½ cup water. Whisk together until there are no lumps and it is the consistency of a light cream soup, adding more water if necessary.

Now for the gravy. First, I am going to add 2 lbs fresh sliced mushrooms to 2 tablespoons hot, melted butter and a tablespoon of oil. Add the seasonings (a handful of garlic powder, thyme, rosemary, and 1/2 cup chopped green onion plus 1/2 tsp each of salt and pepper. Seasons are optional because you have flavoring from the roast and its pan juices). Sauté over low heat for 3 minutes (you want it to come to a soft boil), then add a ½ cup white wine or dry sherry, along with pan juices, and cook 5 minutes longer. Slowly whisk in the roux and continue to soft boil another 5 minutes.
Slice the roast diagonally in 1/4"slices. Arrange slices on a serving tray and ladle merlot-mushroom sauce over it. Serve remaining sauce in a gravy boat. Put orange cranberry cups on or beside the serving tray and you are ready to begin.

Cranberry Sauce

Take a 1lb. package of fresh cranberries and wash in cold water and drain. Pick out any impurities. Add cranberries, 1/2 cup of water to a saucepan and bring it to a boil (cranberries will start to pop open). Lower heat, add 1 1/2 cups sugar, juice of a fresh orange, 1 cinnamon stick and a jigger of gin (1/8 cup) and cook with a slow boil for 1/2 hour, stirring occasionally. The cranberry sauce will thicken like a jelly. Serve at room temperature or chilled. More sugar can be added for extra sweetness. Cranberries are a fall product and can be frozen as is for up to a year. I usually buy a few bags of them and keep them in the freezer for use when I want them.

Harvard Beets

I don't know where the name came from but I am assuming it originated somewhere in England where the name Harvard came from. Otherwise I would think some dormitory cook came up with the idea at the famed Boston University, trying to get the students to eat beets, which were a great New England staple. Harvard

Beets consist of beets, sugar, vinegar, the zest of an orange, a tad of salt and a thickening agent of flour or cornstarch. I prefer flour.

Take a can of beets (or a package of frozen), add to a saucepan with half the juice and bring to a boil. Add 2 to 3 tablespoons of sugar and the same amount of white vinegar. Add orange zest, salt and a flour thickener.* Bring back to a boil and simmer for another 10 minutes and serve.

*To make flour thickener just take a teaspoon of flour and add a teaspoon of water and whisk together until smooth. Add to mixture and stir quickly to prevent lumping.

Chocolate Pudding and Bananas

This recipe is absolutely foolproof, easy and fun. Everyone always asks for the recipe and I am chagrinned to tell him or her (if I do tell at all) that it's a package of instant pudding, but that's what it is. Light, fluffy, and delightful.

Take a package of instant chocolate pudding and mix it according to directions. Once you have done this add 2 cups Cool Whip and blend in. Add 4 to 5 scoops of vanilla ice cream and mix until well blended. Add 2 tablespoons of brandy and blend. Scrape sides of bowl and mix until fluffy (3 to 4 min). Cut 2 bananas into 1/4" slices. Add to pudding and stir thoroughly. Garnish with strawberries or cherries and chill until ready to serve.

To ensure success with this it is essential that you do this in steps to achieve the right amount of fluffiness, which gives it a lightness in taste and texture. I have seen this recipe bastardized by people who have thrown it all together at once. That's a mistake. Take the time with it and blend each item separately and you will get results. Throw it all together at once and I will say "I told you so" and not eat it!

You may also use any other flavor and add to ramekins, baked pie shells and pastry cups. When we have groups of younger people I like putting it in clear plastic cocktail glasses, filling them to about an inch from the top, adding a dollop of whipped cream** and topping with a maraschino cherry. Set it on a nice tray with doilies and you have a hit on your hands.

**I like using Rich's Whipped Cream, which can be found in the frozen dairy section and comes in a plastic style pastry bag with a pastry tip on the end of it to give you a decorative design. The other nice thing about it is that it holds its shape for hours in or out of the refrigerator whereas regular whipped cream will melt and run after a few minutes. 'Course it doesn't taste as good as the real thing, but only you and a fancy chef would know.

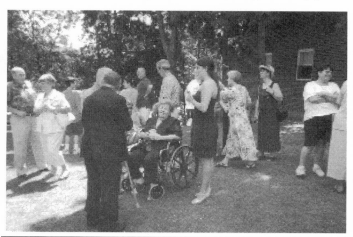

Birthday party for June
Lewis Scheiffer at the
Retreat House

No Salt - Lousy Flavor!

This week has been an experience, with a couple of vegetarians staying with us. They are on a restricted non-salt, low fat diet, and after a couple of days of rice, pasta, and plain vegetables I made a vegetable stew, which came out rather nicely. I would have preferred a teaspoon of salt to bring out more of the vegetable flavors, but our guests said they were fine. So be it. Three of the guests had seconds. If you have or want to eat low fat and no salt I think this mid-February stew is for you.

I started out by sautéing a coarsely chopped Spanish onion, then adding celery, carrots and sweet red pepper. After a few minutes cooking I added garlic, white wine and water. Then came dried Italian herbs and black pepper. After cooking the mixture for about 15 minutes I took a taste and it was terribly bland. With the addition of cumin, cinnamon, and allspice and some quartered potatoes it started to come to life. Some mushrooms cut in half and a handful of chopped parsley added more oomph! I simmered for another hour and thickened it with a little cornstarch diluted with water. An hour later I ladled the stew into bowls and served the guests. As they broke apart chunks of crusty bread and dipped it into the stew I knew I had a hit on my hands. Good as it was, it still needed salt...

February Stew

1 large Spanish onion, coarsely chopped
4 large carrots, peeled and sliced into 1 inch rounds
4 stalks celery cut into 1 1/2 chunks
1 sweet red bell pepper cut into 1" slices
10-12 mushrooms cut in half
2 cloves garlic sliced thin
3 tablespoons of dried Italian seasonings
1 tablespoons dried thyme
1 handful fresh chopped parsley
Black pepper to taste
1 cup white wine
2 - 3 cups water cups water
1 1/2 tablespoons cornstarch blended with 1/4 cup cold water

Method:

Sauté onion in olive oil 3 minutes, add celery, carrots, peppers, herbs, pepper and sauté. Cook for 15 minutes, stirring occasionally. Then add white wine and cook 5 minutes. Add potatoes, tomatoes, mushrooms, parsley, and herbs and cook for another hour, stirring occasionally. Thicken with diluted cornstarch and simmer another 10 minutes and serve. It's better the next day.

If you use salt add about 1 tablespoon when you add the pepper.

Meatless Friday

Another meatless dish I decided to make one evening happens to be a peasant dish that was a family favorite for generations and served in most Lebanese households every Friday. This was because everyone was Maronite Catholics and back then Catholics didn't eat meat on that day. Also, most of our people were poor, meat being a luxury used sparingly when cooking. But no matter how poor you were you could always find an onion, some rice and a handful of lentils and thus came Madjudrah, a staple dish that could feed and nourish your family. Today in "trendy" Mediterranean restaurants you might pay obnoxiously high prices for a dish not nearly as good as my Sitto's (grandmother). If Sitto only knew.

Madjudrah (lentils and rice)

1 large onion chopped and finely diced
2 cups long grain rice
1 cup lentils
1/4 cup olive oil
1/2 teaspoon salt
5 cups of hot water

Method:

In a large saucepan add olive oil and onion over medium-low heat and cook until the onion turns dark brown, almost black. Usually about 5 - 7 minutes. Stir occasionally during this time. (If your onions start to burn lower your flame a tad)
Add lentils, stir them around for about a minute
Add water and salt and continue to cook for about 20 minutes or until lentils are tender (al dente)
Add rice, stir around and put the lid on the pan. Bring your flame to low and cook slowly for another 25 to 30 minutes. The rice will be a little moist. Don't worry about it, it's supposed to be. Let the pan sit with the lid on for 5 minutes, stir lightly and serve.

Now that the restaurant public is discovering old-country food, and paying upwards of 25 to 30 dollars per plate, my grandmother must surely be rolling around in her grave. Being wise and keen, she could make a meal on a few pennies. Sitto would not tell you that she would top it with a couple dollops of homemade yogurt, fresh Till-ah-mee (pita) and make Salatto, a salad of watercress, mint, tomato, cucumbers and chopped green onion, tossed together with olive oil, lemon juice and salt.

And there you have a classic peasant meal. No, Sitto wouldn't tell you about the extras, (which compliment the dish nicely). After all the price of lentils and watercress* might go up. And she couldn't cope with that!

*Back then, watercress and mint grew wild in and around the brooks and streams and were safe to consume. My dad would pick it in late spring when he fished for trout and suckers. The cress would grow along the banks and then crawl along the edge of the water. Different varieties of mint also grew along the banks, but my mother and her people preferred spearmint because it had a fresher taste and was a nice contrast to the horseradishy taste of the cress. I really like fresh peppermint, which has a really nice bite to it and clears the body and sinuses. Really refreshing.

Suburban Snob

The fine looking lady should have said "No thank-you", and I wouldn't be telling you about going into a minor rage. But the lady looked, upped her nose, and piously said, "I don't do eggplant." I said, "Ya Oppy Shoom" - Shame on you. A chance to eat some of the same food Christ ate, and while her mind was hungering for spiritual fulfillment she could have sophisticated her palate, experiencing food that was prepared similarly to what was eaten in the bible times. That would have given her religion. Tsh-Tsh!! What the good woman missed was this:

Butt-en-jaan Zay-Toom, Eggplant with Garlic

5 or 6 baby firm eggplants **
Slice eggplants at an angle into 1/8 to 1/4 inch slices
Sprinkle salt over slices and let set 20 minutes (if watery, drain)
Mix 1 tablespoon garlic paste with 1/4 cup olive oil and toss thoroughly with eggplant slices.

Brush a large cookie tray with oil
Lay eggplant slices side by side in rows. (don't over-lap)
Sprinkle with paprika and dried grated goat cheese and black pepper.***
Bake in pre-heated 350° oven for 10 to 15 minutes, or until the ends of the eggplant start to wilt.
Remove from oven and re-arrange on heat treated platter, making overlapping slices all around the plate.
Keep warm in low heat oven until ready to serve. Give them another sprinkling of grated cheese before the plate gets to the table.

**I like firm, dark purple eggplants about the size of a croissant. If they are firm they won't get watery when you mix them with the oil and garlic.
***You can make your own grated goat cheese just by leaving it unrefrigerated for a day or two covered with a cloth towel.

Zucchini and yellow squash work well done this way too. Just substitute squash for eggplant and prepare the same way. A much better squash is a Lebanese variety called "Koo-Saa." A light green squash that has a sweeter taste. It can be found at the farmers market in the summer. It may also be spelled "Coosa."

Author working in the Retreat House kitchen

20

Chicken George

I have cooked this chicken dish a thousand times or more. I am bored silly with it, but each time I do it, it gets rave reviews. It's a great party favorite and holds up very well in any buffet line it has ever been in. Recently after catering a good friend's daughter's wedding, her father, who had eaten the same chicken at my house for the last 20 years, asked me what kind of chicken it was because it was the best he had ever had. Astounded I said "Chicken George." For some reason it gets better each time I do it. I have altered it, doctored it, tried to give it a new twist and it still comes out good. It's a twist off the Italian recipe Veal Picatta that I found some 40 years ago in "The cooking of Italy," by Waverly Root, who by the way apparently committed suicide over the publication of the series because he came under heavy criticism that the recipes were not accurate. He probably should have added more salt. Poor soul.

Recipe:
Take 6 boneless chicken breasts and trim any excess skin. Rinse under cold water, drain. Coat each side in plain bread crumbs and set aside.
Melt 1/4 cup olive oil and 1/4 stick butter, bring to a medium boil**, and then add chicken. Cook each side 3 to 4 minutes. They will start to turn a crusty brown. Remove and set on a warm plate. Return pan to a medium flame and add 2 tablespoon butter and 1 lb. mushrooms, sliced 1/4" thick. Bring to a boil and add 1 cup dry white wine and continue to cook 2 to 3 min longer. After, add cornstarch/water mixture ***and cook slowly for another 3 to 4 minutes and then add chicken to pan and stir thoroughly until chicken is totally covered. Transfer to serving dish and keep warm until ready to serve. Great party dish.

** When melting butter and oil together I bring them to a boil over medium heat and continue to cook for another 30 seconds so that the butter is bubbling all over. Then I am sure that for whatever I am cooking the pan is ready.

*** Take 1 tablespoon cornstarch and 3 tablespoons cold water and whisk/stir thoroughly. Add to sauce to thicken. Make sure your mixture is boiling or the cornstarch will not thicken for you.

Cavatelli With Broccoli

One spring afternoon "Katie", one of our sanitation engineers, came down to the kitchen and wanted to know what I was cooking and I told her mockroomtoom - homemade macaroni and garlic. Katie became ecstatic and said "that's what I want for my son's graduation party". "Wull-la, Katie" (well?) That's an awful lot of flour and water, especially for 150 people. The old Lebanese people would take 5 lbs. of flour and mix it very slowly with cold water until it started to form into a dough that would stick to your hands. Then they would dip their hands into the flour, cut off a piece of dough and roll it into foot long ropes, cut the dough into 2" pieces, and roll it over an overturned basket to shape its design. Next, they would drop it into boiling water and cook for 1/2 hour, drain and toss with garlic and olive oil, and serve it in the wooden bowl they pounded the garlic in. You would smell for days. One garlic clove is aromatic but try about 30. And back then from about 1920 to the 1960's we were the only people in our town that ate garlic. No wonder people thought our race was strange...

But was it good. I can remember back in the late 40's going to the river on Sunday's in the early summer when the men fished and the women would build a fire and cook the mockroomtoom there. They would cut off green willow branches, sharpen the edges, and we would use them as forks. What a treat it was. Now in the 2000's this dish is just a memory to the countless Lebanese who left their mothers' tables in pursuit of the American way, and will tell you that cavatelli is a good substitution in their commercialization of this dish.

With the addition of some broccoli and sliced black olives, our dear "Katie" has a nice dish to go with her Kielbasa and rolled cabbages...

Take one bunch of fresh broccoli and cut into 1" flowerets. Drop in boiling salted water and cook about 2 min. Drain and run under cold water until cold. Pound 3 cloves of garlic to a paste. Drizzle in 1/4 olive and whisk thoroughly. In 6 quarts of boiling salted water add 3 lbs frozen cavatelli and cook about 8 minutes, stirring often to avoid sticking. When the cavatelli starts to float to the top you know they are done. Drain cavatelli and add to garlic. Add broccoli, 1/3 cup sliced black olives, and 1 cup fine chopped scallions. Stir together, coating thoroughly. Give it a little sprinkling of salt and squeeze the juice of 1 lemon over it. Stir again and serve. This can be served at room temperature.

Remember to stir before serving. Black pepper to taste can be added for extra zing.

Cooking Chicken George!

Sister - Sister

"The sisters are coming, the sisters are coming." The engineers of sanitation are cleaning the house. Up, down and in every direction. Lawns are mowed and walks are swept. Maintenance technicians are tenaciously sprucing up and bringing the building and grounds up to code. Even Father Ireland comes down from his penthouse suite and makes his presence known. We can't get him to vacuum the pool or put out chairs on the deck in proper proportion but that's excusable since he himself is the one in charge of things when the Father Director goes away. Hooly Ki-Beer is very excited since all the flowers in the gardens are in full bloom, showing off his years of toil for tilling the soil. I'm excited!

The sisters - 2000

The sisters - 2001

Sisters like light lunches and well prepared dinners. In fact, having the sisters for a few days is wonderful and fulfilling. Years ago, before the "liberalisms", convents were strict and food was more of a necessity than a luxury; hence anything that was put on the table you ate, some of it good and some of it grueling. Consequently anything we prepare here for them always gets a welcoming response. We're overwhelmed! Alls we did was to take food from its lowest form and bring it to its highest elegance. I guess it's the work of God?

The lunch for today is cold - Crab Salad. Simple and easy and sinfully light. And on a hot day in July, a heavenly delight.

Crab Salad

Take a 2 ½ lb package of imitation Crab Meat, chop it up very fine and put it in a large mixing bowl.

To this add:
1 cup of finely chopped green onion
1 tablespoon each of vinegar, mustard and Worcestershire Sauce
3 tablespoons sweet relish
4 to 5 tablespoons mayonnaise
1 clove garlic mashed to a paste
1 cup finely chopped parsley
1 teaspoon fresh or dried thyme
Salt and pepper to taste and 1 teaspoon sugar (optional)

Mix thoroughly and refrigerate until ready to serve.

When I do this for a party I usually mound it to look like a fish, outline it with shredded carrots and surround it with either pita or garlic bread chips to spread the crab on. It also makes a nice filler for mushroom caps. Cucumbers sliced in 1/4" rounds cut at an angle provide another edible garnish.

Silence is Golden

A new group of sisters have arrived for a week. The difference between this group and the others is that this group is on "silent retreat" – they don't talk. Nor do I when the situation presents itself. They observe the grace of silence and so does the staff and everyone else. The problem with that is you don't know whether they're enjoying their food as they sit there and eat in silence. A couple of them do talk a little bit - in hushed tones and whispers with an occasional nod, hello or thank you. The only salvation one can surmise is if the food is not good, you're not going to hear about it...

I must say though that I was talking to another group of sisters that were leaving and told them about this group coming in. One of them looked at me and knowing how I liked to talk said "good luck next week George, I'll pray for you." Immediately I retorted with "thank-you sister, but not just a prayer – how about a novena?"

After a few days of this one of the sisters came into the kitchen and wanted to know what I did to the corn. Not wanting to fib to the good sister, I said, "I cheated." Inquiring minds wanted to know, so I proceeded to tell her how I took the leftover corn from last night's dinner, diced up an onion, and added some vinegar, oil and sugar and corn relish. That isn't the way to make it except when you're in a hurry and need something in a pinch (they weren't going to complain).

Recipe: to the leftover corn I added:
1 small onion diced up
2 tablespoons of olive oil
a dash of salt and pepper

I mixed this thoroughly.

Then I took a cup of red wine vinegar and a ½ cup of sugar, added it to a pan and brought it to a boil on the stove. Next I added it to the corn, mixed it together again and refrigerated it until ready to serve. Simple and easy and I had used frozen corn. Normally I would dice up an onion and sauté it with a diced up red pepper, add some fresh corn, cinnamon and allspice and sugar and cook it down. I prefer the version I did for the sisters. Easier and again the same results. Either way is good – it just matters how much time you have on your hands.

Incidentally I served more sweet corn this year than I ever have and for some reason everyone ranted on how good the corn was. I think I may have learned a new secret to cooking it and that is instead of plunging the ears into boiling water I added the corn just before the water came to a boil and when the water started to boil I turned the water off and let the corn sit in the water for 15 minutes. It comes out very nicely this way and has a very nice crunch to it. Try it - our guests were satisfied. (Prior to that I would bring the water to a boil and drop the corn in and simmer for 3 minutes. It comes out okay that way too, but I think I prefer the other way)

Another sister story:

One hot August morning and the temperature was around 90 degrees. I was cooking breakfast for the sisters when one of them came in and said, "Ah, but George 'tis way too hot for you to be cooking today." Nodding my head and agreeing with her I retorted, "Ah, but sister, I agree but 'tis one of the prices one has to pay for sleeping in every Sunday for the last forty years."

Zucchini - Zucchini

It is the month of August and time again for our annual family picnic. We have a mass on the lawns and then feast away at hamburgers, hot dogs, salads and chicken. This year I decided to spice it up a little, economize (the diocese would love that) and use the bounties that nature has provided us with. Enter zucchini! Everyone I know is bored with it and I cannot even get a laugh anymore with a joke about it. Even possessing a prized and secret recipe for the green monster doesn't carry any merit like it did ten or fifteen years ago when it was all the rage, with social acceptance depending on one's knowledge of the squashy thing. Not being socially adept I still serve the silly critter and everyone around still goes gushy and continually asks: 'what did you do to the zucchini?'

Recipe: Take 4 to 5 zucchinis and slice them at a slight angle into 1/8 to 1/4 inch slices and put them into a bowl. Add about 2 teaspoons of garlic paste mixed with about 3/4 cup of olive oil, heavy salt and pepper to taste, pour over zucchini slices and mix thoroughly, marinating overnight in the refrigerator. Pre-heat oven to 350° and add 2 cups of your favorite tomato sauce and toss thoroughly together. Put the mixture in a baking dish, cover with foil and bake for an hour to an hour and a half or until the zucchini is tender. Serve at once or at room temperature. Believe me your guests will be wowed and you will be acceptable socially once more.

Another unique way of preparing them is to go through the same procedure of slicing them and marinating them in garlic and olive oil overnight and then take the zucchini slices and grill them. I use a wood fire outdoors but you can do this on your grill. Just get your fire where you want it and lay the zucchini slices on it and cook them about 1 1/2 minutes on each side. Then remove them to a plate and sprinkle with grated cheese, salt and pepper. Be careful not to burn them. You just want them to start to char but not be completely black. Plus, zucchini will continue to cook after they are removed from the grill so it is good to take them of in the al dente stage. (when they are a light brown). Otherwise they will get mushy if cooked too long.

One other way, especially in the midst of winter when your outdoor grill is covered by a foot of snow, is to bake them in the oven or put them under the broiler. Just lay the zucchini slices on a lightly oiled baking tray and sprinkle them with paprika, salt, pepper, and grated cheese, and bake until they start to brown. Remove from pan and arrange on a serving platter and serve. I find that these are equally good served lukewarm and even cold.

Blueberry Buckle

Another August favorite is blueberries. Not the usual commercial type you find in the supermarkets that are mass produced in New Jersey but the real fine and sweet berries that are home grown in Upstate New York and available at local farmers markets and roadside stands. I have a humongous bush in my back yard that usually yields me 4 or 5 quarts and another 25 or 30 quarts for all the birds that converge upon it. Never have I tasted such freshness and nor have the birds. I probably could pick more but it's fun to watch them work away and it's easier for me to buy them at $2.50 a quart and keep the birds fed and the local economy rolling.

Anyhow, I made a blueberry cobbler and the first reaction from one of the guests was "Blueberry Buckle." Inquisitive, I looked into a turn of the century cookbook and found a recipe for it. Apparently it got its name from the fact that when you baked it the blueberries would flow over the pastry dough and bubble over the pan and spill onto the stove, creating havoc as it would harden like lava and become an unsightly mess to clean - consequently BB Buckle.

2 to 3 quarts blueberries
1 1/2 cups sugar
1 teaspoon cornstarch
1/8 teaspoon salt
Juice of 1/2 lemon
1/4 teaspoon each of cinnamon and allspice
1 box of biscuit mix (48 ozs)
2 teaspoon sugar to sprinkle on uncooked buckle

To begin with you will need a 9 x 12 pan to bake the cobbler in. Then you will need 2 to 3 quarts of blueberries mixed with 1 1/2 cups of sugar. To this add 1 teaspoon cornstarch, 1/8 teaspoon. salt and the juice of 1/2 lemon. Mix thoroughly and line the bottom of the baking dish with it. Give it a sprinkling of cinnamon and allspice.   Mix up a standard box of biscuit mix (48 ozs.) or use your favorite biscuit mix. Drop by spoonfuls onto the blueberry mix until all is covered or roll out your biscuit dough and lay on top of the blueberries.   Lightly sprinkle top of dough with sugar and bake in a 350° oven for about 45 minutes or until the top starts to brown and the blueberry mix starts to bubble over and "buckle."

Stuffed Eggplant Rolls

One recent Friday evening I needed a meatless dish for a group that still observed the 'no eating meat on Friday'.   Seafood became my first thought until I received a memo that a few people were allergic to fish and that squelched that idea. Pasta would have solved the problem except that I was serving it to this group and two others the next day. Eggplant was foremost on my mind but I knew if some people realized it was that purple stuff they would immediately take a dislike. On the other hand every time I served moussaka and people didn't know what they were eating they loved it. Had they known – well, that could be another story. But I served this a while back, and one of the guests asked what did I serve and when I told her eggplant, she replied that had she known she would never had eaten it willingly and was heard to say "I can't believe I just ate eggplant and enjoyed it."

You will need:

2 Eggplants sliced lengthwise 1/4" thick. Lightly salt the slices on each side and let sit for 1/2 hour (salting the eggplant will take the bitterness out of it)
2 cups plain bread crumbs
3 cups each of ricotta and mozzarella cheese
1 cup grated parmesan cheese
1 cup shredded cheddar cheese
3 eggs
1/2 cup fresh chopped parsley
2 cups tomato or marinara sauce
Salt and pepper to taste

Bread the eggplant on both sides and lay out on a cookie sheet and bake for about 5 minutes in a 350° oven. Remove from oven and let slices cool.

Mix together the ricotta, mozzarella, parmesan, parsley, eggs, salt and pepper thoroughly.
Working lengthwise, take 2 tablespoons of your cheese mixture and spread evenly on one end and roll up. Repeat the process until all the slices are rolled.

Lightly oil the bottom of a baking dish and lay your rolled eggplant next to each other in a row seam side up.

Cover with foil and bake at 350° for 45 minutes.
Remove from over and ladle tomato sauce over the eggplant.
Sprinkle cheddar cheese over the eggplant and serve.
The cheddar cheese will melt lightly enough to offer a nice presentation and taste.

Your friends will rave and who knows? You may have made a convert out of a non-believer – of eggplant, that is!

The Boss is Coming

Being a conscientious chef, it is always good to do ones research to make sure all the guests will be happy to eat what you serve them. Working for a highly political organization as I do, I did mine. One of the "hierarchy" who has the power over others who sign my paycheck is very fond of onions. Strangely enough a hellacious number of other people are acutely in favor of these bulbous aromatic edibles too. As a result, after a bit of experimenting I was able to infuse the entire house with the odor of onions, which have a sweet smell as they cook and keep everyone guessing as to what you are cooking. And that was encouraging enough to know the recipe was going to be successful.

Boss's Onions

6 to 8 Vidalia or Spanish onions
1/4 cup of olive oil
3 tablespoons butter
Salt and pepper to taste

Take onions, peel them and slice them into 1/4" rings.
In a large frying pan sauté olive oil and butter and bring to a light boil.
Add onion slices, salt and pepper and sauté 5 to 10 minutes, stirring occasionally.
Onions will become soft and limp and that's the desired doneness you will want.
You can cook them longer if you desire but they will start to caramelize and brown.
Once they are done set aside and serve when desired. They will hold 3 or 4 days in the refrigerator.

Pickled Onions

Repeat the same process as the above. As you start to sauté add 1 cup of sugar and 1 cup of red wine vinegar, stirring as you go. Sauté about 5 minutes longer than the above recipe. These work very nicely as an addition to red meats and seem to taste better at room temperature.

Caramelized Onions

Take same amount of onions as in the above and peel and slice.
In a large frying pan take 1 1/2 cups of sugar and melt over low heat.
Sugar will caramelize (turn brown)
Add onions and continue to sauté until limp, about 10 to 15 minutes. Again serve hot or lukewarm.

Judge Ye Booze – Um

Back in the late 1920's my mom and dad came to Sherburne, a little village about 30 miles south of Utica, N. Y. The big draw was Utica Knit, a knitting mill that drew many unskilled immigrants to its doors. My grandparents on my mother's side, Sitto and Jiddo, were already living there and urged my parents to come to the mill and work, with plenty of opportunity. My mom was dead set against it. They were living in Utica with all the modern conveniences – indoor plumbing, running water, electricity and street cars. When they visited Sherburne my mom hated it. None of those modern conveniences existed. No electric – God forbid. I remember her saying that when she wanted to go to the bathroom they literally had to go out back to the outhouse. And if it was winter it was cold. At night they had to take a lantern to see what they were doing. I guess the men didn't have it too bad – but the women? Anyhow, one night my dad came home and told my mother that he had quit his job and had been hired at the mill in Sherburne. My mom was mortified. Her biggest fears were realized and she started to cry. Back to the dark ages and such. Finally my dad calmed her down and told her it wasn't going to be that bad for the mill had built these new houses with indoor toilets and electricity and they were going to live in one of them. She wouldn't have Woolworth's Five and Dime but at least the toilet would flush. (Incidentally, that's where they met - at the Woolworth's lunch counter. They would secretly continue to meet there until they eloped because my grandfather didn't like my father).

Wedding picture of George Lewis and Mary Meelan Lewis, circa 1925

Thus was the start of many years of the Lewis's family involvement into the food and alcohol business. Actually, we got started in the booze business first during the prohibition with my dad putting out some of the finest bootleg whiskey in the county. The way I understand it, one day he came home sick from the mill and went to the doctor, who sent him to a specialist. My dad was diagnosed with an enlarged heart and could not work any more. He was devastated. Having a big family he had to support them someway, and with no disability available he turned to the illegal art of distilling alcohol. I guess moonshining then was a means to an end. Because the whiskey he made was of good quality, his clientele were local people of the higher standing.

A story in particular I would like to share involved a prominent local farmer who was an alcoholic and whose son was a county magistrate. One day the local judge came to the house to get whiskey for his father who was badly in need of a drink and banged on the door. With the curtains drawn and the window shades down (as was always the case) no one would answer the door. The judge kept banging on the door and finally my father opened it. He said he wanted some whiskey and my dad said he didn't know what he was talking about because he wasn't in the business. The judge told him he and everyone else knew he was selling hooch and he had to have it for his father and he wasn't going to prosecute. Reluctantly my dad sold him the whiskey and about a week later the head of state police paid my dad a visit and told him there was going to be a raid that night and to hide the booze. My sister recalls they took the moonshine and hid it in the garden under the tomato plants. In fact she was so scared that she ran down the street to my aunt's house and hid under the bed in their bedroom. Ironically all the other bootleggers in town got busted that night. Perhaps they should have had better booze.

If you didn't have money they would trade butter, sugar, meat, eggs etc., for the booze, which gave them a means to survive in the depression.

The reason I wanted to share a little of this history is the fact that a number of the recipes in this book got their foundation as my mom and dad progressed in their livelihood. One day before I was born my family was having dinner and my brother wanted another slice of bread. Well, there wasn't anymore and they couldn't afford another loaf that day. My dad left the house and went over to his mother's house and started to cry. My grandmother asked him what was the matter and he told her he couldn't afford to feed his family. My grandmother, being a strong woman, told him to go and rent the gas station down the street. It had an apartment above it and they could live there. The rent was $18.00 a month and my grandmother pulled up her long skirt and dug down into her stocking (that was the bank in those days), pulled out some bills and gave my dad the money to start his business. To my knowledge that's how it all started.

They sold Esso Gas and the station had a little room that had five tables and a kitchen behind it. One day my dad was sitting at the table eating a dish of rigatoni with lamb meat. A man came in and asked him if he would sell him some. My dad said no but would share with him what he had. The next day the man came in with his wife and kids and asked if he could buy some of that "eye-talian" food. Thus, the birth of the family restaurant, Lewis' Restaurant, in Sherburne, NY (still in operation and run by my youngest brother Rich).

Lewis' Restaurant, Sherburne, NY, circa 1942

At this time, World War II had started and the knitting mill was working 3 shifts. The workers would get done with their shifts and sit on the steps of the grocery store down the street and drink beer. My mother begged my father to get a beer license and he refused. He had managed to put a hundred dollars in the bank and didn't want to part with it. My mother won out and every night became "Saturday Night" at the gas station. They would sell spaghetti and fried chicken in the basket with home-made French fries (ungodly and unheard of today) that were fried in olive oil (which was cheap then and only used by immigrants) along with the chicken for about 35 cents with a salad and bread included. Beer was 10 cents a bottle.

During that time President Roosevelt had established the CC camps (Core of Conservation Camps) and many young Jamaican and Bahamian men worked there. For $1.00 each way my dad would go to these camps, fill his '31 Chrysler with them, and bring them back to the gas station where they could cavort, drink beer and carry on. It became quite profitable, let alone entrepreneurial. These men were not too fond of spaghetti and one night they brought some pork chops with them and asked my mother to cook them. They told her that in Jamaica they would cook them with tomatoes, onions, carrots and potatoes. The only way my mother ever cooked pork chops was to fry them, but she recalled a stew her grandmother had made in Lebanon using lamb and similar vegetables.

Not wanting to offend her customers, she created a dish which came to be known as "Sun-Nee-Yah" (Arabic for any dish baked in an oven), which soon became and still is a family favorite. Back then pork was a cheap cut of meat and many of the poorer families took advantage of it.

Sun-Nee-Yah (Baked Pork Chops)

6 to 8 medium sized pork chops
2 16 oz. cans of tomato sauce or puree
4 large onions, quartered
6 to 8 carrots, peeled and cut in 2'' pieces
6 to 8 potatoes, quartered
3 stalks of celery cut in 1" pieces
2 cups water
1 teaspoon each of salt and pepper

Heat oven to 350°
Take pork chops and brown on each side for about 5 minutes
Remove chops and put in a large Dutch oven or baking pan
Cover with tomato sauce or puree and bake uncovered for 20 minutes
Add water, carrots, celery, onions, potatoes, salt and pepper, stir in and continue to bake for another 20 minutes to 1/2 hour.
Remove from oven, arrange pork chops on a large serving platter and ladle the vegetables and sauce over them and serve when ready to eat. Again another great dish that gets better as it sits. But you do want to eat it hot or at room temperature.

We had this every Sunday and I hated it. It wasn't the taste that turned me off but the onions and celery and carrots. I would try to get a pork chop without any of the other gook on it. Such was the unsophisticated palate...

If my mother was having you over for dinner of you would get a salad and bread of course. And if she had her way she would charge you too. The bread you would get would be homemade pita, fresh out of the oven - not like the awful stuff in the markets today.

Rigatoni with Lamb Meat

1 lb. rigatoni
2 cups lamb meat, cut into 1/2" chunks
5 cloves garlic, sliced thin
2 cups prepared spaghetti sauce
2 tablespoon olive oil
Salt and pepper to taste

Sauté garlic and lamb meat in olive oil until meat is nicely browned
Add spaghetti sauce, salt and pepper and continue to simmer for 1/2 hour
Cook rigatoni according to the directions on the box
Mix 2 tablespoons sauce with cooked rigatoni and stir thoroughly
Spoon rigatoni onto serving plate and ladle meat and sauce over pasta

Grated cheese may be added if desired - thus the dish that launched the restaurant where I learned to cook.

Garden Fresh

Along with all the Lebanese people in our neighborhood (more than I would care to count) we had a lot of Italians and Polish people. We all lived in a part of town that they called the "quarter", which encompassed about one square mile. Not that our community was huge but we "Furriners" (non-English-speaking, as we were referred to) comprised about 1/3 of the population in a town of about 800 people. We also had a lot of Irish (Anglaise, as we called them) and rumor has it that because of our large garlic consumption and the way the smell permeated, they petitioned the town fathers and had us quartered in the north part of town, hence the origin of the name 'quarter'. I truly believe we purposely quartered ourselves to get away from the odor of the corned beef and cabbage they were cooking...

On any given Sunday you would smell the Poles cooking kielbasa, the Italians cooking lasagna and the Lebanese grilling their shish kabobs. They all had gardens that were huge. Everyone had plenty to spare and many of them would share their bounty. The Italians especially. The Poles were a bit more frugal but occasionally they would give you something but not too often. And from the Italians we would get zucchini. We never grew it because we grew another type of squash called coosa, which we would stuff with rice and herbs. But my mother would make good use of the zucchini by turning it into a casserole with the other fresh vegetables available.

Zucchini Casserole

6 to 8 zucchinis cut into 1/4" slices
3 to 4 peppers, cut into strips
4 large onions cut into 1/8" slices
2 lbs hot sausage, removed from casings and broken into 1" pieces
6 to 8 large tomatoes cut into 1/4" slices
1/2 cups each of fresh chopped mint and parsley
1 teaspoon salt and 1 teaspoon pepper

Method:

In a large baking dish add a layer of zucchini
Next add a layer of tomatoes and repeat with onions and pepper and sausage.
Continue to repeat this process until all are gone, sprinkling 1/3 of the mint, parsley, salt and pepper on each layer.

Bake at 350° for about an hour. Remove from oven and let sit 1/2 hour before serving.

Yum-yum and thank you Italians.

George and friend Beth at a
garden party at the Retreat House

e is any food in the world that I would trade my life for regardless of how good it is. But that _____ment I received one cold winter afternoon when I had two guests to feed and couldn't decide what to give them. I had a freezer full of food and was too lazy to go through the thawing process and all that. On the other hand it was cold as blazes out – my car was covered with snow and wouldn't get warm until I got to the supermarket. Forget that noise. I thawed out some leftover chicken, combined it with some frozen mixed vegetables, added a package of chicken gravy, made it fit for a king and the rest is history. The next day one of the guests just raved about the chicken. Like a fool I said "what chicken?" and she said "last night's chicken - it was simply to die for." Well, well, people have died for their religion; I guess they could do the same for a good meal…

Chicken A La King

1/4 cup olive oil
1 1/2 tablespoons each of granulated onion and granulated garlic powder
1 teaspoon chicken bouillon powder or 1 chicken bouillon cube (chicken base)
4 to 5 cups frozen mixed vegetables
4 to 5 cups cooked chicken meat, diced
1/2 cup diced pimentos
2 tablespoons butter
2 tablespoons poultry seasoning
Salt and pepper to taste
1 package of chicken gravy mix, prepared

Sauté onion and garlic in oil for 2 minutes. Do not burn.
Add chicken base and stir in
Add mixed vegetables and stir-fry for 3 to 4 minutes
Add chicken meat and pimentos and stir thoroughly
Add salt, pepper, poultry seasoning and butter and stir
Add prepared chicken gravy, mixing everything together
Simmer for the next hour, stirring occasionally
Remove from stove and serve warm with biscuits and mashed potatoes

Just a recipe to die for!

Blessed Are

Recently I went to a culinary fest put on by a group of nuns and ironically called "Nun Edibles." Needless to say the victuals were simply mouth watering and sustaining. One particular booth was labeled "Sultan's Delights" and a friend of mine with me at the fest asked "Grape leaves?" The sister behind the table said "yes, and are you Lebanese?" My friend said "no, but I am going to bring someone over to this table that is". After tracking me across the room, he dragged me over to this table, whereupon I introduced myself and noticed the sister's last name. I asked her if she was in any way related to a cousin of mine who shares the same last name. To my surprise and delight she said "yes - she is my sister-in-law." Well, I don't have to tell you the rest, but in addition, she was coming to the Monastery the following week for a retreat. I retorted that I would cook a treat for her, which I did. After a fun day and sharing many stories I made Tabouleh, a classic Lebanese salad that people seem to die for with their oohs and ahs and all those crazy things that people do to describe something exotic or out of the ordinary. Myself, I hate the dumb stuff and hate it even more now that you can find it in your local supermarket's deli cooler. If I ate the grocery store version it wouldn't be to die for but to die from...

Tabouleh (Ta-boo-lee) is best served in the summertime when all the vegetables and herbs are garden fresh – a fragrant bouquet of springtime, mounded atop a bed of romaine lettuce leaves and scooped up with fresh pieces of warm Tillamee - pita bread. Well I did exactly that, made Tabouleh for her and the other nuns, and as they scooped up the salad with their pita bread the good sister replied with an old Lebanese proverb, "Salaam-dye-at-Tick," or in English, "bless the hands that prepared this."

"Salaam-Salaam."

Tabouleh

1 1/4 cups Bulgur wheat (available in Mid-East or gourmet food stores)
4 large tomatoes sliced and diced into 1/4" pieces
4 cucumbers sliced and diced into 1/4" pieces
1 bunch radishes sliced and diced into 1/4" pieces
4 bunches green onions (scallions), chopped very fine
3 bunches fresh parsley chopped very fine
3 bunches fresh spearmint chopped very fine
1 cup olive oil
Juice of 6 fresh lemons squeezed
1 1/2 teaspoon each of salt and pepper

In a colander rinse bulgur under cold water, drain and add to large bowl
Add the next 6 ingredients
Pour olive oil over evenly
Add lemon juice, salt and pepper and mix thoroughly, making sure it is mixed well

Serve after mixing or refrigerate until ready to use. The longer it sits with the dressing on it the soggier it will get (like the supermarket kind).

I have found it is easier to put all the ingredients in a bowl and add the dressing just before I am ready to serve. It always remains fresh. It can also be done ahead of time and refrigerated. Just remember to add the dressing, salt and pepper just before serving and it will be fresh and crisp.

Shame oh Shame

For some odd reason mashed potatoes are a "No No." Word has it that when our director was in the seminary studying for the glorious pampered life in the priesthood all the cafeteria ever seemed to serve was mashed, mashed, and more mashed potatoes. So one day when I served a lovely turkey dinner with the 'no-no' spuds he stormed out of the kitchen, telling me I ought to be ashamed of myself, and no more of those mashed. He had been smashed, mashed and bashed, and that was an order. No ands, ifs, or buts. No more mashed. Bewildered, I looked at myself and immediately thought of my mother, who would say "Ya Oppy Shoom," – "Shame on you!"

Well, after a few choice words under my breath and a couple of libations - "Ya Oppy Shoom, Ya Oppy Shoom," I wasn't ashamed anymore! That same week we had a group of sisters from England and I promised to do them a dish from their country - a special treat. After all the sisters were well deserving, probably being the only Catholics in Protestant England; God only knows they had their work cut out for them. As a result, Sheppard's Pie. I thought "J - Mary and J. How do you make it without those awful 'M' things? Diced, sliced or julienne potatoes just won't cut it."

George and Fr. Michael Carmola

Well, after talking to all the staff and asking their advice, which was overwhelmingly negative, I was really perplexed. I then pondered a future on the unemployment line for defying the boss and doing the right thing by preparing the dish the proper way and getting the sisters approval and trying not to break the fundamental culinary rules. Then it occurred to me that this was the 21st century: priests no longer condemned anyone to hell anymore.

It was then that I got some divine inspiration. I thought 'what would God do?', and then it came to me. God would do the right thing. Not wanting to offend the English or Mr. Sheppard I muttered what every one of my un-atheist friends are constantly reminding me: "God is good." With that premise and the thought that lightning wasn't going to strike on a sunny day I made the mashed potatoes, completed a perfectly wonderful dish, raised my hands to the heavens, breathed a sigh of relief and said, "God (without the "D" word) is Great," and to hell with "Ya Oppy Shoom!"

Footnote: The sisters loved the dish, said it was fit for their queen and complimented our director for having a kitchen with a sophisticated cuisine. Ah Men, Ah Men.

Shepherd's Pie

2 lbs. ground beef or ground chuck
1 1/2 teaspoon granulated garlic and 1 1/2 teaspoon granulated onion powder
1 16 oz. package of frozen carrots * (diced)
1 package of frozen peas **
5 cups of whipped mashed potatoes (real or instant)
1 to 2 teaspoon of Worcestershire sauce and a dash or 2 of Tabasco sauce
Salt and pepper to taste (1 teaspoon each)
1 cup of prepared brown gravy

Method:

Add ground beef or chuck to frying pan and stir in onion, garlic, Worcestershire, and Tabasco. Sauté until browned
Add salt and pepper and drain fat from the pan and set aside
Cook peas and carrots until tender
In an oblong baking dish 13" by 9" spread meat evenly on bottom of pan until all is covered
Add carrots and peas and spread evenly on top of the meat
Drizzle gravy over vegetables and meat
Spread mashed potatoes evenly over the vegetables mix
Cover loosely with foil and bake at 350° for 1/2 hour
Remove foil and continue to bake another 20 minutes or until potatoes start to brown.
Remove from oven and serve hot.

This goes great with some good crusty bread and a green salad.

** Fresh carrots and peas can be used in place of the frozen. I use the frozen as a matter of expediency and because there are only 2 of us in the kitchen and our time is limited. With a bigger staff the vegetables would all be fresh as I am a purist in this form. But I have done this dish with fresh and with frozen vegetables and our guests have enjoyed it either way. You be the judge.

Sitto and Jiddo

Illyayus Saad, Jiddo (Grandfather in Arabic), was our grandfather. His first name was Elias. In Arabic it was pronounced Ill-yay-uss. He was born around 1870 in a remote village called Beqerzla, nestled in the northern mountains of Lebanon, known as the Akkar region. Other than its scenic beauty, changing seasons and mountainous terrain, it had one other notable distinction: it was, as was the region, inhabited by Maronite Catholics, perhaps a throwback to the Crusades when 40,000 or so Lebanese from the Akkar region sided with the Crusaders and drove out the Muslim infidels. About the only difference between them and the Roman church is that the Maronites still speak the language of the bible, Aramaic or Syriac, both dead languages, and the Maronite priests can marry and have families. Other than following God's law versus man-made doctrines, they and their Roman Catholic counterparts all adhere to the same philosophies.

Saad family. Women: Sitto Immee-Jhuazz and Umpta Gemelia. Men: Ummo Sam, Joe Shaheen (Gemelia's son) and George Lewis

Not too much is known about Illyayus. As well as we can figure it he left Lebanon when he was 25 or 30 and headed for America. He was going to send for Sitto (grandmother) Immee Jhuazz (mother of George, as we called her), and their three children as soon as he got settled and established. Two months later they received a letter from him saying he was going to send for them soon and that Allah was the only thing that could keep them apart. The letter was postmarked Santiago, Santo Domingo. Well, God kept his word for he was never heard from again. Efforts to locate him were in vain and the only remnant of him that they had was his name.

Jiddo and Sitto had 3 children: Gemelia, George and Sam. Gemelia was the first to come to the U.S., my father 2 years later, my grandmother the following year and then Sam, three years later. Interestingly enough, it was odd that Sitto left Uncle Sam behind. Unfortunately Ummo (Uncle in Arabic) Sam was the victim of circumstance. From Lebanon their next stop was Cherbourg, France, where they booked passage for the United States. Ummo was swindled by a man who took his money, offering to buy him a cheaper ticket and then took off with his money. At 12 years old he was stranded in France. My grandmother had to go and get him and bring him across.

She hated him for it and never forgave him. She wasn't a happy person, saddled with three kids and having a husband who left for America, promising to send for them, who disappeared into the jungles of South America, never to be heard from again...

All efforts to trace him were futile. It's no wonder she was miserable the rest of her life. She spoke no English, constantly complained of being sick and was 95 when she died. What more can I say, other than she was a good cook and was stuffing her baked potatoes with a fusion of garlic and yogurt long before modern day chefs knew what it was all about. I guess some of that rubbed my way. Both the love for being miserable and also being a good cook.

My father's story is also quite interesting. He emigrated in 1911. He spoke no English, had no money, and was screaming, crying and fighting his uncle, who put him on the boat for America. When they were 10 miles out of the Port of Beirut the boat's captain made an announcement that if anyone wanted to return to Beirut they would need a quarter, 25 cents, to return. My father didn't have a quarter. When he arrived he was quarantined for 2 weeks in New York Harbor with dysentery before he could get off the boat. He was picked up by his sister, who was waiting to take him to Utica, N. Y., where he eventually settled. But a funny thing happened to him while he was being processed at Ellis Island. My dad's name was George Saad and when the immigration clerk asked him his name he replied, "I am George, son of Elias (Illyayus). In the Arabic world when introducing a male member they would always use their father's first name. Hence, I am George, son of Elias. Well the clerk got George right but when it came to Elias, or Illyayus as my dad would pronounce it, it sounded like Lewis and with no interpreters back then the clerk recorded him as George Lewis. Next!

Sitto, as I mentioned before, was a wonderful cook. Back in Lebanon around the 1900's when she was in her early twenties she would work for different families in exchange for food, money, etc. If she baked their bread, they in turn would compensate her with a few loaves for her services. Whatever the job she would be paid with food, clothing, money or such. She wasn't a domestic but was forced to hire out after my grandfather left her and their family. She had to raise and feed three children. They would go to the olive groves and pick olives, pack them in crocks full of brine and sell them in the village. Years later I can remember eating them with fresh pita out of the oven and dipping the bread in the brine, as the story of how they all picked olives in the old country was told over and over again. "Zaytoon, Zaytoon!" - Olives in garlic. Hence the olives are one of our favorite appetizers and we still serve the bread with it – unfortunately it's not home baked anymore.

Zaytoon (olives in garlic)

2 lbs of mixed green and black Mediterranean olives
2 cloves of garlic mashed to a paste
3 tablespoon olive oil
1 1/2 tablespoon of Balsamic or Tarragon vinegar
1 teaspoon Dijon mustard
1/4 teaspoon crushed red pepper (cayenne)
2 tablespoon of fresh finely chopped parsley
2 tablespoon of fresh finely chopped thyme or summer savory (or dried)
1 tablespoon fresh chives or green onions finely chopped
The juice of one lemon
3 thinly sliced lemons cut like a pie into 8 slices
1 teaspoon each of salt and pepper

Mix the whole batch of ingredients together and let marinate refrigerated for a few hours before serving. I let them sit tightly covered in the refrigerator for a few days before serving and then the flavors really begin to build.

They will hold up to a month in the refrigerator as long as you keep them tightly covered.

Recipe Please!

One afternoon a lady came into the kitchen and said "I must have that recipe". My assistant politely told her that we didn't give out our recipes but eventually it would be in our cookbook. Indignant as "H", she tipped up her nose and walked out of the kitchen and said "I've had meatloaf all over the world and I want to know what you did that was different." My assistant retorted he thought it was the mint. "Mint?" she said. "I've never heard of such a thing." Probably not – but it gives it quite a bite.

Meatloaf

3 lbs of ground beef
2 garlic cloves mashed to a paste
2 bunches green onions chopped fine
4 eggs
1 cup of grated parmesan
2 cups dry bread crumbs
1 tablespoon dried crushed mint
1 teaspoon of salt and 1 teaspoon pepper
1 cup ketchup

Mix all the ingredients but the ketchup together thoroughly, until blended together nicely.
Mold the mixture and shape into something that looks like a loaf of bread.
Lightly oil a baking dish and put the meatloaf in it.
Spread ketchup evenly over the top and cover the sides like you would if you were frosting a cake.
Bake at 350° approximately 45 minutes. The ketchup will start to brown or darken.
Let the meatloaf rest for about 10 minutes. Remove from pan and cut into slices and serve.

This can be served with a prepared brown gravy for extra moistness.

Such a fuss made over a little meat!

George and Fr. Michael Carmola in front of the Retreat House

Sauce of the Pommodoros

When I first started working here I had the rare opportunity of tasting the spaghetti sauce of the fellow I replaced. His sauce, like his cooking, was simply awful. Ragu™ could be considered gourmet in comparison. Working on a budget and not wanting to toss three gallons of this glop out in the garbage I resorted to an old trick I learned years ago when I was cooking at a sorority and had to use up a case of prepared spaghetti sauce that too was simply awful. I doctored it up and the Gamma Kappa girls were simply ga-ga.

Before you start this sauce it is essential that you not burn the onion and garlic powder or the sauce will have a bitter taste. Also adding the pork and sausage is optional, especially if you're vegetarian - I add it for extra added flavor which it gives.

2 tablespoons granulated garlic powder
2 tablespoons granulated onion powder
1 cup olive oil
2 no. 10 cans tomato puree (or 8, 16 oz. cans)
2 1/2 tablespoons Italian seasonings
1 1/2 teaspoons sugar
1 tablespoon each of salt and pepper
2 lbs. Italian sausage (sweet or hot) - optional
4 or 5 pork chops or pork steaks - optional

In a large saucepan add olive oil, onion and garlic powder and sauté briefly for about 2 minutes. Let it turn a light golden brown but do not burn.
Add tomato puree and stir thoroughly.

(At this point your sauce is very thick. I prefer a thinner sauce so I add a can of water to every can of puree and this gives me the consistency I want. This again is optional as you might prefer a thicker sauce and if you do add less water.)

Add salt, pepper, sugar and stir.
Add sausage and pork and continue to cook and bring to a boil. Lower the heat on the stove and continue to simmer for another 1 1/2 hours.
Remove meat from the sauce and set aside for your pasta or another use. (meat left in the sauce is OK but it will absorb the sauce gradually and thicken it.

You can refrigerate the sauce for up to a week. Otherwise it freezes very well.

Needless to say I still prefer a sauce with fresh green onion, garlic and basil, which I make quite a bit. But this version will do in a jiffy and to this date I have received no complaints, plus it gets the approval of some of the older Italian ladies who come here for retreats. They should know; they learned from their mothers and grandmothers and when they made their sauce, there was no Ragu™, which by the way in Italian means "gravy". I'm not about to argue with them when they tell me the gravy is good. And they emphasize it with "I should know for I'm Italian! Bouno - Bouno, appetito."

Friends of the author Angie and Vince. Angie used to say "The best Italian restaurant in town is at George Lewis' house."

Other than "Campbell's"

We do pork here at the Retreat house at least once a week, especially pork loins. Inevitably I cook more than I need, which leaves me with a lot more pork than I care to deal with. It being a sin to waste food, and me being a person with no sins to spare, I invented (with divine guidance) a "what-to-do-with-the-left-over-pork" recipe, which actually turned into a sinless delight. So much for the above.

Pork and Beans

2 lbs cooked left-over pork, diced up
2 cans red kidney beans
1 cup tomato sauce
1 1/2 cups tomato ketchup
2 tablespoon mustard
1 tablespoon Worcestershire sauce
1 teaspoon hot sauce (preferably Tabasco)
1/2 cup brown sugar
1 large onion, diced fine
1 tablespoon garlic powder
1/4 cup olive oil
1 teaspoon each of salt and pepper

Method:

In a large sauce pan sauté onion until it starts to brown
Stir in pork and sauté for 2 minutes
Add tomato sauce, ketchup, mustard, Worcestershire, Tabasco, brown sugar, garlic powder, salt and pepper. Stir ingredients thoroughly.
Pour mixture into a large oven proof baking dish
Lay strips of bacon on top of beans and put pineapple on top of bacon.

Cover with foil and bake in pre-heated oven at 350° for 1/2 hour
Remove foil and bake until the bacon starts to crisp (about another 1/2 hour)
Remove from oven and let sit for 15 minutes before serving.

This is a great buffet, picnic or party dish and can be served hot or cold. It's good either way and goes well with corn muffins, green salad and/or good crusty bread.

Goldwater Beans

Years ago, all the way back to the late 50's when nuns were still in habit and Catholics were observing meatless Fridays, I was part of the new frontier that JFK was talking about and interested in politics. Religion was waning, Pope Pius XII was on his way out, and you weren't going to hell for missing mass on Sunday. That was a relief for an impressionable young man, not having to worry about being scorched for an eternity. Then came the assassination of President Kennedy and our world was in turmoil. We had this goofy Texan in the White House and Jackie was going to Greece to be married. Lo and behold that was enough for one to start rethinking ones politics.

Along came a man who made the statement "Defense in the pursuit of liberty is no vice," and he lost the election. I was dating a young lady from a local college who happened to be a next door neighbor in Buffalo to the vice presidential candidate. Begging an invite to the next political rally and volunteering to do anything landed me in the backyard of the VP hopeful where my restaurant background was put to good use: washing dishes for the caterers. There were a lot of dishes. The bad news was that I never got to meet the candidates. The good news was that I got this recipe hand-written before it was mimeographed and given to the newspapers with an ingredient omitted that was truly essential for "Goldwater Beans"!

Goldwater Beans

1 lb dry pinto beans
1 8 oz. can tomato sauce
1 16 oz. can plum tomatoes chopped up
2 large onions chopped fine
1 clove garlic minced
1 teaspoon ground cumin
2 hot chili peppers chopped fine
1/2 green bell pepper chopped fine
2 teaspoons chili powder
2 lbs ground chuck - optional
2 teaspoons salt
1 teaspoon black pepper

Soak pinto beans in 6 cups of cold water overnight
Drain and add beans to 6 cups of fresh cold water
Add onion and bring to a boil
Cook over low heat for an hour, adding more water if needed
Add tomatoes, tomato sauce, garlic, cumin, chili's, green pepper, chili powder, salt and pepper and simmer another 1 to 1 1/2 hours
Sauté ground chuck until brown, drain fat and add meat to mixture
Cook over low heat for another hour or two.

This gets better the longer it sits, so using it the next day gives you added flavor.

LBJ won the election, the pope went back to Rome, and unfortunately we got stuck with Texas Chili - "Oh Home on the Range."

Beans and Beans

"Beans, beans the musical fruit,
The more you eat the more you toot!
The more you toot, the better you'll feel
So eat your beans at every meal!"

I'm sure that wasn't a major radio or television commercial but more like a slogan we used to sing back in grade school every time they were on the menu at lunch time. It was one way to get revenge on the cafeteria staff for their terrible way of turning a wonderful vegetable into a woeful legume. No one was ever punished for the students' tumultuous outburst, it being a bit difficult trying to fit 400 students into the principal's office at once. The cafeteria staff was always a bit chagrinned but would boldly take a bow in response to our trivial but potent song.

So if you're one of those people who are mindfully timid and hateful of beans, here's a green bean recipe that will bring back those tastes of summer and a Lima Bean Bake that will warm your tooters on a cold fall night.

Bedouin Green Beans

2 bunches green onions, chopped fine
1/4 cup of olive oil
3 garlic cloves, minced fine
2 lbs fresh green beans, with the ends trimmed and cut in half
1/2 teaspoon each of ground cinnamon, allspice, and cumin
1 cup of fresh parsley, chopped fine
1 cup fresh mint leaves chopped fine
1 1/2 teaspoon salt and 1 teaspoon black pepper
1 cup of water
2 cups fresh tomatoes chopped or 1 16 oz. can chopped up

Sauté onion in large cooking pan in oil over medium heat until lightly browned
Add garlic and continue cooking another minute or two
Add green beans and stir thoroughly
Stir in remaining ingredients except the tomatoes and bring to a boil
Add tomatoes
Lower heat on stove and simmer for another hour and a half
Add more water if necessary because you want a little juice with the beans

** For an extra added touch fresh sliced mushrooms can be added the last half hour of cooking. I sometimes also add sliced water chestnuts for a bit of a crunch.

***This recipe was originally created for a sauce to put over your rice and is very popular in the Middle-East. It also contained diced pieces of lamb that gave it extra flavor and more substance for those cold Bedouin nights in the desert.

More Western Beans

This is a great dish for one of those nights when the rain is pounding on the windows and the chill outside is colder than the wind chill. I think it may have originated somewhere on the prairie with everyone huddling under blankets and trying to keep warm over a campfire. And if you didn't have a nip of brandy to give you a tingle this was definitely a pot sticker.

Western Lima Bean Bake

1 large package Lima beans
1 lb ground beef
1 large onion chopped fine
18 oz can tomato sauce
2 ham hocks
1 teaspoon brown sugar
1 1/2 teaspoons salt
1 teaspoon poultry seasoning
6 cups water
1/2 cup bean liquid

Method:

Soak beans overnight in 6 cups cold water
Drain beans
Add fresh water (6 cups) to sauce pan, and then add beans, ham hock and onion
Bring to a boil and continue to simmer 1 1/2 to 2 hours until tender
Drain beans, reserving bean water. Set aside
Sauté ground beef until browned
Add tomato sauce, 1/2 cup bean water, brown sugar, poultry seasonings, salt and pepper and simmer for a few minutes
Remove ham hock, pick meat from bone and add to sauce
Place lima beans in casserole dish
Cover with sauce and ground beef mix
Bake 30 to 35 minutes at 350°

Another dish that gets better with age. Salt pork can be used if preferred over the ham hock. A hot pepper can also be added for an extra bite.

** The remaining bean liquid becomes the basis for a good hearty bean soup. The broth is perfectly seasoned and thickened. Usually while the beans are baking I usually treat myself to a cup of the broth which is so good by itself.

If you want it freezes well for soup or the basis for a soup. It doesn't hold well after a couple of days in the refrigerator, so freeze it soon.

Saint Rocky

Years ago when most of you weren't born and Nelson Rockefeller was on his last term as governor of New York I was living in NYC, jobless and broke. I happened upon the San Gennaro Festival that is held each year in "Little Italy" at the end of summer. Well, it didn't cost any money but you pay a hellacious price to attend, especially when you're broke – everything smells good, looks good, and seemingly tastes good. I did get the chance to meet the governor (imagine that, the richest man in the world saying hello to the poorest man at the festival). I should have asked him to float me a loan, for the $2.00 I had in my pocket could not buy me a sausage, pepper and onion sandwich, Italian ice, or one of those wonderful bracioles the street vendors were selling, with their aromas permeating the streets.

The only possibility of getting a bite was to crash the procession of the local Knights of Columbus, who were carrying a flower bedecked statue of San Gennaro through the narrow streets and grabbing one of those $5.00 bills all the faithful patrons were pinning on the statue. As it passed by they would rush up to it make the "sign-of-the-cross" and put their money on the platform. Thievery was out of the question for you surely were going to hell in a hand basket stealing from the church (especially the Italian Church), but when no one noticed the little dollar bill that fell off the statue and onto the ground, like an earthquake I considered it an act of God. It must have been for not only was I blessed by San Gennaro as his procession went by, when I inconspicuously scooped up the bill I knew the Lord was on my side - it was a ten spot and I was in heaven. By the time I realized what had happened it was too late to return it for the procession was halfway down the street and the crowds following it were too thick to penetrate. Lord oh lord, as all my friends keep reminding me - "God is good." So was the sausage, the bracioles and the Italian ices...

Sausage, Peppers and Onions

3 lbs hot Italian sausage cut in 2" pieces
2 large onions sliced thin
4 green peppers, cut in half, seeded and cut into 1/4" strips
Salt and pepper to taste

Method:

In a large frying pan cook the sausage pieces over medium heat and brown evenly
Add salt and pepper
Add onions and peppers and lower heat and sauté another 1/2 hour
Serve on or make a sandwich with fresh Italian bread.

For extra added taste and flavor add a tablespoon or two of marinara or your favorite tomato sauce.

Bracioles

1 to 2 lbs. rare deli roast beef sliced into 1/8" slices
3 cups each of finely diced carrots, celery and chopped green onion
2 lbs. fresh mushrooms (dice up 1/2 lb. and cut the rest into 1/4" slices)
1 package bread stuffing or 6 cups of stale bread cubes cut into 1" pieces
1/4 stick butter or margarine
3 to 4 tablespoons olive oil
1 tablespoon each of sage thyme, Italian and poultry seasonings (fresh if you have it)
1 tablespoon garlic powder or 2 garlic cloves minced fine
2 cups cold water
1 teaspoon each of salt and pepper
2 tablespoon olive oil for brushing
2 cups Merlot Wine
1 package of beef gravy mix
1 8 oz. can of tomato sauce

Method:

Add oil and onion to a large pan and sauté for 2 to 3 minutes
Add carrots, celery, garlic, seasonings, salt and pepper and cook until vegetables are tender (about 5 minutes)
Add diced mushrooms and sauté about 3 minutes longer
Add water and stir thoroughly
Add breadcrumbs and mix together.   Cool and set aside
Lay beef slices out on flat surface
Take 2 tablespoon of stuffing mix, mound on edge of beef slice and roll up
In a large baking dish lay the beef rolls down in a row
Brush each beef roll lightly with olive oil
Bake in 350° oven 1/2 hour or until beef rolls start to brown

To make Merlot mushroom sauce, melt butter or margarine in large skillet
Stir in remaining sliced mushrooms and sauté over medium low heat, 1 to 2 minutes
Add Merlot and bring sauce to a boil.
Add tomato sauce and cook another minute
Add gravy mix, salt and pepper and continue to sauté over low heat for another 15 minutes.
Pour sauce evenly over beef rolls and serve.

Give Ye Thanks

It's Thanksgiving time and it's time to give thanks. Probably more so considering I have been forbidden to serve mashed potatoes (see: Shame oh Shame) and asked by the staff as to what I was serving and I said "French Fries!" That brought about a few raised eyebrows, with everyone in unison exclaiming "French Fries?" I retorted with a touch of cynicism that if I couldn't serve mashed potatoes then French Fries it was. Well, the director got wind of it and told me I was nuts and to serve Sweet Potatoes. I said I would like to but it would look like the opposite of heaven considering I was also serving Butternut Squash. The two would look alike on the plate, both being orange in color and that could be confusing. I might add that priests are never wrong and never have heard of compromise - but I must also add that our director is beginning to progress. Reluctantly he gave the OK with the stern warning - "Just this once."

"Oh God, I just love your wondrous ways and miter-less priests and their liberalism..."

Roast Boneless Breast of Turkey

This is a great recipe for those who don't want the fuss and muss of doing an entire turkey. Quicker and easier and less time and mess.

3 to 4 lb boneless breast of turkey
Rub turkey all over with 2 tablespoon of Olive Oil
Mix together a dry rub of:
> 2 tablespoon of garlic powder
> 2 tablespoon of onion powder
> 2 tablespoon of thyme
> 2 tablespoon of poultry seasoning
> 1 teaspoon cumin
> 1 tablespoon each of salt and pepper

Rub dry mix all over the turkey evenly
Pre-heat oven to 350°
Put turkey in baking dish and add 2 cups cold water to bottom of pan
Add 3 carrots cut into 2" chunks and 1 large onion cut into quarters
Bake for 1 1/2 hours, basting occasionally
Insert food thermometer and when it registers 165° remove turkey from oven
Take turkey out of baking dish and set on warm plate 20 minutes before carving

Take pan juices and add to a sauce pan to make your gravy (I usually scrape up the little brown bits in the baking dish, add 2 cups of cold water to the baking dish, swirl it around a bit and add it all to the sauce pan for the gravy. This way you get all the essence and flavor). Bring pan juices to a boil. Make a paste of 2 tablespoons of cornstarch and 3 tablespoons of cold water and swirl into pan juices. Add more salt and pepper if desired and lower flame and simmer for 10 minutes and its ready to serve.

Use cooked carrots and onions to garnish the turkey.

Acorn Squash

Cut squash in half and scoop seeds out of center cavity
Brush cavity with butter
Add 2 tablespoons either honey or brown sugar
Lightly salt and pepper
Put in baking dish skin side down
Bake at 350° for 30 to 45 minutes or until inside of squash is tender

Butternut Squash

Cooking for a crowd makes it impossible to do fresh butternut squash. If you prefer to use the fresh then you want to cut it in half length wise and scoop out the seeds in the cavity. Then I lay the squash pulp (yellow orange color) face down and cut across the squash to get 1 1/2 pieces. Then I put them in a microwave dish and cook the squash on high for 15 minutes or longer until the pulp is tender. Let cool and then with a paring knife cut the skin off like you would if you are peeling an apple or cucumber. In a bowl mash the pulp like you would mash potatoes. Mix in 2 tablespoons butter, 3 tablespoons honey, 1 teaspoon each of cinnamon and allspice, a dash of salt and pepper and bake in baking dish at 350° for 1/2 hour and serve. At the retreat house I generally use the frozen squash because of the amount of work involved and the lack of prep cooks, but I still use the same seasonings and bake it the same way and the results are great. Either way it works well with the turkey.

Stuffing

1 package bread stuffing or 2 quarts dried or stale bread cubes
1 large onion diced fine
3 cups each of finely chopped carrot and celery
1 lb fresh mushrooms diced fine
2 garlic cloves finely minced or 2 tablespoons granulated garlic powder
1 tablespoon each of sage, parsley and thyme (fresh if possible-otherwise dried)
2 tablespoons poultry seasonings
1 teaspoon each of salt and black pepper
2 tablespoons butter or margarine
2 cups cold water
1 cup of dry white wine

Sauté onion and garlic for 2 minutes in butter or margarine and then add celery, carrot, seasonings and white wine and cook over low heat for 20 minutes, stirring occasionally. Add mushrooms and sauté 5 minutes longer.
Remove from flame and add bread crumbs
Gradually add water, stirring as you go until all is absorbed
Put stuffing in baking dish and bake in 350° oven for 1/2 hour
Remove from oven and serve.

Melt-Aways

Filling:
2 cups crushed walnuts
1 1/2 cups brown sugar
1 teaspoon of vanilla
1 teaspoon cinnamon
1/2 stick of melted margarine
(mix all these ingredients together and set aside)

Dough:
1 lb of cottage cheese
5 cups flour
1 lb chilled margarine cut into small pieces

By hand mix 3 dough ingredients together until mixture is of crumbly texture

2 egg whites lightly beaten
2 cups of flour to dust the work surface

Refrigerate overnight.

Lightly flour a working surface
Cut pieces of dough about 1/2 size of your fist
Working with a rolling pin roll out dough into rectangular shapes creating a ribbon effect about 12" long and 3" wide (dough should be about 1/8" thick)

Put a line of the walnut mix all the way down the middle of your laid out dough

Just cover the walnut mix with the long side of the right hand side of the dough. You should now have a log of dough in the middle, and on the left side you should still have more of the original dough, flat.

Brush this long, left side of the dough lightly with egg white.

Now, take the left side and fold it over the log you created earlier.

Cut the log into 1 1/2 inch pieces
Repeat the process and lay cookie pieces on a cookie sheet lined with parchment paper
Brush cookies with egg white mixture lightly

Bake at 375° for 15 to 20 minutes or until lightly browned.
Remove from pan and dust lightly with confectionary sugar.

Store in air tight container up to 3 weeks.
Will freeze indefinitely

Plenary Indulgence

It was close to St. Valentine's Day and I had made Chocolate Rum Balls to compliment the fresh, first of the season Florida strawberries for our dessert table. A woman walked in, spotted the table and with shrieking delight renounced her sinful ways for the indulgence of chocolate. Using that typical choc-o-holic phrase that she could "give up her life for chocolate but couldn't pardon herself for the sin of indulgence", she took one anyway and exclaimed again that "it was to die for." Not wanting to elicit the services of the local funeral director I told her if she was planning to die for her sins she was in luck because there were three priests in residence and she had her choice if she needed the last rites. We all found that to be quite humorous. The real laugh was on me about two weeks later, when on the front page of the local newspaper was her picture, proclaiming her the newly elected Lutheran Bishop of the greater Northeastern United States. She reminds me of my antics every time she comes on retreat. I always oblige her with chocolate and remind her that it's not a plenary indulgence.

Chocolate Rum Balls

1 standard sized box of Vanilla wafers
1 cup light corn syrup (karo)
1 cup pecans finely chopped
2 cups shredded coconut
1 tablespoon vanilla
1 cup confectioner's sugar
2 cups cocoa powder (reserving 1 cup)
2 ozs rum

In a food processor add wafers and crush them to fine powder

In a large bowl add the finely crushed wafers and the rest of the ingredients and mix thoroughly together.
Using a teaspoon scoop out a teaspoonful of the mixture and roll into a ball about 1 1/4" round.
Lay the ball on a tray lined with parchment or waxed paper and continue the process until all are rolled.
Refrigerate for two hours and then roll the balls in cocoa powder and serve.
Store in airtight container or freeze until ready to use

Makes about 40 balls.

Cromwell's Chocolate Chewy Cookies

1 6 oz. package Bakers semi-sweet chocolate
2 egg whites
1/8 teaspoon salt
1/2 cup sugar
1/2 teaspoon white vinegar
1/2 teaspoon vanilla
1/2 cup shredded coconut
1/4 chopped nuts

Melt chocolate over hot water. Cool and set aside
Beat egg whites and salt until foamy throughout
Add sugar to egg whites, 2 tablespoons at a time, beating after each addition until sugar is blended
Then continue beating until mixture will stand in stiff peaks
Add vinegar and vanilla and beat well
(entire beating process should take about 10 minutes)
Fold in coconuts, nuts and chocolate
Drop from teaspoon onto greased baking sheet
Bake at 350° for 10 minutes
Makes about 3 dozen cookies.
Store in airtight container.

Absolutely scrumptious!

Heavenly Chocolate Flakes

1 6 oz. package of semi sweet chocolate
4 to 5 cups of cornflakes

Melt chocolate over hot water
In a large bowl add cornflakes
Pour chocolate over them and mix together
Line a tray with parchment paper
Using a soup spoon scoop out chocolate covered flakes and lay them about an inch apart on the tray

Store in airtight container until ready to serve.

Garnish This

Apples

Another nice garnish for roast pork, turkey, ham or lamb is spiced apple rings. Simple to make, delightful to eat and pleasing to the eye. Although a number of different apples can be used, I prefer the red delicious kind. They are firm and if you don't cook them to death they hold up very fine and have a crunch to the bite.

6 red delicious apples cut into 3/4" rings.

(Lay the sliced apples out on a cutting board and with an apple corer cut the seed part out of the center of the ring.)

Place apple rings in a bowl and toss lightly with a cup of pineapple or orange juice
Add 1 teaspoon each of cinnamon, allspice and ground cloves and toss lightly
In a large skillet melt 2 tablespoons butter and add apple rings evenly. Reserve juice
Add 1 teaspoon red food coloring or 1/2 cup cherry brandy to juice and pour over apples
Sprinkle 1 cup sugar over apples and sauté over low heat, stirring evenly for about 15 minutes or until the apples are tender but still hold their shape
Remove apples onto a plate with a slotted spoon and let cool

Garnish your roast with the rings and pour remaining juice over them.
These will hold in the refrigerator for a few days.

Pineapple

You can also do the same thing with fresh pineapple. If you don't want to bother with the peeling and coring of the pineapple you can buy them already cleaned and cored and slice them yourself. Green Crème de Menthe can be substituted for red food coloring for another nice taste. But the seasonings and process is the same as the apples.

Pears

Fresh pears, either halved or quartered or whole, are another nice garnish. The green Crème de Menthe works nicely with them. Again, peel, slice and core. The same process as the above applies except that you only want to cook the pears for about 8 to 10 minutes. Just remember not to drink too much of the green stuff – it can get awful minty...

Oranges

Sliced oranges, about 1/4" thick, are also quite tasty. The only thing different with them is that I don't peel off the rind and I eliminate the cinnamon, cloves, and allspice (the spices darken their color and make their appearance a bit unappealing). Just give them a squeeze of lemon and cook them for about 5 minutes with a cup of sugar and a cup of peach brandy and let them cool in their syrup.

Slurp - Slurp - Slurp!!

Foods You Love To Hate

For some reason every time I make pickled beets everyone under the age of thirty-five makes a weird face and gives you a concocted story of why they dislike them or cannot eat them because they hallucinate, puke, get violently ill and such. But anyone born before 1950 – look out! They love them. So for that crowd out there and anyone brave enough to try them, here is a delicious pickled salad that is a nice compliment to any dinner.

Pickled Beets

If you are using fresh beets there are two ways to do them. One way is to boil them and the other is to bake them. Either way cut the greens (beet tops) off at the top. If boiling drop beets into 6 cups boiling water and over medium heat cook until the beets are fork tender. Remove from water and cool. At this point you want to peel the beets. Actually the skins slide off rather easily by hand, or else use a peeler. If baking brush with olive oil and put in a baking dish and bake at 350° until fork tender. Again the same process applies for peeling them. Then rinse the beets under cold water to get rid of the bits and pieces of skin.

Slice beets about 1/8 to 1/4 inch thick.

1/4 cup olive oil
2 tablespoons of red wine vinegar (or your favorite vinegar)
2 tablespoons sugar or honey
1 cup green onion chopped fine
1 large onion cut into 1/8" slices
1 teaspoon garlic paste
1 teaspoon each of salt and black pepper

In a large bowl add the sliced beets, green onions and sliced onions.
Add remaining ingredients and toss together lightly.
Refrigerate until ready to serve. Mix gently again and serve.
This will hold in the refrigerator 4 to 5 days.

Carrot Salad

4 cups shredded carrots
1 cup raisins
1 cup finely chopped pineapple pieces
1 cup of maraschino cherries sliced and diced
1/4 cup olive oil
1/4 cup honey or sugar
2 tablespoons red wine vinegar or your favorite vinegar
1 tablespoon orange zest (optional)
1/2 teaspoon each of salt and pepper

In a large bowl add carrots and remaining ingredients

Toss together thoroughly, refrigerate and allow to chill before serving.

Cleanse Thy Soul

This is Advent season.   Ignorant of the holidays of the church, other than the major ones, I asked the director father what Advent was and he said it was a time to clean within – the spirit and the body, examine oneself and so on. I would also add that if you were Catholic you really had your hands full. It's also ironic that my mother, at this time of year in December, would cook a certain chicken and rice dish called "Jugh-edd Mishee." I can't recall if she did it on Advent day (December 8th) but I do remember she would mutter a prayer in Arabic, make the sign of the cross and say "Ya Mart Moura."   Mart Moura was a young pagan girl who took up Christianity and became the patron saint of all the Maronite Catholics in Lebanon (Mart is saint in Arabic). I don't know what Mart Moura had to do with Advent but I think the prayer was said and the saint invoked to make sure the dish came out right. And it always did and was what the Lebanese would consider comfort food.

I'm not certain whether it was a meatless day in the Roman Church but it was observed by the Maronite Catholics and in our hour house that meant "meatless" whether it was a Friday or not. Hence, to save all our souls from going to hell without a stopover in Purgatory and to keep the holy day meatless we always ate my mother's Buttenjan Yaknah, or eggplant stew, served with Lebanese rice and yogurt. I always hated the dish and sure as hell would have traded my soul for the fires of Hade's and a hamburger back then, but since have sophisticated my palate and serve the dish quite often.   I add a little chili pepper to give the dish some heat and to show me what I might have missed at those burning gates.

Eggplant Stew

2 Eggplants cut into 1" pieces
1 large onion cut in half and sliced thin
2 green peppers cut in thin slices
1 lb mushrooms sliced in half
4 tomatoes cut in 1" quarters
2 cans garbanzo beans drained of their water
2 cloves garlic sliced thin
1/4 cup olive oil
2 cups fresh chopped parsley
1/2 cup fresh cut mint or 3 tablespoons dried
1 teaspoon salt
1 teaspoon pepper
1 teaspoon cumin
1/2 teaspoon each of cinnamon and allspice
2 cups water
1 small (7 oz) can tomato paste

Lightly salt eggplant pieces and set aside

In a large skillet sauté onions in olive oil over medium heat until limp
Add green peppers and garlic. Stir and cook for a few minutes until they become soft
Add all remaining ingredients to skillet except tomato paste
Bring to a boil and then simmer for 1/2 hour
Add tomato paste, stirring thoroughly and cook slowly for another 15 minutes.
Adding the tomato paste will thicken the stew.

Okra is another vegetable that my mother would use to thicken it. Unfortunately no one in the family other than my mother liked okra so she wouldn't use it to appease us all.

Serve immediately nice and hot

Oh Ye Judas

There was a restaurant in Greenwich Village whose food was fabulous and its recipes were closely guarded. It was called Keneret and had very strong Turkish-Greek origins. They had a Green Goddess salad dressing that was the rage of the city. The food editor of Gourmet Magazine tried unsuccessfully to get the recipe, but to no avail. The restaurant wasn't sharing its ingredients or preparation. Nor would they sell a jar to you. In broken English they would tell you to come into the restaurant and buy dinner and you would get the dressing on your salad. It was their house dressing and the only dressing they had to offer. Very entrepreneurial! The only thing I could figure out was it had avocado, parsley, thyme, mint, oregano, olive oil, lemon juice and yogurt. After many attempts at trying to recreate this recipe and many failures I was on the right track but still couldn't get the taste the restaurant had to offer.

But alas to no avail. One night as I was having a drink in a unique village bar called "Casey's," which was renowned for its Eggs Benedict, Bloody Mary Brunches, out of work actors and many disgruntled restaurant employees. Luck was in my corner when I spotted Jam eel, a busboy from Keneret who had just been fired and was cursing the place into damnation. Offering a sympathetic ear with an endless supply of drinks, I plied the recipe out of him. Ethical, probably not – but I'm able to share it with you.

Green Goddess Keneret

2 cups olive oil
Juice of one lemon
2 tablespoons tarragon vinegar
1 ripe avocado, mashed to a paste
2 garlic cloves, minced finely
1/2 cup yogurt
1/2 cup parsley, chopped fine
2 tablespoons fresh mint leaves, chopped fine
1 teaspoon fresh thyme
1/4 cup fresh oregano
1 teaspoon cumin
1 teaspoon sumac powder
1/2 teaspoon dried mustard
1 1/2 teaspoons each of salt and pepper

Add all ingredients except the oil into a blender and start to blend on slow speed. Drizzle in olive oil slowly until all is blended. Increase the speed to medium and blend another minute. Scrape from blender into a bowl and refrigerate until ready to serve.

Because of the heavy nature of the dressing you wan to spoon it over the salad rather than toss it together with the salad.

Unfortunately the restaurant is long gone but the salad dressing lives on. My version is good but still not as good as theirs and that's what you get for copying...

More From Keneret

Another favorite from Keneret was their Greek Lasagna, better known as Moussaka. Theirs was good but I like this adaptation a little better thanks to a little help from an Armenian friend who claimed the dish was stolen by the Greeks when they and the Turks occupied Armenia. I have had the Greek and the Turk versions and can only relate that if you ate with the Armenians you would understand their superiority in the preparation of this classic. The dish is of Middle Eastern origin but can be found in any Greek restaurant in the country. What is particularly interesting about the dish is the many variations: whereas all the Mediterranean countries from Spain to Greece tend to layer it and overload it with cheeses, the Middle Eastern countries tend to stuff it with the likes of pignolia nuts, currants, and mint leaves. This is my version, altered for the home cook who doesn't want to spend the day in the kitchen preparing what will be devoured in 10 minutes.

Before doing this recipe there are a few things you should know about eggplant. First of all, you want your eggplant to be dark purple and firm. If not it's not fresh. After you cut or slice the eggplant you should lay the slices out on a tray and lightly salt them and let them sit for 20 minutes. This is known as bleeding the eggplant and taking out the bitterness in it. Then you want to drain off the juices. A lot of chefs when preparing this dish generally flour the eggplant slices and sauté them in hot oil until they lightly brown and then drain on paper towels. You can do this but it's a lot of work.

I have made it easier by flouring the slices on both sides, laying them on a plate (one layer at a time) and microwaving them for 2 to 3 minutes on medium. This makes them tender and omits all that oil. I then let them cool until I am ready to assemble the dish. You can also use bread crumbs instead of flour and bake them in the same manner. I prefer flouring them. Or sometimes I cheat and get the eggplant slices already prepared from one of my food distributors. You could probably find them in your supermarket freezer department. And they're very good.

A Grecian Lasagna: Moussaka

4 firm eggplants cut diagonally into 1/4" slices
3 cups flour for dredging

1 cup olive oil
3 bunches green onions chopped fine
3 cloves garlic minced
2 cups each of finely chopped carrots, celery, and mushrooms
3 cups ground raw lamb
1 teaspoon each of cinnamon, allspice, salt and pepper
2 cups dry red wine
1/2 cup each of chopped parsley and mint mixed together
16 oz. can of tomato paste
3 cups of milk mixed with 1 pint of heavy cream
2 cups Parmesan cheese

2 cups each of shredded Mozzarella and shredded sharp cheddar mixed together

Flour eggplant slices and microwave them according to above directions, setting aside.

Sauté onion, celery, carrots, mushrooms and garlic for 15 minutes or until vegetables are tender.
Add lamb meat, cinnamon, allspice, parsley, mint, salt and pepper and sauté until browned
Add red wine and continue to sauté 10 minutes longer
Add tomato paste and milk. Mix and let it simmer for 1/2 hour, stirring occasionally
Add Parmesan cheese, stir thoroughly and set aside

Lightly oil a 13" by 9" baking dish

Eggplant and meat sauce

Add a layer of eggplant to the bottom of the pan until all is covered

Spoon on 1/4 of the vegetable/meat mixture spreading over eggplant evenly
Sprinkle with 1/4 of the shredded cheese

Layering the eggplant with the cheese and meat

Repeat this procedure 3 more times, starting with another layer of eggplant, meat/ vegetable mix, and shredded cheese.

Ready for baking

Cover tightly with a layer of plastic wrap and then cover tightly with aluminum foil over the plastic.

Bake in a 350° oven for about 45 minutes, covered with the plastic and the foil. The plastic wrap helps steam the Moussaka and keep it moist. Just be careful that the foil completely covers the plastic and isn't damaged in any way. The cheese will start to bubble and brown and you will know it is done.

Let the dish sit for 10 to 15 minutes before serving.

When The Lettuce Doesn't Get Washed

In the course of a year I had three different cooks work for me and eventually walk out on me. All three had previously worked for celebrity status chefs at locally prominent restaurants and all three had the same habit, which I had the darnedest time breaking them of. They never washed the vegetables they would put into the salads they were making. This may be the current atmosphere in these local eateries but it was totally intolerable in our kitchen. After many arguments I would wash and drain the vegetables, reserve the water they were washed in and show them the dirt that had accumulated in the bottom of the sink. Nor did I have to say, "I told you so!"

Unfortunately I personally think it's a common practice in most restaurants, which generally leads me to ask when I am out to dinner whether the vegetables have been washed when ordering a salad. Be careful if you plan to follow this procedure – it can get you labeled pretty fast in a restaurant, prior to receiving your dinner.

So when the lettuce doesn't get washed and you're in a hurry here is a nice salad substitute. It's better in the summer when everything is fresh but it works well in the winter even though the flavors aren't as intense.

Tomato, Cucumber, and Olives

2 red and 2 yellow** tomatoes cut into wedges
2 cucumbers*** scored and cut into 1/8" slices
10 green and 10 black olives cut into slices
1 bunch green onions chopped fine
1/4 cup each of fresh chopped parsley, mint, and oregano
1 tablespoon fresh thyme chopped fine
3 tablespoons prepared vinaigrette (below)
Salt and pepper to taste

Toss together lightly and serve on washed lettuce leaves.
For added flavor, squeeze the juice of 1/2 lemon over it.
If you want you can prepare the salad ahead of time and the toss the vinaigrette on it when you're ready to serve.

**If you can't find yellow tomatoes use all red or cherry tomatoes cut in half
***To score a cucumber, wash it first. Using a fork, from the top of the cucumber, working lengthwise, take the prongs all the way down, piercing the skin and making lines. Then cut the cucumber into slices.

Vinaigrette

1 cup olive oil
Juice of 1 lemon
1 teaspoon Dijon mustard
3 or 4 tablespoons of your favorite vinegar
½ teaspoon salt
½ teaspoon pepper

Whisk together, refrigerate until needed

Dips For The "Dips"

We were having a cocktail party for a group of influential people. They were quite demanding on what they wanted to eat but financially were about as forthcoming as one would be when dipping into one's pockets for a third collection during mass. Anyhow the person in charge sent me a memo and gave me my "marching orders." I was told to exclude the hommous (Arabic dip) and guacamole (Mexican dip) because no one liked them. Taken back by their tenacity I won't repeat what I muttered but thought there is never any left when I serve it and this particular person didn't like it. With my feathers ruffled, I singled out the individual before the party and in my nicest sarcasm told her it was too bad she scrapped the hommous and guacamole because the Archbishop's office had called earlier and had hoped we were serving the omitted dips because they were his favorites. 'By all means please serve it' was their reply. Too late, too late for me to comply - the menu is set and the party's at five. Touché, touché, I hastened to say, I hope the Archbishop has a nice day...

Guacamole

3 ripe avocados (soft to the touch)
3 cloves garlic, mashed to a paste
Juice of 1 lemon
2 tablespoon olive oil
1/2 teaspoon Tabasco sauce
1/2 teaspoon each of salt and pepper

Method:

Cut avocados in half, remove pit and scoop avocado out of its peel
Mash avocado to a pulp and it becomes smooth
Add garlic, oil, Tabasco, lemon, salt and pepper and mix until smooth
Chill about an hour before serving

Garnish with diced tomato and lemon wedges

Hommous

3 cans of garbanzo beans
3 cloves garlic mashed to a paste
Juice of 1 lemon
3 tablespoon of tahina (sesame see paste, available in Middle Eastern import stores)
2 tablespoons olive oil
1/2 teaspoon each salt and pepper

Method:

Drain the water from the garbanzo beans, reserving one cup of bean liquid.
In a food processor add the beans and reserved liquid and blend until smooth
Add tahina, garlic, olive oil, lemon juice, and salt and pepper and blend another minute
Remove from food processor to a bowl and refrigerate an hour before serving
Garnish with chopped parsley and a sprinkling of paprika

Dip in with fresh pita bread cut into triangles.

Poor Man's Delight

While we are on the subject of parties here are a few appetizers that are easy, fun, economical and a good source of conversation, especially if your host is too busy with other guests and you don't know anyone else. Been there and done that and when the server passes you a slice of cucumber with some tiny shrimp and a dollop of cocktail sauce you can at least voice your enthusiasm and say, "now, isn't that clever?" That will give you the opening to express yourself to whoever is standing next to you, since you read the New York Times that morning and are loaded with bits of things to talk about.

Cucumber Shrimp Cocktail

2 cucumbers, scored and cut into 1/4" slices
1/2 lb of salad shrimp or English Prawns (these are very tiny shrimp)
1 1/2 cups cocktail sauce
Take 4 to 5 shrimp and arrange them on the cucumber slice pinwheel style
Put a 1/4 teaspoon dollop of cocktail sauce in the middle of each pinwheel
Arrange on garnished tray and refrigerate until ready to serve.

This makes about 40 individual appetizers

Cocktail Sauce

1 16 oz. bottle of ketchup
3 tablespoons prepared bottled horseradish
2 teaspoons Worcestershire sauce
Juice of 1/2 lemon

Mix all ingredients together in a bowl thoroughly and refrigerate until ready to serve.
This will hold at least 2 weeks refrigerated.

Herbed Cream Cheese Bread Rounds

(For this hors d'oeuvre you will need a 2" round cookie cutter)

1 loaf of good whole wheat or rye bread
Take a slice of bread and cut rounds out of it (you will get 3 per slice)
With a knife spread top of bread round with either soft butter or mayonnaise

Mix the following ingredients thoroughly in a bowl:

1 package of softened cream cheese
1/2 cup of finely chopped chives
1 teaspoon finely chopped chives
1 teaspoon thyme
Dash of Tabasco sauce
1/8 teaspoon salt

In a pastry bag fitted with a star tip add cream cheese mix
Pipe onto bread rounds and make a fancy design
Garnish with a 1/8" diced piece of red pepper in the middle of cream cheese
Arrange on tray and refrigerate until ready to serve. This also freezes well.

Salmon Stuffed Eggs

2 dozen hard cooked eggs
1 lb cooked Salmon Fillet, flaked or 1 16 oz. canned Salmon, flaked
3 tablespoons mayonnaise
2 tablespoons prepared horseradish
1 teaspoon Dijon mustard
1/2 teaspoon sugar
1/2 teaspoon each of salt and pepper
1 jar red caviar (optional)

Slice hard boiled eggs in half, remove the yoke and put it in a mixing bowl
Take a damp cloth and gently rub the egg cavities to clean

In a food processor:
Add flaked salmon, horseradish, Dijon, sugar, mayonnaise, salt and pepper and blend to a thick puree

Take mixture and fill into a pastry bag fitted with a star tip and pipe mixture into egg cavity, giving you a fancy design

Add a little dollop of red caviar on top (about 1/4 teaspoon) for added color, garnish and taste.
Arrange on serving dish and refrigerate until ready to use.

** Because eggs and other hors d'oeuvres tend to wobble and not stay straight on a tray I usually like to take a head of Iceberg lettuce or red cabbage and shred it thinly and spread it all over the tray. It not only gives you an attractive bed to lay things on but it also helps to keep the hors d'oeuvres in place, preventing them from rolling or falling all over the place.

Asparagus Sandwiches

2 bunches asparagus or about 3 lbs, washed and trimmed to 3" spears
(cut asparagus about 3" long, discarding the stalk end)
1 loaf of good white bread

Meanwhile mix together:
1/4 cup melted butter
1 tablespoon bottled horseradish
Juice of 1/2 lemon
Set aside

In boiling water with 1/4 teaspoon salt cook asparagus about 3 minutes or until tender
Drain and run under cold water for a minute until they are cooled. Set aside.

Take a slice of bread and cut off the crusts. Repeat this until all the bread is trimmed
With a rolling pin flatten the bread and get it as thin as you can get it
Cut in half, lengthwise and lay out on flat surface
Brush top side of bread with butter
Take an asparagus spear, put it on one end of the bread and roll it up

Lie on a garnished tray seam side down and attractively arrange.
Refrigerate until ready to serve. This also freezes well tightly wrapped.

S.O.P.

Another popular hors d'oeuvre that I really hate, cannot stand the taste of and inevitably fill with the contents of the kitchen sink are stuffed mushroom caps. No matter what I put in them, nor how horrible they appear to me the tray always come back empty. Like Mikey in the commercial, "they like them." So if they like them they get them.

My good friend Stella (Stash) is no longer with us, but with her Borja (Polish for God). She would go out into the woods, pick mushrooms, stuff them and feed them to her guests. In her ninety some odd years on this earth she never poisoned a soul. Me thinks there were a few mortals out there she may have liked to but being a kind soul she would gently curse you in Polish because she knew you couldn't understand it. But we all knew what "dupa" meant. Her daughter YonYuu (Janet) was and still is one of my best friends, from whom we all learned the kind of Polish we weren't supposed to. And Stella never called you an S.O.B., but an S.O.P. - Son of a Peach Basket.

Stella kept the cleanest house in town. One day I was driving by and there she was up on a ladder washing her windows. I stopped and invited her to have a cup of coffee with me. She said she would love to but she had to finish the windows (which were already clean, but not to her standards) and then go inside to dust and vacuum. The inside was impeccably clean but not clean enough for her. By the way, the day she was up on the ladder cleaning her windows she had just celebrated her 88th birthday.

An even crazier story about her that didn't and still doesn't make any sense is the story of the Sacred Heart. Stella had a hard but blessed life. She was very poor in finances, always claiming poverty, and she did

struggle, yet managed to give her family all the necessities in life. As she would always say and then make the sign of the cross, "Borja will provide." She was confident of that. When she was in her late 80's her sister-in-law had passed away and bequeathed to her a sum of around $10,000. She gave her son and his family a third of it and another third to her daughter and her family. So I said to her, "Well, now you can take a vacation." She said "Oh no - I bought a statue for the church." No ordinary statue but a five foot statue of the Sacred Heart, to the tune of about $3,000. I said to her "Are you 'blank, blank' nuts?" She calmly replied, "No," and smiled a bit. She said her brother Peter said the same thing and he was mad as hell at her. She said "but Georgie, the money didn't belong to me." So when you go to confession at St. Malachy's, make sure you don't trip over her statue on the way to the confessional but do look to see that it says "In memory of Ray and Stella Cosens." Her Borja would be proud.

Stella was deeply religious and the day they elected the Polish Pope she was so proud that she wore a sterling silver crucifix around her neck, so heavy that it darned near strangled her (see photo).

Stash's Mushrooms

1 lb firm medium sized mushrooms
3 cups cooked chicken meat
1/4 cup finely chopped green onion
1/2 cup green seedless grapes diced fine
3 tablespoons mayonnaise
2 tablespoons sweet relish
1/4 cup red sweet pepper chopped fine
1 teaspoon sugar
1 tablespoon mustard
1/2 teaspoon garlic paste or powder
1/2 cup finely chopped parsley
1 teaspoon Worcestershire sauce
1/2 teaspoon each of salt and pepper

Remove stems from mushrooms. With a melon ball cutter scoop slowly, removing the membrane from inside of the cap, working diligently so as not to break the mushroom but to remove as much of the inside without damaging the cap.

Mix remaining ingredients together thoroughly
With a teaspoon fill each mushroom cap and set on serving tray.
Refrigerate until ready to use.

It must be noted that the mushrooms Stella found in the woods and horse pastures were far superior to any of those you will find today in any market. Her secret for picking the best non-poisons mushrooms was simple: Make sure the mushrooms you pick match the color of the palm of your hand and you can't go wrong. If you try this method, by all means I would love to hear from you and how you made it.

I have also stuffed mushrooms with egg salad, crab and shrimp salad, Tabouleh, guacamole, curried ham, olive tapenade, eggplant relish, clams casino, lobster thermidor and what have you. They're versatile and ready to be filled with your best imagination. And if they don't match the color of the palms of your hands – don't buy them!

Funeral Chicken

Not that you are going to die but if you went out and picked your own mushrooms and didn't follow my instructions they might be cooking this dish for you. All joking aside, just about everyone has a favorite ritual that is served at funeral dinners and mine is no different. Thank God the woman that was in charge of cooking the chicken after the funeral is no longer with us for her chicken wasn't "to die for" but "to die from."

Way back when in the 50's and 60's the Lebanese community was quite thick. Tail end cousins and friends were still close, with the church being the major unifying factor. We had all started out in Utica, N. Y. but eventually strayed. One group migrated to Sherburne, N.Y., which was 40 miles away, and another moved to Clark Mills, N.Y., which was about 10 miles from Utica. The church was still the focal point and when someone from Utica died all of Sherburne and all of Clark Mills came to pay their respects and funeralize for a couple of days. Or if the shoe was on the other foot and someone in Sherburne passed on the Utica and Clark Mills people would show up in droves and the same for the Clark Mills. That poor Irish undertaker in Sherburne, he knew more Arabic than he wanted to tolerate. And everyone wore black. It was the order of the day. But alas that's all gone with the wind. Arabic is hardly spoken, no one wears black, no one sings to the dead anymore, and even that hysterical wailing is a thing of the past. Everything has been modernized and the poor corpse is lucky if they get three calling hours today.

But the funeral dinner has remained intact. Some things have changed. For instance, back then the food was all Arabic and a group of women would prepare feverishly on end for a feast that would be devoured in an hour. They would have the Lebanese dip, hommous, along with classic salad of Tabouleh, and then there would be Kibbee Naya, (a lamb version of Steak Tartar heavily spiced), Dolmades (stuffed grape Leaves), Mishee Coosa (stuffed squash with rice and lamb and tomato), Mishee Malfoof (rolled cabbage leaves), fried Kibbee (meat pies), Fah-toy-eed (spinach turnovers), Loub-ya (green beans in tomato sauce), Madjudrah (rice with lentils), eggplant marinated in garlic, labeen (homemade yogurt), Mediterranean olives and cheeses, and the usual dates, figs, salted almonds, homemade Pita bread and Baklava. It was a feast to be feasted upon. Oh God, I almost forgot - chicken. Aunt Muriel's chicken.

Aunt Muriel was a great lady and a great organizer and although she spoke Arabic she was fluent in English. You see, she was born in Utica so she was actually second generation Lebanese and a bit more modern than the old ladies in the kitchen. Whereas they were all dressed in black she wore black too but the collar had white trim. I guess you could call that a liberal rebellion. She was unmarried and always drove a fancy car. She had striking features. For instance, she had the most beautiful black hair and olive complexion you ever laid eyes on. Her teeth were perfectly white and her figure would make you take a double look. There are two things that make Lebanese women unique - either they are extremely beautiful or horrifically ugly. And Aunt Muriel had a face with a mole on her left chin, a moustache that wouldn't go away and a nose the size of an elephant. God rest her kind soul.

But her chicken. If she would only pull it out of the oven. She had the best intentions and she also had the driest chicken in town. And you had to eat it and tell her how good it was. Well, here's the recipe, minus the three hours or whatever the amount of cooking time she would keep it in the oven. No matter how dry it was and how many times we came close to breaking our teeth on it we still loved her…

Aunt Muriel's Baked Funeral Chicken

8 to 10 chicken breasts with the bone in
10 cloves of garlic sliced thin
1/2 cup of olive oil
1 lemon sliced thin
2 teaspoons each of salt and black pepper
2 teaspoons paprika

Preheat oven to 400°
Rinse chicken breasts under cold water
Remove and pat dry
In a large baking dish or Dutch oven add garlic and olive oil
Add chicken breasts skin side down
Sprinkle with half the salt, pepper and paprika
Bake in oven uncovered for 20 minutes.
Turn chicken breasts over and sprinkle with remaining salt, pepper, and paprika
Add lemon slices around the chicken
Continue to bake another 30 minutes basting occasionally.
Remove from oven and serve when ready.

Notes:

The garlic and lemon pieces are extremely tasty so you might not want to discard them.

You can also bake cut up chicken pieces the same way and in the same amount of time.

If you're baking half a chicken follow the same procedure but I find it usually takes between 1 1/4 to 1 1/2 hours when baking

The same procedure would be followed if you were baking a whole chicken but you might want to bake it 1 1/2 to 1 3/4 hours. If in doubt with a whole chicken use a food thermometer and cook to the poultry setting (165°).

Let's Have That One Again

Fr. Ireland is a good judge as to whether a dish is good, bad or indifferent. He never has a negative comment on any of the food but after his first bite or two the expression on his face usually tells you whether or not you have a hit on your hands. If he likes it he roars his approval with the perennial expression of "put that one on the menu." So these simple stuffed shells are on the menu and easy to prepare.

Baked Stuffed Shells

1 box of large jumbo shells

Filling:
2 16 oz. containers of ricotta cheese
2 lb. mozzarella cheese, shredded (reserve 1 cup)
1 cup grated parmesan
4 eggs
1 cup fine chopped parsley
1 1/2 teaspoons salt
1 teaspoon black pepper

1 quart of Marinara sauce**

Cook shells according to directions on the box, drain and rinse under cold water
Remove and set aside

Lightly oil the bottom of a large baking pan/dish
Mix the filling ingredients together thoroughly
With a tablespoon fill each individual shell with the cheese mixture and lay them in rows, top side up in the baking pan.
Cover with foil and bake for 20 to 30 minutes or until the cheese starts to bubble
Remove foil and pan from oven

Top with hot marinara sauce and sprinkle remaining mozzarella cheese over shells
Serve immediately or soon after. (if this sits too long after cooking the cheese and shells tend to get a little hard)

**If you prefer you can sauté a little broccoli in butter to pour over shells.

Broccoli Sauce

2 tablespoons butter
6 cloves of garlic sliced thin
3 tablespoons olive oil
2 cups of broccoli flowerets
1/4 cup of grated Romano cheese
1/2 teaspoon each of salt and pepper

Melt butter in pan. Add olive oil and garlic and sauté 1 minute
Add broccoli and stir fry 3 to 5 minute or until broccoli is tender
Add grated cheese, salt and pepper and pour over baked shells and serve
Red or green peppers and/or mushrooms can be added or used in place of broccoli.

Before Veal Became Scaloppini

The Italians in our neighborhood were poor enough to know that veal was the food of kings. If they were lucky they would get a shoulder blade (chop), which was usually an undesirable piece of meat and a scrap cast off to the dogs, bone and all. Quite a feast for the dog and such a waste to people who were hungry. An old Sicilian lady in our town told the story of her great grandmother who worked for an Italian Count. Instead of giving the chop to the dog she would trim off all the viable meat, throw the bone to the dog, take the meat home and make a Stuffato (Stew) and feed her family. The Stuffato she made was excellent. As to the authenticity of her story let me tell you she would attend early mass every Sunday, sit in the front pew, take communion and remain in her pew reciting the rosary until the next mass began an hour and a half later.

Stuffato

2 lbs. veal stew meat
2 cups flour for dredging
1/4 cup olive oil
1 large onion finely diced
3 cloves garlic minced
2 cups dry white wine
4 large carrots cut into 1/2" pieces
4 stalks of celery cut into 1/2" pieces
2 tablespoons fresh oregano chopped fine
3 tablespoons fresh basil chopped fine
1 teaspoon fresh thyme
1/2 cup fresh chopped parsley
2 bay leaves
1 1/2 teaspoons each of salt and pepper
1 lb of sliced or button mushrooms (optional)
1 6 oz. can tomato paste

Dredge veal pieces in flour until all are coated, set aside
Add oil to a large kettle and cook over medium heat for 3 minutes
Add veal pieces a few at a time until all are added and brown on all sides
Add onions and garlic and sauté for 2 minutes
Add white wine and bring to a boil
Add carrots, celery, basil, oregano, thyme, parsley, bay leaves, salt and pepper and continue to cook slowly for another hour.
Add tomato paste and mushrooms, continuing to simmer for a half hour or until meat is tender.
The longer it simmers the better it gets. If the stew is too thick and loses most of its liquid add a little cold water to thin it to the consistency you like, cooking as you go along.
I like serving this over wide noodles like papardelle or the bowties, farfelle.

Mangia Mia - she cooked liked she prayed. With love!

Potted Luck

Whenever I have a large group and I am uncertain as to what to give them to eat a good old fashioned Yankee Pot Roast does the trick. This is one of those recipes that uses a cheaper cut of meat that gets better the longer you cook it. A chuck roast works best.

1 Chuck Roast 4 to 5 lbs.
2 cups flour for dredging
1/4 cup olive oil
2 bunches green onions chopped fine
3 cloves of garlic, minced
6 carrots cut into 1 1/2" pieces
6 stalks of celery cut into 1 1/2" pieces
6 large Yukon Gold potatoes, quartered
1 lb mushrooms, quartered
1 1/2 cups of dry red wine
1 1/2 teaspoons thyme
3 bay leaves
1/2 cup chopped fresh parsley
1 1/2 teaspoons each of salt and pepper

Method:

Take chuck roast and dredge in flour until completely coated
Heat oil in large skillet or Dutch oven over medium flame for 3 minutes
Add chuck roast and brown each side for 5 minutes
Add onions and garlic and sauté 2 minutes longer
Add water, scraping sides of pan to get all bits and pieces
Add celery, carrots, thyme, bay leaves, salt and pepper and cook over low heat for 1/2 hour
Add red wine, parsley, bring to a boil and remove skillet from stove
Place skillet in a pre-heated oven at 350° and bake for 1 hour
Add potatoes and mushrooms and bake for another hour or until the meat breaks apart
Remove from oven and serve

Turkish Discipline

When you walked into a room full of elders and didn't bother to say hello or acknowledge anyone the adult with the most clout would call you into the middle of the room, reprimand you and make you go from person to person, shake hands and say hello.   Thus, for your own good sense, you learned to say hello.   Such was the case at my dad's house.   1948, 1950, somewhere around there the council was in session. My dad and his friends were sitting around the table drinking Turkish coffee, munching Lebanese cookies of almonds called Ca'aak, and eating diamond shaped delicacies of Baklava. And always there was a bottle of Arak, a licorice tasting liquor around 95% alcohol that had quite the lethal effect if not consumed in moderation. In our case it was used as a sweetener for the thick bitter tasting coffee, which added fuel to their heated conversations that covered everything from the greatness of President Roosevelt to the holiness of the Pope. The older you were the more clout you had in the group. One such man was Ummee Muharib. Most of the older men were called Ummee (Uncle) whether we were related or not. It was more or less a title of respect which he wore very well. Connoisseur and Judge. And Ummee Muharib's word was generally construed as law.

A big heavy kind of man with a protruding belly and long ear lobes, he was always at our table and everyone else's and ate his fill, but no one was ever at his. In fact no one was ever invited to his house nor can anyone ever remember getting a cup of coffee there. Even so, a place was always set for him at the table and when he had the floor you listened and didn't argue. One such instance revolved around a conversation about a neighbor's daughter and my sister, who had just graduated from high school. Our neighbor and my dad were contemplating sending the girls to college (a big step in those days) and Ummee Muharib, who had daughters of his own, said that women don't go to college and everyone heeded his word and they didn't go. Instead they stayed in the kitchen waited on the men and learned the art of making Ca'aak and Baklava. Such a pity, because most of the Lebanese families didn't send their daughters to college until the 1960's. Thank you Ummee Muharib for such insight. One little foot note about him before we get to the Baklava recipe.

Ummee Muharib's story is quite unique. When he migrated from Lebanon at the turn of the century his boat was quarantined at New York Harbor and its passengers were shipped to Mexico and let off the boat there. By a strange twist of fate he befriended a revolutionary group who guaranteed him passage to New York in exchange for a few pesos. The group got his pesos, Muharib was swindled, arrested, charged with stealing and shipped off to prison near the Texas border where their wagon was apprehended by the revolutionaries who had swindled him. They locked him in a shack and by another twist of fate he managed to escape. As he was about to cross the Rio Grande into Texas he was accosted by the man who was guarding him. Being the stronger of the two he killed the man and eventually made his way to the Lebanese community in Utica.

His troubles still weren't over. The local Maronite priest had heard of his ordeal and denied him absolution and refused to allow him into the church. Totally dismayed and deceived by his ouster and ostracism he became quite despondent and bitter. My dad, realizing his plight, went to the priest and belligerently pleaded his case until the priest relented, offered forgiveness, and welcomed him back into the fold (or so the story goes). By the way, Ummee Muharib raised a fine family of 5 or 6 children and the girls didn't go to college nor did he ever invite you to his house for a cup of coffee…

Ca'aak

for the dough:

4 cups flour
1 cup unsalted butter cut into cubes
3 tablespoons of rose or orange blossom water
5 tablespoons milk
Confectionary sugar for sprinkling

for the filling:

1 1/2 cups walnuts chopped fine
1/2 cup blanched almonds ground very fine, or 1 tablespoon almond paste
1/2 cup granulated sugar
2 teaspoons ground cinnamon
1 teaspoon ground allspice

Mix all filling ingredients together and set aside

Place flour in a food processor fitted with the dough blade
Add butter and turn machine on and process for 10 seconds
Add rose or orange blossom water and milk and process the mixture until it starts to form a ball. Turn off machine and remove dough
Take half dollar size lumps and roll into a ball and hollow with your thumb
Place a small teaspoonful of the filling in the hollow and then press the dough back over the filling to seal.
Arrange the cookies on a large baking tray about 1 1/2" apart.
Press them lightly with a fork to flatten them a little

Bake in 325° oven for 15 to 20 minutes, not letting the dough turn brown or the cookie dough will become hard

Let cool slightly and sprinkle with powdered sugar

Store in air tight container for a month, or freeze until ready to use.

"B'Laaywaa"

This section contains a recipe for the familiar diamond shaped Baklava as well as for an alternative. With the alternative recipe I make 1 1/2" rounds. I would caution you that if you are unfamiliar with working with phyllo dough it can be quite tricky. You have to work fast with it – otherwise it dries out and starts to break apart.

Bi-Laay-Waa, But-Lull-Waah, Ilhumdillah !!!!!
Baklava, Baklava, Thanks be to God!!!!!

Those were the words my mother would throw-up her hands and shout after she pulled her tray of Baklava from the oven. There on the kitchen table was her Bi-Laay-Waa, this large round pan with golden brown phyllo cut into a sea of diamond shaped squares, the aromas of nuts roasted in butter and sugar mixed with the scents of rose and orange waters filling the air. And "don't touch!" she would yell as you tried to nibble at the crispy air-like phyllo leaves. Then she would slowly pour the "attar," a deliciously syrupy mix of sugar and water, over the entire tray. She would let sit for a couple of hours before cutting out the diamond squares and serving. And you never cut into the B'Laaywaa until your mother had cut into it. If you took a piece, a lone cut up empty diamond square would give you away. What a ritual, every holiday.

B'Laaywaa (or Baklava)

1 package phyllo dough
1 lb of butter, melted

Filling:
2 lbs walnuts, chopped fine
1 cup sugar
1 tablespoon vanilla
1 tablespoon of rose water
1 tablespoon of orange water

Mix walnuts with 2 tablespoons of melted butter and the remaining filling ingredients.

Remove phyllo from package
Working quickly, lay a sheet of phyllo dough in the pan and butter it lightly.

Take another sheet and lay it squarely on top of the other and butter it lightly
Repeat until half the dough is in the pan.

Next, take the walnut mixture and spread it over the dough.

Repeat the above procedure with the remaining phyllo dough.

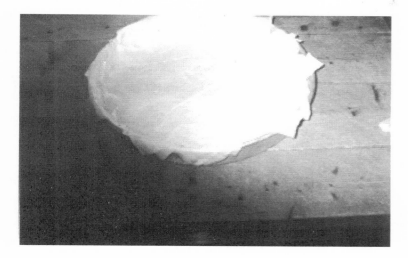

Cut the dough into diamond shapes.

Bake in 350° oven about 45 minutes or until the B'Laaywaa turns golden brown.
After the pan comes out of the oven, drizzle the syrupy attar slowly and evenly over the phyllo

Attar (sugar syrup)

2 cups water
2 cups sugar
1 tablespoon rose water

Bring mixture to a boil, lower heat to medium low and cook until the mixture gets silky on the edge of a spoon and gives a ribbon effect when you dip a spoon into the mix and pull it out.

Alternative to traditional recipe:

Working quickly, lay a sheet of phyllo dough on work surface and butter it lightly.
Take another sheet and lay it squarely on top of the other and butter it lightly
On the edge of the buttered phyllo add a row of walnuts about 3/4" round
Tightly, roll the phyllo like a cigar and butter lightly. (It will be a foot long)
Make a 1/4" deep incision into the phyllo every 1 and 1/2 inches working left to right
(you should get 10 incisions per roll)

Repeat the above process

Transfer to a large ungreased cookie tray and space them 1/2 inch apart and not touching
Repeat the above process. You should be able to get 9 to 10 'cigars'

Bake in 350° oven 20 to 30 min. or until the phyllo roll turns golden brown
Slice the roll all the way through at the incisions and keeping the phyllo intact
Drizzle the syrupy attar* slowly and evenly over the phyllo

Arrange on trays and serve. I like putting them in muffin wrappers. Makes them easier to handle.

Store in air tight containers. They will hold on the shelf for 2 to 3 weeks, store up to a month and a half refrigerated, and freeze about 1 1/2 years.

Midfudlack - Eat and enjoy

Upsee Daisy

There is a funny story regarding B'Laaywaa. In 1950 or 1951 my cousin Daisy, a new bride, made a tray of B'laaywaa to send to her husband Louie, a soldier in the U.S. Army, stationed in Korea during the war. When it arrived, Louie and a bunch of buddies eagerly awaited digging into it. When they unwrapped the package and cut into it the nuts were green. Without tasting it they surmised it was spoiled and threw it into the garbage. Little did they know that poor Cousin Daisy had run out of walnuts and used pistachios instead. I guess the boys figured that after crossing the ocean and two continents it was just too much for the pastry to endure. What they didn't know was baklava has a shelf life of three to four months if properly covered.

Daisy Joseph, in the middle (author is 4th from the left)

Daisy was Uncle Sam's daughter. Uncle Sam didn't like her husband Louie because he thought he was too short for her. They had five children and were as true as any Lebanese family could have been. After Uncle Sam died in 1953 they came to Sherburne for Christmas dinner every year until the kids rebelled and refused to leave their home and presents. Plus, they said my older brothers thought of them more as nuisances than cousins. That might have been partially true, but my younger brother Rich and I really enjoyed having them. I can still see them pulling up in their Mercury station wagon and someone yelling, "here come the Josephs."

Daisy died in 1983, a victim of breast cancer and to this day is sorely missed. Louie is the grand patriarch of the family today and just recently turned 80. The family wanted to throw a huge birthday party for him and he told them if they did he wouldn't show up. Daisy once said to me, "we didn't have a lot of money but we managed to raise a fine family," and thus they did.

I still wish she was around for then I would be able to get to the bottom of who coined the phrase, "Sherburne, Sherburne, You are It. S.H. for Sherburne, I. T.!" Her daughters, Theresa, Eva and Mary, say I coined it but I know damn well it was them…

Eva and Louie Joseph

Theresa Joseph Fitzsimmons, George, Louie Joseph, Rich Lewis, Mary Joseph Tomaselli

A Lettuce Story

My Dad had a grocery store in the 1930's and one day he went out and bought a case of lettuce and put it outside the store and put a sign up that said 10 cents a head. At the end of the day he hadn't sold a head. A bit discouraged by the lack of sales he put the lettuce out at 10 cents again. Uncle Tony Mody (on my mother's side) came by and he asked my father what was wrong and he told him about the lettuce. Uncle Tony yells at my father and says "What are you, crazy? You can't sell it at 10 cents a head. You gotta get for them 2 for a quarter." An hour later my father had sold all the lettuce.

Our House Salad

1 head of Romaine Lettuce
1 head of Iceberg Lettuce
1 Head of Leaf Lettuce

Soak Lettuce in Cold Water 15 minutes, remove and drain in colander for 1 hour
Cut lettuce in nice 1 to 1 1/2" pieces and add to salad bowl

On top of that add:
1 Red onion cut in 1/8" slices
3 Tomatoes cut in wedges
Cut 1 Cucumber in half lengthwise, scoop out seeds and cut into 1/4" slices
Drizzle 3 to 4 tablespoons of olive oil over the salad
Sprinkle 1/2 tablespoon salt over it
Add 2 to 3 tablespoons of cider vinegar

Toss together lightly, but thoroughly.
Serve immediately.

Every once in a while I add about 3/4 cup of crumbly Bleu cheese

The secret to our house salad and its crispness is that the oil is poured over the lettuce then the salt and then the vinegar and in that order. The oil marries lettuce and the salt and vinegar enhance it. If you don't follow that order it won't be as good.

Fresh herbs like mint, basil, thyme, and oregano are great additions and I generally use about 3 to 4 tablespoons of them. Sometimes separate and sometimes mixed.

A Couple of More Salads

One salad I find particularly well received is our Shredded Carrot Salad. It's a crowd pleaser and a big hit with ladies, especially in the 40 to 70 age group. It's appealing, vegetarian, Vegan and invaded by Middle-East herbs and spices. A couple of things you can do - shred your own carrots or buy already shredded carrots from your local market.

Shredded Carrot Salad

5 cups shredded carrots
1 cup of regular or golden raisins
1/2 cup of maraschino cherries cut into quarters
1 cup of pineapple chunks chopped up
1 cup mandarin oranges
3 tablespoons olive oil
2 tablespoons cider vinegar
1 tablespoon sugar
1/2 teaspoon salt and 1/2 teaspoon pepper
2 tablespoons mayonnaise (optional)

Mix all the above together in a bowl and toss thoroughly. Refrigerate until ready to serve. Mix again before serving.

Rice Salad

This was created with left-over rice and vegetables. After putting it together and serving it to the guests they really gave me mixed reactions.

4 to 6 cups of cooked rice
2 cups left-over vegetables, diced, or 1 package frozen mixed vegetables (cooked)
1 cup chopped green onion (any diced onion will do)
1/2 cup fresh chopped parsley
1/2 cup of grated or shredded cheese
3 tablespoons olive oil
2 tablespoons cider or tarragon vinegar
1/2 teaspoon each of salt and pepper

In a large bowl mix all the above ingredients together. Chill until ready to serve. Remove from refrigerator 1 hour before serving.

As I was removing the near empty salad bowl one guest surprisingly remarked that it was an interesting use of leftovers. She was an overnight guest and we had served rice and vegetables for dinner the night before...

Unappealing and Unappealing and Unappealing!

If I ever encounter another of those spiffy trays of baby broccoli, carrots, cherry tomatoes and ranch dip I am going to trip up the well-meaning, thoughtful person who brought it and let it spill all over the place, only to clean up and dispose of the mess, apologizing profusely for bumping the person over (before his or her deli platter disrupted the food on my table).

This recently happened at a funeral reception. It wasn't the first time this had happened but this time around I handled a situation that could have become delicate very quickly by setting up a smaller table for all the foods that weren't on the menu. Not that food is unwanted; it's more that the reception was being overwhelmed. Three separate trays of broccoli, carrots and such. And none of it gets eaten, never. Then come the meat and cheese platters garnished with green kale and giant Kaiser rolls, and cheese, pickles and olives.

Imagine this: Baked Virginia Ham, glazed with honey mustard and cloves, garnished with fresh sliced peaches. A hand carved roast turkey and roast beef and horseradish sauce. A bowl of cavatelli with garlicky broccoli and roasted red peppers. An old fashioned potato salad, asparagus and tomatoes in a vinaigrette of fresh mint and chives, French crusty bread, chilled melon balls with strawberries and chocolate dipping sauce. In come the aforementioned deli platters. Setting up the smaller table worked very nicely. If you didn't want the foods on the buffet you could go to the deli platter table, make a sandwich and a few of that sub-sandwich culture did just that and thought they were in hero heaven. Those that ate from the laden out buffet table were the real connoisseurs of food. My table wasn't as upset as I would have been had all the food made its way to the head table.

My suggestion to the people who want to send food in a situation like this is to continue to send food. The families not only can use it, but they're grateful for your thoughtfulness and will consume it. No one is in the mood to cook so food prepared becomes a blessing and one less thing to deal with. But use a bit of imagination the next time and send a ham or pasta or a casserole, a green salad, a fruit platter or even a pizza or two, but please omit the veggie plate, the cold cuts and such, just like the obituary asks you to do with the flowers.

Remember there is always someone out there who will send those platters and that's great. You just send something that's tasty. That's the difference.

Uh Lan Wan Suh Lan

A traditional Lebanese welcome – hands extended out with hugs and kisses. That was the custom. These were our cousins, "The Saads". Although that was our last name too until it got changed at Ellis Island they were able to retain theirs. How they got through the gate is a mystery. There were three first cousins: Michael, Elias, and Najib, all with the last name of Saad. When they came to America my cousin Mike got the last name of George, my dad got Lewis and Najib retained Saad. Kind of confusing but they all remained very close.

Najib married Catherine Koury and they had five children. We referred to her as K'net Umee (cousin on your father's side). We never knew her husband because he passed this world around 1929, leaving her pregnant with her fifth child who was born a few months later. They were very poor and my dad kind of became the grand patriarch of this clan. One day somewhere in the 1930's Louis and John Saad wanted to purchase this auto garage and start a business. They couldn't get a bank loan anywhere. Hearing about this my dad went to the bank president in Sherburne, explained the situation and was able to secure a business loan for them on his good word. Thus began their road to good fortune and the rest is history. They went into the hearing aid industry and became successful, bringing the whole family into the business. It still flourishes today with their children now running their business. Whenever one of them phones nowadays I usually answer and say "what, I can't hear you? Hello?"

They are a classy bunch. Generous, hospitable, fine cars, expensive jewelry, trendy clothes and the like. We get together every couple of years for a reunion and they're great to be around. They are also musically inclined, with a talent of great voices that continues today. So when you get together you can always expect a music fest of some sort. My cousin, Jimmy Jr., really has one hell of a voice, which causes the church to shake with his rendition of the "Our Father." About the time he reaches "Give us this day", the tears start to roll and by the time he gets to "And deliver us from Evil" there isn't a dry eye in the place. I can't remember the rest of the prayer but when he gets done you can call it 'mission accomplished.' I've already booked him for my funeral.

One quality they lacked was that they (according to my mother) were not good cooks. I never had their Arabic cooking but my mother was a good authority on that subject. They did make great feta cheese chunks, which were generally a delight served with breakfast.

Beatrice Bach Saad, Jim Saad, George Lewis, Louis Saad, John Saad, Jenny Saad Eddo, Mike Eddo

Marinated Feta Cheese Chunks

3 to 5 garlic cloves peeled
1/2 cup fresh lemon juice
1 lb. fresh soft feta
5 to 6 sprigs of summer savory or thyme
2 or 3 bay leaves crushed
1 tsp black peppercorns
Zest of 1 lemon (optional)
1 1/2 cups olive oil

Soak garlic cloves in lemon juice overnight, 24 hours
Drain and pat dry the garlic cloves
Let feta drain for an hour and cut into 3/4" chunks (squares)
Layer the feta, bay leaf, thyme, garlic, peppercorns and lemon zest in a half quart canning jar with a tight fitting lid
Fill the jar with olive oil
Seal the jar and refrigerate for 7 to 10 days.
Keep refrigerated for 3 weeks after opening.

Ummee Saad

Ummo or Ummee is uncle in Arabic. Ummo was my father's younger brother and known as Uncle Sam. Uncle Sam lived in the city and would usually come and stay with us on weekends. I would absolutely hate it because his bedroom was next to mine and he would loudly snore all night long. But I liked him because he would always bring me and my younger brother presents when he came. Mostly he would come by bus but other times he would come with friends and my mother would prepare something Arabic and rightfully delicious.

One time he brought this friend of his, an Italian guy who was a chef in Utica at the then famous Grimaldis restaurant. After eating a Lebanese dinner that my mother had prepared, to show his appreciation, he taught her how to make pizza and lasagna. At this time (late 1940's) these now ubiquitous Italian specialties were virtually unheard of in the Sherburne (Chenango Valley) area. The pizza was thin crusted and just served with tomato sauce on it – no cheese. That came years later. Little did that man know that in 1948 or '49 people in the Chenango Valley and the surrounding areas got their first bite of pizza and their introduction to lasagna from Lewis' Restaurant in Sherburne.

Lewis' Restaurant today

They became main staples at the family restaurant, along side Spaghetti, Chicken-In-The-Basket, and T-Bone Steaks. As for the lasagna it took a bit longer to catch on but rumor has it that in 1950 my mother went to a covered dish supper and mesmerized everyone with the now famous dish. It became popular on the menu and cost 10 cents more per order than spaghetti and meat balls.

For the longest time the Lewis' were the only ones serving those two dishes. Then in the late 50's, Gary Steffenelli of Norwich started serving both of the items in his restaurant, Grove Park, the same exact way that we did. My mother always chided him for stealing the dish from us. There is an irony here and that is that Norwich was 30% Italian and those in the restaurant business did not start serving these items until Grove Park put them on their menu. For years Lewis' was known for the best Italian food around...

The other funny thing about Lewis' serving this Italian food was that we did one hell of a business from Norwich, especially with the Italian community. Back then my sister June and I were waiting on tables and 'Norwich Italians' would come in and order our sizzling steaks and always have a baked potato or French fries. June and I could never figure out why they would never eat our spaghetti because we had the best. Eventually we found out that that's all they ever ate at home and the steak and potato were quite the treat…

Back to Uncle Sam. He was quite the maverick. He ran a coffee shop that specialized in gambling and illegal booze, catering to all the top officials in the city. In fact he was on a first name basis with all of them. You wanted a favor, you went to Uncle Sam. You needed a driver's license he sent you to see the motor vehicle commissioner, who had you drive around the block then took you upstairs to get your license. You took care of Uncle Sam and he took care of the commissioner. And for the sake of a good bottle of whiskey another bad driver hit the road.

And garlic. He reeked of it. He ate it with everything. That's to say he did after he peeled a few cloves, pounded them with a little salt to make a paste and then drizzled two or three tablespoons of olive oil into the paste and swirled it around.   That was his condiment for everything. He would toss it with home-made macaroni, pour it over tomatoes with mint and green onions, dip his chicken into it or pour it over his Marook (Arab flatbread) when he made a wrap sandwich back then.

Ummee's Zayit B' Toomb (olive oil and garlic)

6 to 7 cloves of garlic peeled
1 ½ teaspoons salt

In a small bowl make the garlic paste with the garlic and the salt.
Drizzle in olive oil and stir around a couple of times.

Serve at room temperature
Refrigerate when not using.

About the only delineation from this would be a squeeze of lemon or two.

Mockroomtoom (home-made macaroni and garlic)

One day in the early 1950's Ummee Saad came over to my sister June's house and told her he wanted her to make Mockroomtoom, otherwise known as homemade macaroni with garlic. She explained that she didn't know how to make it. He told her that all she needed was flour, water and salt, and that it was a simple dish to prepare. What he didn't tell her was that it would create one hellish mess and half the day to prepare. But back then when a male member of the family wanted something, especially an uncle, you did it and with very little argument. Male hierarchy was the rule and women still accepted their second class status. If you went for a ride the men sat in front and the women to the rear. Just like priests the men ate first and were dutifully waited on by the lot of females in their lives. Kids didn't really count; you ate if there was a place available or ate with the women. Not until the 1960's did mothers start feeding the kids first. (unless the house was orthodox; then all males ate first). The hierarchy was breaking.

Method:

Homemade macaroni is easy. You take 5 lbs of flour, put it in a large bowl and make a 4" by 4" well in the middle of the flour so it resembles a large donut. Sprinkle with salt.

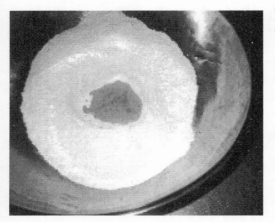

Next, you gradually add 2 cups of water to the well (optionally, this water can be combined with 2 lightly beaten eggs).

With a fork or with your hands slowly cave the sides of the well into the water, continuing to add the water slowly to the flour mixture.   Work vigorously until all the water is absorbed into the flour. When the water is all absorbed, the dough should have a consistency a little stickier than pizza dough.

Sprinkle a handful of flour over a large surface. Flour your hands. Cut a 2" by 2" piece of the dough off and roll it out between your hands until it gets 4 to 5 inches long.

Lay it on surface and continue to roll it until it resembles a large tootsie roll.

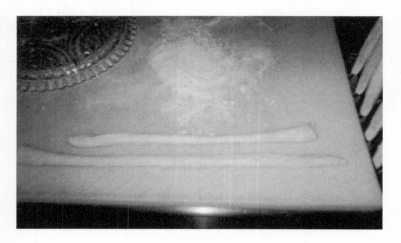

Cut off 1" pieces.

Turn a ribbed basket or a cut glass dish upside down, sprinkle it with flour and take a piece and roll it over the glass to get a ribbed look and lay them in neat rows on lightly floured waxed or parchment paper. Continue the process until all the dough is gone.

In a large kettle bring 7 to 8 cups of water to a boil and add 1 tablespoon of oil and 1 teaspoon salt. Drop the ribbed macaroni's into the water 1 or 2 at a time, working very quickly until all are dropped. Stir the kettle lightly but thoroughly and continue until the macaronis float to the top. Remove from stove and drain in a large colander and transfer to a large bowl. Pour Zayit B' Toom (garlic and oil) over macaroni, mixing it thoroughly.

At our house we mix it in an aged old wooden bowl and a dish filled with halves of lemons for you to squeeze over the Mockroomtoom, and cut willow branches into little spears to eat it with. Not only do we like it hot but it's as good the next day cold. What a wonderful Arabian delight.

Small Town Girls, Won't You Come Out Tonight?

Once upon a time there were two sisters that lived in a tiny, tiny village called "the four corners", which was half way between somewhere and nowhere. One sister was beautiful, wonderful, stylish and wise. The other sister was also beautiful, flirtatious, garishly trendy and was dubbed "wicked." Woe for the "good sister" who didn't follow the latest trends, nor flirt outrageously with the other sex, nor dress outlandishly, nor hang out with girlfriends that made spectacles of themselves. The good sister was content to be a free spirit, design her own wardrobe, immerse herself in good literature, pick wildflowers and enjoy one or possibly two mint juleps on Derby Day. She was a connoisseur of fine wines, good foods and a gourmet cook of her own, being a graduate of the George Lewis Cooking Classes in the 1980's, in which she successfully completed 14 courses.

One day the good sister left the tiny, tiny, village went to a big city, became the head honcho of a quality arts and crafts store and met her "prince charming". She is living happily to this day, offering the fine décor accessories one would find in Architectural Digest to the folks of the big city, making everyone's lives a little more chic.

Joanne, Vince Quinn, Patti, and Cindy Lewis (Rich Lewis' wife)

On the other hand, Sister Wicked has had her ups and downs. She too left for the big city after breaking the hearts of a few of the "local boys" and also became a successful businesswoman, continuing all her outlandish, garish ways, breaking the hearts of a few of the big city boys and having more than 2 mint juleps on the day of the Derby. But alas, the wicked sister reformed her ways, married her old childhood sweetheart, became a respectable member of society, shed her garish outfits, started wearing cardigans, quit going to K-Mart to get her hair done and the rest is history. But she still can be deceiving. On the day of my 67th birthday she called me up at 3 in the afternoon to wish me a happy birthday. I was wondering how in the hell she knew it was my birthday as we talked away for a half hour. Later that night she showed up for my surprise birthday party, acting like nothing had happened. Now you see why we dubbed her "wicked".

Even though she wasn't a graduate of my cooking school (still don't think she could pass the boiling water entrance exam) she made a wickedly good Baked Lasagna. All who ate it lived to tell about it. She never gave me the recipe but I figured out what she had in it and she never argued the point when I confronted her. Both girls are very close, devoted to each other and their elderly parents, Betty and Carl. What more can one say about the sisters from that tiny, tiny, village of Sherburne Four Corners that still doesn't have its own zip code. By the way the wicked sister's name is Patti. JoAnne is still as heavenly as one of God's angels.

Baked Lasagna

1 package lasagna noodles cooked or 10 sheets of frozen pasta 9" by 13"

2 lbs. of ground chuck
2 lbs of hot sausage
Salt and pepper to taste

1 quart of Ricotta cheese
2 lbs. of shredded mozzarella cheese
2 cups of grated Parmesan or Romano Cheese
4 raw eggs
1 cup fresh chopped parsley

1 quart of tomato or Marinara Sauce

Crumble and sauté the sausage until browned
Add ground chuck and continue to sauté until it browns.
Add salt and pepper
Drain the juices from the pan and add 1 cup of tomato sauce, stir and set aside.

Mix together Ricotta, Parmesan, parsley, eggs and half of the mozzarella cheese
Stir thoroughly

Lightly oil the bottom of a 13" by 9" pan
Lay a sheet of pasta in pan
Spread 1/3 of cheese mixture over this and sprinkle 1/4 of mozzarella cheese over it
Put another pasta sheet over this
Cover with 1/3 of the meat mixture and sprinkle 1/4 mozzarella cheese over it
Repeat this process until you reach the top of the pan
Lay a final sheet of pasta and spread tomato sauce evenly over it.
Sprinkle remaining mozzarella cheese over this.

Cover with foil and bake in 350° oven for 45 minutes.
Remove foil and bake another 15 minutes.
Remove from oven and let it set for 10 to 15 minutes before cutting into.
Serve by cutting into squares 3" by 3"
Have extra sauce on hand to pour over individual servings.

If you cannot find the frozen pasta sheets cook the ribbons of Lasagna according to the directions on the package using about 4 of the wide ribbons per layer.

If you have leftovers, cut into squares and wrap individually and freeze them.

This can also be made a day or two ahead of time and baked when ready to serve. You can also freeze the whole tray unbaked and bring it out, thaw it and bake. You won't lose any of the flavor.

Aunt June and Anchovies

Whenever my sister June would order a pizza she would always tell them to omit the anchovies. They would make her deathly ill. She wasn't a big fan of seafood and she was overly fond of Italian food. She knew her pasta and she knew how it should be cooked. Her favorite was stovepipes, better known today as rigatoni. She always ordered it "al dente" or firm to the touch. If it wasn't to her liking, lord there was hell to pay.

One particular day, with the whole family gathered, I decided to do my famous Linguine with Anchovy Sauce. I wouldn't have made it but when June had said she wasn't coming I went ahead with it. It's another one of those simple sauces that you can prepare while the pasta is cooking. Kind of like the Roman version of "Salsa de Harlot", where the ladies of the night would cook this simple tomato sauce and serve it with spaghetti, as it was the custom to feed the men who were paying for their services. Kind of like going to a dinner dance where you get two for the price of one.

Anyhow, to make the anchovy sauce:

Warm 3 tablespoons of olive oil in a pan
Add 3 to 4 cloves of garlic sliced thin and sauté until very lightly browned
Add 4 or 5 anchovy fillets and mash with a spoon into the sauce
Continue to sauté and add 1/2 cup of sliced black olives and 1/2 cup of fresh chopped parsley
Season with 1/2 teaspoons red pepper flakes
Add a cup of dry white wine and simmer for another 5 minutes
Cook linguine to al dente stage, add linguine to the sauce, stir lightly and top with fresh grated parmesan or Romano cheese or both and serve.

June Lewis Scheiffer

And that's exactly what I was proceeding to do when Aunt June, who had changed her mind and decided to join the festivities, came to dinner. She never refused any kind of pasta. Well, we were all chomping along, June being on her third plate, enjoying every morsel, when the 'hudda' hit the pan. A friend of mine asked her to please pass the linguine with anchovy sauce. I can still see her now. She jumped up, made an awful face, pushed the plate to the side and said "I can't eat this." My friend, who knew the June didn't like anchovies, started to smirk and we have all laughed like hell over that story ever since. It was really a mind over matter scenario but you couldn't tell her that. She never got sick and never mentioned the story to anyone and hated anchovies with a vengeance.

Poor June, may her soul rest in peace, had been duped. If it hadn't been mentioned she would have gone for another plate and truly enjoyed her dinner. She never trusted pasta with a white sauce ever again...

Coosa - Coosa

If you're a frequent visitor to the farmers market there is a light green squash that is relatively new to the American vegetable scene but as old as the culture of the Middle East. It's called coosa.** Like a zucchini it is much shorter and a bit fatter. The ideal size is about 5 inches long and 1 1/2 inches wide.

But a funny thing happens to the coosa if you don't harvest it at the ideal size. Like zucchini it gets pretty big if left to grow. My mother always let a few grow for two reasons. One, to collect the seeds for next years planting and the other to make slices about 1/4" thick to deep fry in olive oil until they were lightly browned, removed from the pan to paper towels to drain and sprinkled lightly with salt and set aside until ready to serve or make a sandwich with. They were good warm, room temperature or cold. I would prefer them between good crusty Italian bread versus filling the pocket of the pita bread. Or they were served as a side dish. The uniqueness of them was the subtle sweetness of the dish that resonated summer. Another nice thing is that the slices freeze well and can be had all year long.

Fried Coosa

2 large Coosa about 10 to 12" long and 3" wide, cut into 1/4" slices
2 cups olive oil (vegetable or canola oil can be substituted)

In a large skillet bring oil to a medium high heat
Add slices one at a time until the surface is covered. Do not lie on top of each other.
Deep fry until golden brown, remove with slotted spoon to a paper towel to drain and sprinkle lightly with salt.

Continue the process until all are cooked.
Serve when ready to eat.

** Most farmers who sell coosa really are at a loss to tell you how to prepare this squash and have relied on their customers to tell them how to prepare them. Most of their customers are Arabic, speak broken English, and leave the farmers perplexed as to how to prepare the coosa. Still, they continue to grow the squash because the Arab people continue to buy them.

P.S. I have cooked and baked them the way I do zucchini and have had good success. They're quite versatile and sweeter than yellow squash or zucchini. Also good with butter and cheese.

Stuffed Coosa

The ideal way to serve coosa is to stuff it. But first you have to hollow out the squash. For this you would need a minqara - a tool used to hollow out cucumbers, eggplants and squash. It is available in Middle Eastern import stores. If you can't find this tool, a good apple or pear corer will do.

To hollow out the coosa, you want to cut off the top of the stem, about 3/4 of inch from the top. Your base should be about the size of a quarter. Insert your minqara and go down to about 1/2" from the bottom and start scooping out the pulp, working in a circular pattern, making sure to leave about 1/4 wall to the skin. Try not to make any holes in the skin. Discard the pulp or mix it with a little butter and cheese and bake until golden brown.

The author, hollowing out the coosa

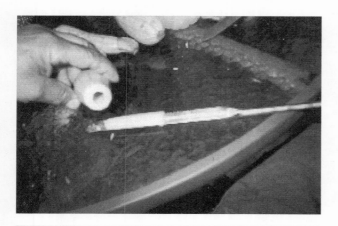

Hollowed out coosa, with tool

Hollowed out coosa

Now to make the hushwee:

2 cups of raw long grain rice
1lb. of raw ground lamb
1 bunch of fresh chopped parsley
1 1/2 cups of fresh mint leaves or 3 tablespoons crumbled dried
1 teaspoon each of cinnamon, allspice, and cumin.
1 1/2 teaspoons of salt and 1 tsp black pepper
 1 16 oz can of tomato sauce
Juice of one fresh lemon.

Mix all hushwee ingredients together thoroughly and set aside.

Take a teaspoon and using the hushwee mix start stuffing your coosa. I like using the handle of a wooden spoon because after the first teaspoon of stuffing is inserted it works great to push the mixture to the bottom. Keep adding stuffing until it is level with the top of the coosa. Repeat until finished.

Using a saucepan or Dutch oven about 10 to 13" in diameter, stand the coosas next to each other upright until the kettle is filled.

Take a can of plum tomatoes and pour it over them evenly. Add enough cold water to come up to 3/4 of the pan. Add 2 or 3 cloves of peeled garlic, cover with a tight fitting lid and bring mixture to a boil. Lower flame to a simmer and cook another 40 to 50 minutes. Remove from stove and using a slotted spoon lay the coosas on a large serving platter and ladle remaining sauce over them. Serve warm, with a side bowl of plain yogurt to spoon over them.

A Dish For All Seasons

One amazing aspect of growing up in an ethnic household was that most of us were poor and a good deal of the food we ate was usually grown in gardens in the backyard. The wonderful thing about it all is that we are still eating and carrying out the traditions of the foods that our grandparents brought over to this country with them. And certain foods to this day are prepared for the seasons. Dandelions are still dug out of the ground in early spring when they are young and tender. Grape leaves are picked in early summer and desserts like Baklava are still made for the holidays. To this day if I don't go out and dig the greens in spring or pick the grape leaves before the 4th of July or make Baklava at Christmas or Easter a certain sense of guilt erodes me and I feel as if I have missed out on an important event. To this day if I don't pick a pail of blackberries by the first week of August it's like committing a mortal sin.

Such customs must be observed in order to be preserved. With the advent of refrigeration, freezers, and green grocers these foods can be had all year long, but I challenge anyone who has not savored the taste of a blackberry picked straight from the bush or tasted a dandelions fresh from the ground versus a bunch bought at the produce department to try this and compare their flavors.

Another trite pet peeve I would like to address is the so called discovery in the last thirty years or so of the 'new American Cuisine', where established and up and coming chefs have discovered fresh and regional victuals being used in their cooking. They and the food writers behave as if they had discovered a new wonder of the world. They probably should have visited the apple and berry groves of the Amish people down in Pennsylvania or been in old Philomena Pepe's kitchen in our town and watched her make tomato sauce with yellow tomatoes or sampled some of my grandmothers Chili Sauce made with plum tomatoes and Portuguese hot peppers. Fortunately, after 60 or 70 years, Gourmet Magazine and the Food Network finally caught up with what they were doing in their kitchens. Garlic, olive oil and basil have been in our cuisines for the last seven or eight thousand years. They probably would have unearthed many more secrets like arugula, chives, wild sorrel, wood mushrooms, fresh young horseradish leaves or tansy leave to make tea with.

Just recently I read an article about ramps (wild leeks) starting to show up at farmers markets. Hell, you didn't dare eat them or you would be ostracized in school for they left such a foul odor on your breath that no one would get near you. But there was an old farm lady in our town who would sauté them and serve them as a vegetable and they were the sweetest green you would taste. It would smell the hell out of the house for days but oh the taste. Again they were one of the first signs of spring, covering the forest floor with their lemony green color. Another was cow slips. These shiny green leaves look like nasturtium leaves. You would usually find them in swamps or wet fields and had to pick them before their bright yellow flowers appeared. We would sauté them briefly with spring onions. I'm afraid all of this will become extinct as not too many people have the know how to recognize what they're looking for. Oh well, so much for sweet potato fries and puréed yucca on a bed of fried plantains....

Sautéed Greens

With the abundance of fresh greens year round I still enjoy cooking them and serving them as a bed for fish or chicken to lie on. Unlike spinach and other greens that used to be cooked to death years ago I find that I like to briefly stir fry them and serve them in an al dente stage with a crunchiness to the bite.

1 bunch fresh greens such as endive, escarole, spinach, Swiss chard or dandelions, cut up
1 bunch green onion chopped fine
2 cloves garlic sliced fine
1/2 cup olive oil
Salt and pepper to taste
Squeeze of fresh lemon juice

In large skillet sauté onion and garlic briefly for a minute or two.
Add greens and stir thoroughly.
Add salt and pepper and continue to stir fry for about another minute or until the greens are wilted.
Squeeze lemon over greens and serve.

The old Italian ladies in our neighborhood would drain the juice from the greens, bottle it and refrigerate it and drink a sip or two to ward off colds and fevers. The first sip was horrifyingly bitter. But then the second sip or two had a gratifying taste that left a certain sweetness in your mouth. Those that practiced this ritual lived long beyond their expected years.

Greens and Beans

Prepare the greens the same as the sautéed greens in the above recipe.
Instead of cooking the greens briefly, stir and continue to cook for three or four minutes.
Add 2 cans of *cannelloni beans, salt and pepper to taste and 1/2 teaspoon of thyme.
Stir and continue to cook over low heat for 20 to 30 minutes.
Give a squeeze of fresh lemon and serve.

*Black-eyed peas, garbanzo or Great Northern beans can be substituted in place of the cannelloni.
Dried beans instead of canned can also be used, following the directions on the package to cook the dried beans.

Chicken and Rice

A popular dish at most holiday dinners that usually sat beside the turkey was Chicken and Rice. Why we served turkey when we had all these other foods is unknown to me, but then when in America, do as the Americans do. Certainly it was quite hard to explain at school that we always had Jaag el Mishee, or chicken and rice. Wanting not to be left out my mother always made turkey although I'm sure most of it hit the garbage can because no one ate it. It was more symbolic than anything else and we could at least tell our teacher that we had the big bird and were right in tune with what the Americans were serving. The Italians had the same problem serving Spaghetti and Meat Balls and Antipasto. I'm positive their turkey hit the garbage can too.

Jaag El Mishee

1 frying chicken, 2 to 3 lbs.
1 medium onion, diced fine
3 stalks of celery, chopped fine
1 cup of parsley, chopped fine
1/2 cup of mint, chopped fine
1 cup of raw lamb diced
1 cup pignolia nuts
2 tablespoons of butter
2 cups of long grain rice uncooked
Salt and pepper to taste
4 to 5 cups of water

In a large stockpot add 4 cups of cold water
Add chicken, onion, celery, 1/2 cup parsley, salt and pepper
Cook chicken until tender and meat is ready to fall off the bones
Remove chicken, set aside to cool and reserve broth
In a large skillet sauté lamb, remaining parsley, mint, salt and pepper until cooked
Remove mixture and set aside

In same skillet add butter and pignolia nuts and sauté until golden brown
Add rice, 4 cups of reserved chicken broth and cook slowly until the rice is cooked
Pick chicken meat from the bones and add to the rice mixture stirring well.
Transfer to large serving platter and serve.

A bowl of plain yogurt is a nice condiment to serve on the side, to be ladled over the rice and chicken.

My mother was heavy on the salt and pepper, which always intensified the flavor of her dishes.

This is a very popular dish in the Middle East with many variations. The distinguishing factor between the Lebanese and the rest of their Arab brethren is that the Lebanese dish it out to you on individual plates whereas in other Levantine countries they serve it on a big tray, put it in the middle of the rug on the floor and everyone digs their fingers/hands into it. Forks? Heaven no - not in the desert!

Malfoof, Malfoof

In the fall the cabbage trucks would come rolling through, with the backs of their trucks loaded with cabbage, heading to the cabbage factory where they made sauerkraut. En route they would stop off at my dad's place for a quick shot and a beer. Probably to take a break from the smell of cabbage. But anyhow, a free "one for the road", offered to the truck driver, would usually yield a bushel or two of cabbage, which would always be put to good use. Cabbage salad for the Friday night fish fries and Mishee-Ma-Foof, stuffed cabbage leaves. Different from the rest of the world, the Lebanese used lamb instead of ground beef and also infused the filling with a little mint to enhance the flavor. That always separated ours from the Gwumpies made famous by the Polish and their eastern European neighbors. It also would produce a lot of arguments as to whose cabbage was original. I think ours had more flavor.

Mishee-Malfoof (stuffed cabbage)

1lb diced raw lamb meat or ground lamb
2 cups uncooked long grained rice, washed and drained
1 cup for fresh chopped parsley
1 cup fresh mint chopped or 1/2 cup dried
2 16 oz. cans tomato sauce, reserving one can
1 teaspoon each of salt and pepper
1 large head of cabbage
4 cloves garlic sliced thin
4 quarts boiling water

In large bowl mix rice, lamb, parsley, mint, 1 can tomato sauce, salt and pepper

Cut around the stem of cabbage (core) so the leaves are loosened. Do not break away leaves from cabbage
Place cabbage in boiling water 3 to 4 minutes until leaves soften
Remove from water and drain
Take a leaf and place a tablespoon of rice mixture on it and roll tightly. They should be about an inch thick. It's important to roll tightly so they won't unfold
Place rolled cabbage in a 4 quart saucepan side by side until you have a layer
Sprinkle a little of the garlic over it.

Continue to add another layer, adding garlic after each layer until you are out of the mixture and leaves.
Add remaining can of tomato sauce over the leaves.
Place a heavy plate on top of rolls and slowly add enough cold water to just reach the top of the plate
Leave plate in place, cover saucepan tightly and bring the saucepan to a boil
Reduce flame to a simmer and cook 1 hour until done.
Remove lid and plate and gently arrange cabbage rolls on warm platter and serve

A bowl of yogurt is a nice condiment to ladle over this.

Fancy Cabbage Salad

1 head of cabbage shredded
1 pineapple cut in 1/2" cubes
2 peaches cut in 1/2" cubes
2 pears cut in 1/2" cubes
12 cups green grapes cut in half
2 apples cut in 1/2" cubes
1 cup cherries cut in half
2 carrots shredded
1/2 green pepper shredded

1 tablespoon fresh lemon juice
1 cup sour cream
2 tablespoons cider vinegar
1 teaspoon salt and 1 teaspoon freshly ground pepper

Take first 9 ingredients (fruits and vegetables) and gently mix together

Blend in sour cream, lemon juice, vinegar, and pepper and salt
Gently fold mixture together and refrigerate a few hours or overnight until ready to serve.

Note: If you find that cutting up all that fruit is too time consuming, canned fruit cocktail can be substituted in its place.

Drain the fruit cocktail and add 1 teaspoon of horseradish to add some zing. Horseradish can be added to the above recipe for added texture

Corned Beef and Cabbage

1 raw brisket of corned beef
3 tablespoons of pickling spices
3 bay leaves
2 tablespoons black peppercorns
2 quarts of cold water
2 small heads of cabbage

In a large kettle add water, beef brisket, pickling spices, bay leaves, peppercorns, garlic and kosher salt.
Bring the water to a boil and then simmer the mixture for two to three hours or until the brisket is tender.

Cut the cabbage in half, remove the core, and then cut into quarters.

Add the cabbage after the brisket has been cooking for two hours and remove the cabbage once it becomes tender.

Remove the brisket from the water and let rest for 10 minutes before slicing
Arrange cabbage and lay corned beef slices on top or aside the leaves.
Pour a little of the juices from the cooking liquid over the top

Serve white vinegar and spicy mustard on the side.

Let's Build Our Church

Back in the 1930's there was quite a large Lebanese community in Utica, New York who spoke very limited English and certainly no Latin. Being Maronite Catholics they felt like foreigners in the Roman Church and if they wanted to go to mass they had to go to one of the churches in East Utica. These churches were predominately Italian, and their masses were in Latin while the Maronite mass was said in Syriac, a dead language similar to Latin. Thus they were unceremoniously welcomed by people they looked like but who spoke a different tongue. It didn't take a cook's assistant to tell them that they didn't belong and were being tolerated because they all made the sign of the cross and genuflected the same way. They needed their own church. They needed their own priests. Their priests could marry and had families. These priests, mostly Irish and Italian, didn't and couldn't understand them, let alone allow them to be worldly. Consequently they decided to build their own church – a task easier said than done.

Stained glass window from the church

First, there was the diocese of Syracuse, which had very little tolerance for a people they knew nothing about. According to the diocese, there was a Greek church in Syracuse. The Lebanese could go there. They were similar and from the same part of the world.

Stonewalled, the Lebanese wouldn't take no for an answer and they were determined. One story has it that they took their families, baby carriages and all, and went down to one of the busiest corners in Utica and literally "camped out" with a sit-in demonstration in the middle of the street. The mayor and police chief were called in but they still wouldn't move. Finally a call was placed to Bishop Duffy who told them if they would disperse he would meet with them to resolve the issue. They complied and met with him, whereupon he gave them permission to build their church. But! Not a cent would come from the diocese. They would have to earn the money themselves. And he also told them that their perseverance, diligence and prayers would get the job done.

I guess all of the above worked for they got their church and ironically the bishop did relent for he or the diocese co-signed a note with the Oneida bank of Utica for $30,000. To pay off the note each family was assessed $100.00. A huge sum back then. Many of them couldn't get near that sum of money and instead held dances, raffles and food sales to make up their share. One of the items sold was Laban, better known as homemade yogurt. They had to sell a ton of it to make up their quota.

Procuring Our Future, A Laban Story

When our people were getting ready to immigrate to America they weren't quite certain whether or not they would be able to make jibbin or Laban (cheese and yogurt). No one had come back from America and they were afraid they wouldn't have that staple in their diet. Being mountain people and descendants of Bedouin tribes they did what their ancestors did and took a culture* from the yogurt and cheese, dried it in their aprons, and re-activated it when they were finally settled in America. Most cheeses and yogurts are made from a starter or culture and that's exactly what they did. Thus they assured themselves that they would have laban. In some households where they made their own yogurt and cheese the culture was perhaps hundred of years old.

Whenever making yogurt they would always reserve a cupful from the last batch they had made. They would add this to the warm milk and this would begin to grow and be the starter you would need to make your yogurt.

Laban (homemade Lebanese yogurt)

1 gallon of whole milk
1 cup of starter (yogurt) at room temperature

In a large sauce pan bring milk to a boil and turn off immediately
Let this sit until the scalded milk has cooled (112' on a candy thermometer)
Another way to check the temperature is to stick your baby finger in the middle and count to ten.
Remove thick film that covers the top of milk and discard

Remove 1 cup of cool scalded milk and mix together with the starter
Add mixture to the remaining pot of cooled milk.

Cover tightly with a lid and take a bath towel folded in half and cover the lid.
Let set undisturbed overnight.
The mix will become thick.
Remove water (whey) that has gathered on top and discard.

Stir the yogurt. It should be thick and creamy.
Refrigerate until ready to serve.

There are good brands sold commercially if you don't care to go through this process. You can get away with it today - the old timers and purists are gone.

Aunty Oh Aunt!

"Here comes Umpta." Umpta is aunt in Arabic. It's a bit confusing because if it's on your father's side she is called Umpta. If it's on your mother's side she is called "B' Holtee." Her real name was Gemelia but we called her Umpta out of respect for her and the position. She was a very good looking lady with beautiful hair that she rolled back into a bun and always wore a pill box that would cover her beautiful face.

Umpta came to this country in 1908 at the age of 14. It's uncertain whether she was promised in marriage but was married soon after she arrived and had five children. She was a strong willed woman, highly judgmental and threw her weight around usually where it wasn't wanted. But she was Umpta, my father's only sister, who would inevitably voice her opinion, which you obeyed regardless of your own feelings. She was married to Ummee (uncle) Tunsy, who was Uncle Husky's and Uncle Habib's brother. Unfortunately he died of a heart attack long before he fulfilled his duty on this earth at the age of 40. They had a grocery store next door to the mill that turned out to be a profitable adventure for the family's fortune.

The mill was a major factor in our town. It employed about 300 hundred people morning, noon, and night and most of our families worked there. After work their store became the social meeting place where you spent your money for groceries, ice-cream, candy, gas, beer and gossip. You heard who was born and who died. Back then in the 30's and 40's they would toll a bell when someone died, with a ring for each year of their lives. As a result you went to the store to find out who died and perhaps bought a sandwich or some other miscellaneous item.

Umpta's store, Sherburne, NY, 1936

My aunt was a good cook. She was also thrifty in her ways. One way she was thrifty and entrepreneurial is she would extend you credit for groceries and sometimes would get paid in eggs, meat and vegetables, which she in turn would sell and/or use to feed her family. She was quite the opposite from her husband Ummee Tunsy. If he sold you an ice cream cone he would give you an extra dip or if you bought a pound of baloney he would give you an extra slice or two but she wouldn't give the extra dip let alone extra baloney. You got what you paid for. She was also highly respected and her opinion was highly adhered to.

One such incident involved old Joe Powell. Joe was a scrawny little rump of a man, always wearing dirty clothes, kind of a ne'er do-gooder. He could never seem to hold a steady job but was always there to do an odd job or dig graves or drink a beer on you. He was married to Flossie, who was short with curly hair and huge as a barn, wearing the same dress days at a time. They were poor white trash but still an acceptable part of the community. And they loved each other.

Well, the mill workers went on strike and there were a lot of bitter workers picketing around the mill, heckling management and drinking. There was a lot of tension in the air with jobless families, friends, and neighbors all riding the same boat. The bosses brought in strike breakers from out of town and also hired a few local people (those who dared) to fill in. And on a hot and humid August Saturday in 1943, Joe Powell broke the picket line and went to work. All of Joe's friends and neighbors were in an uproar with one of their own going against them. They all congregated in the store and decided Joe's fate. Word got out that they were going to get Joe.

When the work shift ended Joe tried to sneak out past everyone, going out the back way and almost made it home but was caught in the street and dragged back to the store by an unmerciful mob. They took him to a platform outside and held a kangaroo court. They asked the mob what to do with him and they said "hang him", and they meant it. They got a rope, made a noose and tied it over a tree and were going to hang him. Joe's fate was sealed. Joe, crying away, begged the mob to spare him. He got down on his knees and pleaded and prayed, but to no avail. The mob was unruly and there was a crowd as word had spread of the lynching.

Flossy came to the store, screaming frantically, cursing at them to save her Joe. The sentence was to be carried out. They pulled Joe from Flossy, who was holding on to poor skinny Joe for his life. Crying hysterically she ran across the street to get my aunt who had just come home from Saturday afternoon confession unaware of the pending crisis. My aunt came across the street and wanted to know what was going on. They told her what was happening and sensing the urgency of the situation she took over the podium. She pondered the situation for a moment or two and then began to pronounce sentencing. She berated Joe and gave him a severe scolding for turning his back on his friends and neighbors and that he should be hung for what he did. She asked him if he had anything to say and he told her he would never do it again, stop drinking, go to church regularly and pleaded on his knees to be saved because he loved Flossy and she needed him.   My aunt stood there for a moment then threw her hands in the air turned and walked into the store. Flossy wailed and Joe cried. The crowd showed no mercy and put the rope around his neck and started to take him away.

As they got to the tree, ready to hoist him up, a voice of authority told them to stop. It was Umpta, standing on the railing in front of the store. She raised her right hand and told the mob to free him. He had suffered his punishment. They obliged. Joe got to his knees, kissed her shoes, flaying his hands, vowing to do good forever with the promises of a sinner redeemed and made his amends.   My aunt, in one of her rare moments of generosity, made Buttenjan sandwiches and fed the crowd. She didn't buy the beer for them though. They bought their own. Thus was the saga of Joe Powell. Thus was the authority of Umpta.

Buttenjan is eggplant. Partnered with tomatoes, garlic, mint, and green onion stuffed in a pita you have a great sandwich.

Buttenjan (Eggplant) Sandwiches in Pita

Take firm eggplant, cut across into 1/4" slices and salt lightly
After you salt the eggplant, let rest 15 minutes and dice up fine
Dice up one large tomato
Cut up 1 bunch green onion chopped fine
Dice up one green pepper
Chop fine 1 bunch of fresh mint (1 cup)
Sauté green onion in 3 tablespoon olive oil until green color starts to fade
Add eggplant, pepper, tomato, and mint
If desired add salt and pepper to taste
Lightly sauté vegetables for 1/2 hour. Remove from stove and cool

Take a loaf of pita and cut in half and open bread to make a pocket
Take a tablespoon or two and stuff it in the pocket
Sprinkle some crumbled feta and squeeze some fresh lemon juice over it and serve

Umpta Pita Sandwich

Another way she would make a sandwich involved filling a pita pocket with onions, peppers and potatoes. A great Lenten favorite.**

Peel 2 white onions, cut them in half and slice thin
Cut 2 peppers in half, clean out the seeds and slice thin
Take 4 cooked potatoes, cut in slices and dice
Sauté onions in 2 tablespoon of olive oil for 1 minute. Add peppers and cook until limp.
Stir in potatoes and black pepper**to taste and continue to sauté for 15 minutes more.
Fill pita pocket with a tablespoon or two and serve.

**Peppers, onions and potatoes was a popular Lenten dish and a good meal for meatless Fridays. What generally happened was they always had leftovers and it became a good source for a sandwich, especially when most of the Catholic population gave up meat for Lent.

Note: Umpta's family had 2 doctors and they very, very rarely salted their food. So salt is optional but needed for a finer taste. Uncle Tunsy salted the hell out of his food and they all figured that's what killed him at the age of forty.

Another common bond of the ethnic people is they ate their own bread. Store bought bread was unheard of. Everyone baked their own. We always had Thilma (pita) Then in the early '40's we started eating what the Americans were eating. Store bought bread. What a novelty – everyone was eating the same loaf as a new era began. You could set your clock to the tune of the Tip Top Bakery Truck rolling into town at 8:45 am. Daily deliveries. A miracle, no? A travesty, yes.

By the 1960's you were rarely treated to the aromas wafting in the air. Fewer were making pita and only at Easter would the Poles make Babka and raisin bread. And nice Sicilian round bread, forget it. You could buy it at the store because the Italian bakery in the city would have the Tip Top man deliver it along with his own product. Thus entrepreneurship entered into it as I'm sure the Tip Top People never knew that their driver had a route of his own in their truck. Also those sandwich fillings stuffing the pita soon made their way to the Sicilian bread and bon appetito.

When Telling A Lie Becomes The Truth

If you can conjure up an image of the old vaudevillians Laurel and Hardy, with emphasis on the heavier character, then you have an idea of our Uncle Husky. Husky's real name was George and he really wasn't our uncle, but we all called him that because that was how we knew him. He was Uncle Habib and Uncle Tunsy's brother, working for them in their stores where he was a fixture. He was short and fat, wore a derby, and he epitomized the Pillsbury dough boy, always wearing a clean white shirt and tie and a clean white apron that went down to his knees. He was a confirmed bachelor but I don't know why, because he had a way with the ladies who would hang onto him, make quite a fuss, bring him gifts trying to court his favor and believe dearly all the tall tales he would tell.

And he could tell them. They said he could embellish the truth to such a point that even St. Peter would have no choice but to open those pearly gates. He was a good man and he always made you laugh. One day the mayor of the city came into the store to buy groceries. He started talking with "Husky" and asked him how his niece (Uncle Habib's daughter) was doing. Uncle Husky said she was doing fine, was going to graduate from Syracuse College at the top of her class and was engaged to be married soon. Sincerely impressed the mayor inquired as to whom she was going to marry and Husky beamingly replied "Oh, Mr. Mayor, she's going to marry a very big famous man. A United States Senator." Uncle Habib, who was standing nearby, tried to interject and cut Husky off, hollering at him in Arabic, telling him to cut out his "blank--blank" lying. But to no avail. The mayor, quite impressed, paid for his groceries, congratulated a chagrinned Uncle Habib and left the store, no doubt thinking of the political and beneficial ramifications for his city. As the door closed Uncle Habib cursed him out royally and asked him why he had to lie and especially to the mayor. Uncle Husky looked at his brother and matter of fact told him that the mayor was a nice man and he wanted to hear a nice story....

"Hey, who you like better – your mother or your father?" That was one of Huskies favorite expressions. Whenever we would go into the store to buy candy or ice cream he would always pose that same question to you, only to change the characters, to your chagrin and his hysterics. On one particular day I went into the store and as chance would have it both my "Sittos" – grandmother in Arabic – were there. As I was about to buy an ice cream he asked me who I liked better, my father's mother or my mother's mother? Wanting the ice cream and not wanting to give him an answer to the embarrassing question I stammered, stuttered, fidgeted, reluctantly telling him my mother's mother, which didn't get me praise from her but "Ya Oppy Shoom" - shame on you and a whack upside the head from my father's mother as she muttered "Ya unnee ah book" - just like your father. You couldn't win. Only Husky and his huge stomach would roll with laughter with his little quirk. That was Husky, he was the winner.

He loved macaroni and would have eaten it raw if you weren't watching. He would ask every customer that came in and bought a box of pasta how they prepared theirs and would generally try to fix it the way they would tell him. He wasn't a great cook but he would eat his creation. On a particular day a rather heavy set woman came into the store with a dish of pasta fagiola or pasta fazool (macaroni and peas), gave it to Husky, and proceeded to tell him how to prepare it as he voraciously devoured it, smacking his lips and graciously thanking her with a "hey shuk-ra, shuk-ra, (thank-You) Miss uh-Misses hey hey hey Hefty. You nice lady. Nice for her pasta fazool and "hefty" because he didn't know her name and being obese it was the perfect fit. If you had black hair he would call you Blackie and if your dog was brown it was natural for him to call your dog Brown. He identified by sight. Don't know if the "hefty lady" ever brought him anymore macaroni and peas....

Huskie's Macaroni and Peas

1 lb Ditalini or elbow macaroni
1 package frozen or 3 cups fresh peas
1 onion finely chopped
2 cloves garlic sliced thin
3 tablespoons olive oil
1 16 oz can tomato puree
2 tablespoons fresh or dried mint
Salt and pepper to taste

Sauté onion and garlic in oil until the garlic lightly browns
Add tomato puree and 2 cups water and bring to a boil
Stir in peas, mint, salt and pepper
Lower flame and simmer another 15 minutes
Cook macaroni in boiling salted water according to directions on package and drain
Put macaroni in a large bowl, add the sauce and mix it all together and serve.

It's a pretty hefty dish!

Linguine With Garlic Butter and Roasted Red Peppers

1 lb of Linguine
3 tablespoon of butter
2 garlic cloves mashed to a paste
1 roasted red pepper diced fine*
1/2 cup sliced black olives
1/2 cup grated Parmesan cheese
Salt and pepper to taste

Cook linguine in salted boiling water according to directions on the package and drain.
While linguine is cooking, melt butter and add garlic, red peppers and olives.
Toss butter sauce with the linguine, add salt and pepper and serve

*Roasted red peppers are available in cans or you can roast your own.

The Syrian Sandwich

Mary and George Lewis

One night a school teacher and his wife came to my dad's restaurant and were sitting at the bar having a draft beer. There were three tables in the bar: two small and one big round. That was considered my dad's table, where he always sat. My dad was eating a sandwich and the teachers at the bar ordered a sandwich like the one my dad was eating. My dad told the bartender to order them a sandwich and thus the "Syrian Sandwich" was born.

Commercially at least. We Lebanese have another bread which we call Marook. It resembles a large flour tortilla and/or the kind of bread they use for wraps today.

In the sandwich you would lay the bread out flat and lightly brush it with a mix of olive oil and vinegar. Add a layer of either thin sliced ham, turkey, or beef.
Then add a layer of thin sliced tomatoes.
Then add a layer of thin sliced onion
Then add a layer of shredded iceberg lettuce
Drizzle lightly a little of the oil/vinegar mix
Add salt and pepper to taste

Then add another thin layer of ham-beef-or turkey
Roll bread into pinwheel and slice diagonally every 3 to 4"
Arrange on plate and serve.
A good mustard/mayonnaise mix works too in place of the oil/vinegar. Russian dressing is another option.

Another dish we used to serve that was laden with garlic was fah-jye-lea, which was the stems of wild mustard that would grow in the fields. You would pick the stems of the wild mustard before it bloomed into its brilliant yellow flowers. Unfortunately, it's very rare today because most of the fields have been plowed under and fertilized with chemicals and I wouldn't advise eating them. But every once in a while I can still find the edible stem, chemical free. The thin pencil-like stems are reminiscent of sweet asparagus with a faint mustard bite. Today I substitute asparagus instead.

Fah-Jye-Lea (asparagus)

1 large bunch of asparagus
5 cloves of garlic mashed to a paste
3 tablespoon of olive oil
Juice of 1 lemon

Trim the asparagus spears, cutting off about 2 inches from the bottom stalks
In a large kettle bring 3 cups of water to a boil
Add the asparagus and cook about 3 to 4 minutes to the al dente stage
Drain asparagus spears and add to a bowl
Combine the garlic and olive oil and toss with the asparagus
Drizzle on lemon juice and toss gently and serve.

This can also sit for a while and be served at room temperature or can be refrigerated and served cold. Just remember to toss gently before serving to get all the juices blended in.

Baked Salmon and Zucchini

1 3 lb. filet of Salmon
3 zucchinis sliced about 1/8" thick or as thin as you can get them
3 tablespoons olive oil
1/4 cup fresh chopped thyme or 1 tablespoon dried
2 lemons sliced 1/8" thick
1 tablespoon fresh garlic chopped fine or 2 tablespoons granulated garlic powder
1 cup fresh grated parmesan cheese
1 tablespoon black pepper
1/2 teaspoon salt

Toss zucchini with olive oil, garlic and black pepper thoroughly
Add grated cheese and toss lightly
Line bottom of large baking pan with zucchini slices, laying them like shingles on a roof covering the bottom of the entire pan

Bake in preheated 350° oven for 10 minutes and remove from oven and let cool to room temperature
Take salmon and sprinkle salt and thyme over it
Cut the fish across making 1 and 1/2" slices until it's all cut
Take the slices and reassemble the filet on the bed of zucchini
Bake in oven 12 to 15 minutes for medium
Top filet slices with lemon slices and serve

Creamy Dill Sauce

2 cups green onion chopped fine
1 clove garlic diced fine
1 sweet red bell pepper diced fine
1 bunch of dill chopped fine
1 cup parsley chopped fine
5 thin lemon slices cut in half, then quartered
1/2 teaspoon white pepper
3 tablespoons butter or margarine
2 tablespoons olive or canola oil
1/2 cup dry sherry
1 cup heavy cream

Sauté onion in butter and oil until the color fades
Add red pepper, garlic and dill and sauté 2 minutes
Add sherry and cook over low flame until mixture reduces in half
Add heavy cream and pepper and continue to simmer 10 minutes
Add parsley and lemon. Stir and serve over salmon

Muhumarah (hot sauce)

When I grill fish over an open flame I get a craving for a hot pepper sauce my mother's mother would make called Muhumarah. It was a blend of garlic, onion, olive oil cumin, hot peppers, walnuts, bread crumbs, and pignolia nuts. It has quite the kick to it but was a nice sauce to dip your fish into.**

** It has to be understood in Middle East cuisine, especially Lebanese, sauces generally were served in a large wooden bowl and everyone would dip their food into the bowl, most likely wrapped in bread or lettuce leaves. If you weren't Lebanese you were kind of reluctant to dip your food into a bowl that everyone else had dipped into.

Muhumarah

5 tablespoons of olive oil
1 medium onion finely chopped
½ cup of walnuts or almonds finely chopped
1 hot pepper chopped fine or 1 teaspoon of ground hot pepper or 1 teaspoon hot garlic paste
1 cup of dried bread crumbs softened with 2 tablespoons of cold water
1 teaspoon of cumin
1 teaspoon paprika
1/2 teaspoon each of salt and black pepper
1/2 cup of lightly toasted pignolia nuts

In a deep skillet sauté onion and garlic in olive oil until very lightly browned
Add the bread crumbs, hot peppers, cumin, paprika and salt
Continue to sauté mixture for 10 to 15 minutes, stirring 2 or 3 times
Remove from stove and put in a large bowl and sprinkle chopped pignolia nuts over it
Serve with lemon slices and a cup of finely chopped green onion and one of parsley.

My great-grandfather, "Jiddo Old Man", would take a lemon slice and put a teaspoon of it on top and then put it on a piece of Arabian bread, sprinkle the chopped onion and parsley over it and eat it with a pignolia on top.

Another old favorite and a good sauce for fish is Taratoor, which we always poured over grilled fish and meats and vegetables.

Taratoor Sauce (tahina sauce)

1 cup Tahina (available at Middle-East import stores)
3 tablespoon cold water
3 cloves garlic mashed to a paste
1/2 cup of fresh lemon juice
1 teaspoon salt
1 teaspoon fresh black pepper
1/2 cup chopped fresh parsley

In a food processor add Tahina and water and blend 30 seconds

Add lemon juice, garlic, salt and pepper and blend another 30 seconds
The sauce will take on the consistency of thick gravy

Pour over fish or grilled meats and sprinkle parsley over it.

Los Ah Lahm (Lamb and Potatoes)

A Monday night special in our house was this dish, which was nothing more than leftover lamb with potatoes - a hash perhaps. Why Monday?   Well lamb was the meat of choice for the Lebanese and every part of the lamb was used in cooking, particularly on the week-ends with Shish Kabobs and Lamb shanks. By Monday all you had left were the breast and the neck bones. The cooks would trim off any excess meat and combine it with something else to make another meal and a good use of the leftovers. They would take any and all available meat from the bones and add it to rice, potatoes or whatever and a meal would come about. Today the shank or the breast are prized pieces of meat but back then they were just scrap pieces that with a bit of ingenuity became a meal for the whole family. Today I guess you could call it a hash made of lamb. Nowadays it's easier to buy a shoulder blade lamb chop and cut it up than to consume all your time nit picking the breast.

Los Ah Lahm

(Lamb and Potatoes)

2 cups of finely diced lamb meat
1 large onion finely chopped or 2 cups finely chopped green onion
6 large potatoes diced in 1/2" pieces
3 tablespoons olive oil
1 1/2 teaspoons of salt
1 teaspoon of black pepper

In a large skillet sauté onion in olive oil until onion turns golden brown
Add lamb meat and cook until browned
Add potatoes, salt and pepper and stir mixture together
Continue to cook over low heat for another hour stirring at intervals until the potatoes have cooked and start to brown.

This is a dish that can be eaten hot or at room temperature. Served with crusty bread, a bottle of ketchup and a green salad, and a pauper's meal becomes a Sultan's delight.

*note: The potatoes may stick to the pan but don't worry about it. Continue to stir and scrape the sides of the pan incorporating it all. A little more oil may be added to prevent sticking.

**It is also common knowledge that potatoes were not a staple of the Middle East but with the advent of supermarkets and such the potato has now become a mainstay in the Middle East diet, especially fried in oil in different forms. It is commonly thought that the potato became a part of our culture in America, where it was introduced and helped supplement Lenten diets along with rice, lentils and beans. Eggs and peppers mixed with potatoes often are substituted for the lamb, especially in meatless households.

Going To The Syrian Picnic

It was July, 1941, and I would be born a month after the bombing of Pearl Harbor. With a war rapidly approaching people were on edge and any cause for a celebration was a welcomed event. The annual Syrian picnic was coming up at the Lebanese church and all our family wanted to go and that was fine, except for the fact that my family owed Ummee Habib's family $28.00. My mother, being an extremely proud woman, refused to allow the family to go unless they paid the money back. She wouldn't dare show her face at a celebration knowing Ummee Habib's family would be there. It was just disrespectful. She said they could go if they paid the money back and one source of extra revenue was picking beans, where you were paid by the number of bushels you picked. Well, the family set out to pick beans and they earned enough money to pay Ummee Habib what they owed him. So they headed out to the picnic, with a detour to Ummee Habib's store to give him his money. After they gave him the money owed he called them back as we were leaving and said to my sister "this is yours", and gave her $5.00. He did the same thing to my three brothers and took $8.00 and gave it to my mother and said this is for the newborn baby (myself). My sister obediently gave the money to my father, as did two of my brothers. My third brother (Jimmy) held onto the money. My father gave him a stern inquisitive look and my brother said he wasn't going to give him the money because it was his and he meant to keep it. Before it was considered child abuse my dad gave him a whack upside the head and took the money. They all went to the picnic, ate Shish Kabob, and had a good time.

About a month later a member of Ummee Habib's family became gravely ill. As was the custom back then my dad would gather everyone together in the evening at home and they would say the rosary for the sick person. With everyone gathered in the living room of our house my dad asked my brother who tried to keep the money why he wasn't joining them in the recitation. He replied that because he had to give back the money he had earned he wasn't going to pray for him. "Oh, but for the love of God and money..."

On of the nice things about the picnic was they always served a salad that is only good in the summer time when the weather is hot and the vegetables are fresh.

Cucumbers and Mint

4 cucumbers sliced into 1/8" slices
2 bunches green onions chopped fine
1 cup fresh mint chopped fine
1 cup parsley chopped fine
1 clove garlic, mashed to a paste
3 cups of homemade or plain commercial yogurt
1/2 teaspoon each of salt and white pepper

Mix all ingredients together in a large bowl, refrigerate for a couple hours and serve. Stir the salad just before serving and garnish with lettuce leaves.

Shish Kabob

1 boneless leg of lamb, trimmed of all fat and cut into 1 1/2" pieces
2 large onions cut into 2" pieces
2 large peppers cut into 1 1/2" pieces
2 cloves garlic crushed
3 tablespoon olive oil
1 tablespoon black pepper

Mix lamb with all above ingredients and let marinate overnight
Using either wooden or metal skewers take a piece of onion and skewer it in the center
Add a piece of lamb and then a piece of pepper. Continue with a piece of lamb, then onion, lamb and pepper until you have 5 to 6 pieces on a skewer.
Continue to do this until all the meat and vegetables are skewered.
Cook over an open flame about 4 minutes on each side for a nice medium rare.
Cook longer for well done.

One way that I like to cook them is over an open wood fire with the flames just touching the meat searing it enough to give the meat a crust and not scorching it.
Another thing I like to do is to occasionally throw a sprig or two of a grape vine branch to flare up the fire and add a fruity flavor.
Let meat sit on the skewers for a few minutes before serving.

A side dish that we always served with Shish Kabobs was grilled plum tomatoes that were superb.

Grilled Plum Tomatoes

6 plum tomatoes cut across into 1" slices
2 cloves garlic crushed to a paste
2 tablespoons olive oil
Juice of 1 lemon
2 tablespoons of fresh mint chopped fine
1/4 cup chopped green onion
2 tablespoons chopped fresh parsley
1 teaspoon each of salt and pepper
Gently toss all ingredients together

2 tablespoons grated parmesan or Romano cheese. Set aside and do not add to mix

Take tomato slices and skewer them in the center (skin side) until you have filled the skewer (5 or 6)
Grill over open flame 3 minutes each side
Remove from skewer and sprinkle grated cheese over them and serve.

Skewered Teriyaki Potatoes

For this recipe you want to use new potatoes about 1 1/2" to 2" round.

18 to 20 new potatoes
2 cloves garlic mashed to a paste
2 tablespoons of olive oil
3 tablespoons butter or margarine
1/2 cup chopped green onion or chives
1/4 cup of teriyaki sauce
2 tablespoons fresh grated Romano or Parmesan cheese
1/2 teaspoon salt
1 teaspoon black pepper

In a medium sized kettle add potatoes and cover them with cold water
Bring to a boil and then simmer for 10 minutes until cooked yet still firm
(you don't want to over cook, but when inserting a wood skewer you want the insides firm to the touch)

Toss potatoes with all the above ingredients and let marinate for a half hour, stirring together 3 or 4 times
Using a wood 10" skewer that has been soaked in water for an hour or two, pierce the potatoes right down the center, placing 4 or 5 potatoes on each skewer
Over an open fire or under a broiler lay the potato skewer on the grill or under the broiler and cook on each side for about 5 minutes or until the skins start to brown, basting occasionally with remaining marinade.

Remove from skewers and serve hot with an extra sprinkling of cheese.

These are also good served at room temperature.

Grilled Eggplant

1 large firm eggplant
3 tablespoons olive oil
1 tablespoon granulated garlic powder or 1 tablespoon fresh garlic paste
1 teaspoon paprika
1 teaspoon salt
1 teaspoon white pepper
1/2 cup fresh shredded Asiago cheese
1/4 cup chopped fine parsley

Cut eggplant across making 1/4" slices
Lay slices out on sheet pan and lightly salt and drain off excess juices 10 minutes later
Brush each side with olive oil and then sprinkle on garlic, paprika and pepper
Lay slices on hot grill over open flame and cook for 3 minutes
Turn slices over and grill another 3 minutes.
Lay out on serving platter and liberally sprinkle with cheese and parsley and serve

*You can broil this in your oven using the same procedure or bake in 400° oven for 8 to 10 minutes.

Farfelle With Chicken or Chicken With Bowties

3 tablespoons olive oil
1 tablespoon butter
2 bunches (3 cups) chopped green onion
4 cloves garlic sliced thin
2 tablespoons fresh basil, chopped fine or 3 tablespoon dried basil flakes
1 cup chopped fresh parsley
1 teaspoon salt
1 teaspoon black pepper
1 16 oz. can tomato puree or 1 16 oz. can plum tomatoes crushed
1/4 cup dry sherry
2 pints heavy cream or 1/2 qt half and half
4 boneless chicken breasts already baked or broiled and sliced into 1/4" pieces
2 lbs of Farfelle Pasta
2 cups fresh grated Pecorino Romano cheese

Sauté onions and garlic in olive oil for 3 minutes
Add sherry and cook for 2 minutes
Add tomatoes, basil, salt and pepper and bring to a boil
Lower flame, add heavy cream and sauté 15 minutes more
(be careful not to burn the bottom of the pan)

Cook pasta in boiling salted water according to directions on package and drain
Add pasta to a large bowl and stir in butter coating the pasta
Add chicken, sauce, and 1 cup of cheese mixing together lightly but thoroughly
Sprinkle parsley and remaining cup of cheese evenly over pasta and serve.

Another pasta favorite especially amongst the high school age kids is our version of macaroni and cheese. Never a complaint, nor an empty plate, with no one being bashful about going back for seconds and more.

Macaroni and Cheese

1 lb box medium shells
1 16oz can of Cheddar cheese sauce with Jalapenos
3 tablespoons butter
3 cups of milk
1 cup parmesan cheese
1 cup of diced roasted red peppers (optional)
1/2 teaspoon each of salt and white pepper

Melt butter in a saucepan and add milk until it is heated
Add cheese sauce and whisk it smoothly into milk and butter
Add cheese, peppers, salt and pepper continuing to cook slowly for 30 minutes

Meanwhile cook shells according to directions on package and drain
Add shells to cheese sauce stirring gently but thoroughly and serve.
Sprinkle a handful more of grated cheese over shells.

The kids just love it. So do the adults.

Porcupine Balls

This recipe comes from a friend of mine's mother who had the knack to take simple ingredients and turn them into a meal that would put the Betty Crocker Cookbook in the gourmet category. This is simply economical and quick. I think she may have got the recipe out of the Los Angeles Times circa 1935 - 1940 or perhaps from the label of the Campbell's soup can.

Porcupine Balls

1 lb of ground beef
1 cup of cooked rice
2 raw eggs
1 regular size can of tomato soup
Salt and pepper to taste
Fresh chopped parsley for sprinkling

Preheat oven to 350°
In a large bowl add ground beef, rice, eggs, and salt and pepper and mix together
Shape into meatballs about 2 inches round
Set in a baking dish about an inch apart
Cover with tomato soup and bake in oven for a half hour
Turn balls over and bake another 20 minutes.
Remove from oven and serve
Sprinkle chopped parsley over balls for garnish

Another one of those recipes is kind of like those made with hamburger helper only this one calls for a can of Campbell's Cheddar Cheese soup, ground beef and onion.

Blank! On A shingle

1 lb. ground beef
1 medium onion chopped and diced fine
1 can of Campbell's cheddar cheese soup
Salt and pepper to taste
6 to 8 toast tips or toasted English muffins

In a large skillet slowly sauté ground beef and onion until the meat is cooked and browned
Drain off excess juices
Add cheddar cheese soup, salt and pepper, stir and slowly cook for 15 minutes
Serve over toast tips or English muffins

Jimmy Lewis' Tomato Salad

My brother Jimmy started growing tomatoes in his early sixties. From that day on you would think that no one else in the world had grown a tomato. From there the fun began. He had learned to make a tomato salad and at every function that gathered a crowd his tomato salad would appear. I don't know if it was any good because I always made my own, but everyone would tell him it was good after he damn near forced an opinion out of you. So when the tomato salad appeared you ate it and that was that. He also learned how to make the classic Lebanese salad, Tabouleh. That in itself was like winning an Oscar at the Academy Awards. An accomplishment everyone of Lebanese descent strived for. Everyone tried, few were successful and I called it the bastardization of an age old dish. I never ate their versions because I'm not very fond of the dish yet I make a very good one and if you tasted it you would heartily agree.

One summer day a few years back when we were all gathered at a house on Lake Tuscarora, where the family has had a summer place since the 1960's, the Bobby Lewis family decided to make Tabouleh. They were chopping the cucumber, tomatoes, parsley, etc., when my brother Jim got involved. He informed them they weren't cutting the vegetables small enough and they didn't have enough of this and enough of that. He was partially right and that set off a series of name calling and arguments that ended up in the same bowl with the age old adage that too many cooks spoil the broth. I didn't have to taste it to know it was awful but with their disgruntled remarks ate the dumb thing. One thing you have to understand is that my brother Rich and I are under the same impression that at any family function you never let the Bobby Lewis clan plan the menu. I won't go any further because I could write another two chapters. But anyhow!

The only thing Jimmy Lewis was afraid of was coming in second. He had such a fear of it that he always came in first. He wasn't afraid of death; in fact, he defied it for five years. He was struck with a debilitating disease which slowed him down a bit but he fought it with a vengeance that defied the odds. The only time I really saw fear in his face was when we both showed up at the same family gathering with a tomato salad. I can remember him looking at his wife and saying, "Damn, Georgie has brought a tomato salad." I don't recall who ate what but that was about the only time I can ever recall him coming in second.

Jimmy Lewis, demonstrating the proper way to make Tabouleh at Lake Tuscarora, summer 2002

Tomato Salad

When selecting tomatoes for your tomato salad I prefer them to be three quarters ripe. To me that is when the tomato tastes the best, especially for a salad. The acid content is high and the sugar level hasn't reached maturation. There is also a certain crunchiness that exudes from this fruity vegetable. Riper tomatoes are generally suited for cooking, broiling and making sauces for they are juicy, meatier, and sweeter. One secret to a successful salad is plenty of salt and fresh lemon juice. I might add that to get the ultimate in taste you want them garden fresh. In New York State that means from July to October. A short season. I have made it in the middle of winter with all different kinds of tomatoes but the flavor is not there.

6 to 8 firm 3/4 ripe tomatoes cut into wedges (about 10 per tomato)
1 bunch green onion chopped fine
1 cup freshly chopped mint
1 cup freshly chopped parsley
1 cup freshly cut basil (optional)
1/2 cup freshly chopped thyme
3 tablespoons of good olive oil
3 garlic cloves mashed to a paste
Juice of 2 fresh lemons
1 teaspoon salt and 1/2 teaspoon of black pepper
1/2 cup of fresh grated Romano or Parmesan cheese

In the bottom of a salad bowl add the olive oil, garlic and lemon juice
Whisk these together thoroughly.

In the order they are written, add:
Tomatoes, green onions, mint, parsley, basil, thyme salt, pepper, and cheese

Toss lightly but thoroughly and serve at room temperature.

With the dressing in the bottom of the bowl, you can mix this when ready to serve. I like to mix it about 1/2 before serving and this gives the flavors a chance to merge.

Add more salt if needed.

This can also be refrigerated until ready to serve but I have a thing about refrigerating garden fresh tomatoes in that they lose a certain content of their flavor once they have been refrigerated.

Cooking Pasta

Today there is a rage to cook and make fresh pasta. Years ago a lot of Italian based restaurants featured homemade pasta on their menus and unless you had an Italian grandmother that was probably the only way you could get a dish of the homemade stuff. But with the advent of numerous cooking magazines, TV shows and pasta making machines everyone has been able to procure this one way or another. That is one of the reasons that I prefer the homemade versions in a restaurant, thus avoiding the time it takes to make, the hanging and drying of the pasta and lastly the cleanup. Especially in a small kitchen.

If you have your heart set on the fresh then you could improvise by going to your local supermarket, where they carry several varieties that are frozen or under refrigeration. I prefer the store bought dry packages of macaroni and one of the main problems I come across is that most people have trouble following the directions and cooking it properly. Either it is cooked too long and becomes mushy or not cooked enough and too crunchy. Or it doesn't get stirred often enough and it sticks together and to the bottom of the pan. I have been cooking pasta for almost half a century and only twice have I had a problem with it. Once while cooking cappellini (angel hair) when I cooked it too long it became mush, and once when I was cooking fettuccine when I put more of the macaroni into the pan than I had water. It absorbed most of the liquid and turned starchy.

But I have found a fool proof way to cook it and never do I have bad results. In a large kettle bring 6 to 8 cups of water to a boil and add 1 teaspoon of salt. Never add the salt until the water is boiling, otherwise the salt will start to cake up on the sides of the kettle and give your water a grayish color. Also I never add oil to the water. I'm a firm believer that once you put your pasta into the water you must stir it thoroughly as this will prevent sticking. And then stir again in a minute or two.

Once the water is boiling add your pasta (a 1 lb. box or package)* and stir immediately. Let cook a few minutes more and stir again thoroughly. Pasta while cooking are a bit like sheep. Every once in a while a few sheep will stray from the flock. This is exactly what will happen with pasta. A few strands will start to float to the top of the kettle. At this point it tells me that it is cooked "al denté" - firm to the touch. Most likely at this point I will give it a final thorough stir, take the kettle off the stove and drain the pasta, giving it the al dente stage. If you want your pasta cooked a little more then wait until perhaps half of the pasta floats to the top and then take the kettle off the stove and drain it. Once drained, remove your pasta to a bowl and add your sauce and stir lightly. I usually add about 1 1/2 teaspoon of olive oil to the pasta and stir it together again with a tablespoon or two more of sauce and serve. One of the reasons I add oil to the finished product is that it keeps it moist and prevents sticking. I find this to be fool proof and if you follow my method you shouldn't have any problems. Once you drain your pasta it is important to coat it with sauce, oil or butter to prevent it from sticking or drying out.

*note: If you plan to cook more than 1 lb of pasta always add 2 more cups water for each pound of pasta you use. For best results never cook more than 5 lbs. at a time.

Where There's Life There's Hope

Helen Harp: That was her maiden name before she married Joe. A strikingly beautiful woman with jet black hair, beautiful blue eyes, good inbred manners, full of life and a yearning for the good old days to return. She had two boys and a girl, was a good mother, good cook and raised her family well. Her only drawback was that she had a temper and when she got mad she would shake the pillars of hell. Helen had a hard life. She married young and I think that may have been a mistake. Joe drank and Helen yelled. The more he drank the louder she yelled and it went on that way for years. One thing was assured though, every week he gave her his paycheck, leaving himself a little to imbibe and her a reason to yell when he came staggering home. Joe was a good man; it's just that the beer can got to him before anything else. The verbal abuse between them was chaotic but that's as far as it went. It didn't get physical. He would call her a "blank-blank" Syrian* and she would call him a "blankety-blank" Pollock. And so it would go.

* Back then we were all called Syrians and that didn't end until 1948 when Lebanon became independent of Syria, but the stigma stuck and we stayed "Syrians" until the 1960"s. Then gradually we started to become "Lebanese."

Helen loved to take walks. On beautiful summer days you could see her and her good friend and cousin-in-law, Shamoona, taking a walk to the river to gather fresh mint. They would pick the leaves and dry the herb for the winter. She always knew where the best mint was. Or you would see her and Shamoona going up the hill to the cemetery. She didn't have anyone buried there but I guess they would go up there to see a lot of their friends who had a permanent address there. She would pick wildflowers and place them on the grave of old Boulous Deep. He shot himself with a double barreled shotgun and was buried way off in a far corner of the cemetery all by himself. Everyone said he couldn't be buried with the rest of the people because he had committed suicide and had gone to hell. But Helen had felt sorry for "the poor bastard" as she would say of him after she said an act of contrition at the grave, hoping to move his soul into a purgatory situation. I always thought that if he didn't pull the trigger he wouldn't have burned forever. But then he would never have gotten Helen's flowers. It's ironic that Helen spent so much time up there. For part time work Joe would dig graves. "Dig 'em and plant 'em" he would always say, and after one of his many verbal battles with Helen he always promised her he would literally "water her grave." Fortunately for Helen Joe died first...

She was quite philosophical. One day in the 1980's an uncle of mine was quite ill and I had told her that he wouldn't last the night. Helen replied with that great wisdom of hers that as long as there is life there is hope. It took him a couple of days to die but her words have stuck with me ever since.

Helen was what you would call a social drinker. After Sunday dinner she and Shamoona would take their usual Sunday walk and by mid afternoon would usually end up at Lewis', sit at the bar and order a whiskey and ginger ale which she never finished. I don't think she liked to drink but it was the fashionable thing to do. Joe was usually in the bar when she came in drinking, with all his Polish cronies and you would never know they were married for they would barely acknowledge each other. Joe would usually mutter his famous "blank - blank Syrians." Or shout a warning to all who would listen that being married to a Syrian was nothing but trouble and he would never understand why he married one. Back then very few woman drove and very few families had more than one car. So when Helen and Shamoona were walking up the street the men at the bar would yell to Joe "here comes Helen you'd better hide under the table" and he usually did. There was a song on the juke-box that was a polka and it went like this; "Helen, Helen, Helen, Helen, we don't give a damn" which some of the guys would play when she walked in. Then Joe would sheepishly come out from under the table. He couldn't stay there forever or his beer would get warm.

You couldn't open the bar until noon on Sunday. As soon as you did there were about 10 to 12 Polish men who would come in and have a "Peevo and Voodka" - shot and a beer. That was the norm. A half hour later they would promptly go home and have their dinner and by two o'clock they would all be back to resume where they left off, playing the juke-box, singing songs and putting down a glass or two. A half hour later their wives and families would join them for a libation. The only rule was that they had to sit at the tables and not at the bar. That was unladylike and unheard of. Helen, being a maverick, would break tradition and set herself right up to the bar with all of the men, with few objections. Nobody dared. I can still see her standing on her stool, cigarette in hand, leading the bar in their rendition of the Notre Dame fight song.

"Shame, Shame on old Notre Dame
Letting the Pollock's ruin your name.
Send those Syrians out for gin
And don't let a sober Irish in.
We never stagger, we never fall
We sober up on illegal alcohol.
While her loyal son keep falling
Drunk on the barroom floor"
da da da da da da da"

That was Helen. Many years later I had returned home for a few weeks and heard Joe was dying of cancer. I went over to their house to see him. Helen was very glad to see me and took me to his bedroom where he was lying in bed with very little strength. Helen had to tell him who I was and he nodded with a faint gesture of recognition. Later as Helen and I were sitting in the kitchen having a cup of coffee she said, wiping a tear from her eye, "you know George after all these years and all the fighting and hollering I guess I still love that old Pollock." I stood up gave her a hug and said "Helen, right on." On my way out I asked to use the bathroom. Closing the door I lifted the top to the commode and all I could say was "God bless you Joe." There were 3 cans of beer in the cold water and out of Helen's sight. To her dying day I don't think she knew where Joe kept his beer. If she did we would have heard her - loud and clear!

Sunday was the day to go to Helen's for dinner. Right after second mass she would lay her table out with rigatoni and sausage, a green salad, fresh baked Arabic bread and her famous Stuffed Peppers. I hated peppers but I loved hers. Simply stuffed with meat, cheese and a simple tomato sauce laced with mint. It was the best.

Helen's Stuffed Peppers

8 medium sized green bell peppers
6 cups boiling water
1 lb of ground beef uncooked
1 cup dried bread crumbs softened in 2 tablespoons milk
1 teaspoon granulated garlic powder
1/2 cup grated parmesan cheese
2 raw eggs
1 small onion finely chopped
3 tablespoons fresh mint or 3 tablespoons dried
1/2 cup fresh chopped parsley
1 teaspoon salt and 1/2 teaspoon black pepper
1 16oz. can tomato sauce

Cut tops off of peppers and scoop out seeds and inside pulp
Blanch peppers in boiling water for 3 minutes, remove and drain under cold water
Place peppers upside down and set aside

In a large bowl mix together all the above ingredients except tomato sauce
Fill the pepper cavities with the meat mixture to the top and set upright in a lightly oiled baking dish
Top each pepper with a tablespoon or two of tomato sauce

Bake in preheated 350° oven for 45 minutes, remove and serve

Rigatoni and Sausage

2 lbs of hot sausage links, diagonally cut in 1 1/2' pieces
6 cloves of garlic sliced thin
1 large onion sliced across in 1/4" rings
3 tablespoons fresh chopped mint or 3 tablespoons dried
2 cans tomato puree salt and pepper to taste
1 lb. box Rigatoni

Heat a large sauce pan and add sausage pieces a few at a time until all are added
Stir them around for a few minutes and then add onion and garlic.
Stir them a couple of times until they have browned on all sides
Add tomato puree, 2 cups of water, salt, pepper, and mint and bring to a boil, then let simmer for an hour

Cook rigatoni according to the directions on the package, drain, add to a bowl and toss together lightly with a couple tablespoons of sauce
Dish out rigatoni to a large platter and top with sausage
Ladle desired amount of sauce over sausage and pasta and serve
Grated cheese can be sprinkled on top, but Helen never did. She claimed it took away from the dish.

Simply prepared and heavenly.

Beit Yousef

House of Joseph. That's what the blue gothic letters said on the front structure over the doorway at cousin Joe's house. Beit, pronounced bait, stood for house and Yousef stood for Joe. Much to the horror of Joe's wife and son it was his way of expressing his Lebanese heritage. Like the Irish who flew their shamrock flags or the Italians with the hereafter outdoor shrines to the Virgin Mary adorning their flower gardens, Joe was just expressing himself, although I'm sure that everyone passing by had no idea of its meaning until he told you. And he would tell you with a quivering smirk, feeling he had put one over on you.

But Joe could afford to be a little bizarre. He made a lot of money and accounted only to God and the angels. Joe was Uncle Tunsy's son. His mother was my father's sister, who we called "Umpta," or aunt. When Uncle Tunsy died Joe took over the grocery store and was a shrewd businessman. Having the foresight to know food would be rationed with World War 2 approaching, Joe bought and hoarded commodities such as sugar, coffee and flour, and sold them during the war when a lot of those foods were rationed by stamps. All of this was legal, buying and storing before the rationing. He also had an airtight lease on his grocery store that rented for $25.00 a month up until the 1960's. One reason Joe was loaded was that he was frugal and had more nickels than the first one he earned. Joe was the epitome of physical conditioning. He walked to and from work every day, didn't smoke, nor use salt, drank lightly, and was just pure healthy. Unfortunately one day he cut his hand, caught a staph infection and was dead a week later. They waked him in the church parlor. One story has it that after finding out the cost of the funeral home rental, the church basement would suffice. And it did. So much for pre-arranged funerals.

It's ironic that I had sent a pasta salad to the house after calling hours. I had never been frugal in my life so it was incongruous when someone complimented me on the delicious salad but was curious as to why I had four different kinds of pasta in it. I guess it fit the mode. I had four half empty boxes of shells, rotini, ziti, and farfelle. Instead of going out and buying two boxes of pasta, I thought, just like cousin Joe, that rather than going out and spending a dollar, I would use what I had in the house and save a buck. I'm sure Joe would have approved.

Pasta Salad

2 lbs of shells, ziti. farfelle or rotini pasta, cooked and drained
2 cloves of garlic, mashed to a paste
1 cup mayonnaise
2 tablespoons of sweet relish
2 teaspoons mustard
1 teaspoon Worcestershire sauce
1 teaspoon each of salt, pepper, and sugar
1 tablespoon red wine or tarragon vinegar
1 cup finely chopped green onions
1/2 cup sliced green or black olives

Put all the above ingredients in a large bowl and stir together
Add cooked pasta and mix together with all ingredients thoroughly.
Chill and serve or serve at room temperature.

Uncle Doofy

Toofeik Jaytanie was our next door neighbor. He was a short, dark, good looking man with a jaundiced face and white hair. It was said that he got yellow jaundice and malaria during WW 1 and the effects never left him. He was married to a large rather robust lady with striking dark features. Mrs. Jaytanie (we never called her anything else) was a gas. Witty and abundantly full of life, she was also kind of strange. She wore her hair back in a bun, always had an apron over her dress and wore her husband's socks. I remember one night when I was about 6 years old and my mother and father had gone to a ballgame. I was sick and couldn't go to the game and she and my grandmother were watching me. I woke up and the two of them were sitting there and I asked them who won the ball game. Mrs. Jaytanie asked who was playing and I replied Sherburne and Greene. She said Greene won and I went back to sleep. When my folks got home Sherburne had won.

Uncle Doofy had a well tended garden with beautiful flowers. Especially his peonies and lilies, which I would always pick, and he would get mad as hell and chase me out of his yard. He and my dad didn't like each other but were civil and always acknowledged each other and that was as far as it would get. My dad always made fun of Toofy (as he was called, but being kids we couldn't call him goofy so we changed it to Doofy) because he was a tightwad. One day my mom, who was good friends with Mrs. Jaytanie, asked her what was wrong. She had just got her electric bill and it was $1.05 and she couldn't believe it. It was normally around 65 cents and she was distraught, especially over when Toofeik would find out. She couldn't understand it because after the sun went down the house was always dark. They would never turn the lights on and they cooked over a wood stove. Such was their frugality. But they were good people. One story has it that in 1949 my dad had bought a new car and Mrs. Jaytanie came over, asked my dad why he bought a new car and spent so much money, and did he think he would live long enough to enjoy it? His replied that he bought it just to drive in her funeral. He wasn't too far off or just speaking off the cuff. In fact she died a month later.

I guess Mrs. Jaytanie's demise was my first real experience with death. They waked her in their house and hung a floral wreath draped with a black ribbon on the front door. Inside the house all the clocks were stopped and pictures and mirrors were covered with cloth. At the head of the casket there was a big clock with the exact time that she had died. All the women were clad in black from head to toe, sitting around the casket hysterically wailing in Arabic every time someone new came in to pay their respects.   Then there was the chanting by women, who would stand at the foot of the coffin and sing to the dead, recalling their life and bemoaning what was to happen to the living having left them and so on. That would usually keep your handkerchief perennially soaked. Meanwhile the men would all gather in another room of the house, smoking cigarettes and cigars that were passed around. One theory was that the men got fed up and tired with the women and their frantic weeping, wailing and carrying on in that memorable sea of black. Another theory I've heard over the years is that the men thought that the women didn't have anything intelligent to offer to the conversation and so they made them sit in the other room.

Sequestered in a room filled with smoke, the men were able to conduct business, make deals, see old friends and converse about everything except the deceased. As they took a smoke from the passed box they would raise their right hand and mutter "Allah Ye Mart Hummo" (may her soul rest in peace) and stuff the smokes in their pockets.   With their left hand raised again, they would curse the women in the other room every time they started crying and carrying on. And so it would go.

There was a cigar box on a table in the middle of the room where the men sat and that was the money box. Each family would give a donation to help defray the costs of the funeral and one of the older men would write your name in Arabic on a piece of paper with the amount you gave and when you had a death in your family the recipient was expected to give back – kind of a loan. I always wondered if everyone got the same amount back that they had put in, but it was all in Arabic and every time I would see the box at a wake I couldn't figure it out. The other irony is that I'm sure their electric bill soared because the lights were left burning for three nights in a row, for the first time in about 30 years...

One thing that Mrs. Jaytanie cooked that was really good was Bulgur wheat and red kidney beans. Cooked like a risotto, bulgur is a coarse grade of wheat that is used in Kibbee (Lebanese meat dish) and Tabouleh, and was cooked mostly on Friday's and during Lent when meat was forbidden to eat. Also, bulgur was really cheap, about a nickel a pound, and Uncle Doof grew the onions and beans in his garden. Economically it was sound.

Bulgur and Kidney Beans

1 lb of Bulgur wheat #2 grade
1 large onion finely diced
2 cans of red kidney beans drained
3 cups of cold water
2 tablespoon olive oil
Salt and pepper to taste

In a large skillet heat oil and sauté onions until lightly browned
Add Bulgur wheat and stir thoroughly
Add 2 cups of water a little at a time until all is used, reserving 1 cup
Add kidney beans, stir and continue to
Cook slowly over low flame until all the water is absorbed
Add salt and pepper
The mixture will start to thicken.

If the mixture starts to stick to the bottom you will want to add the remaining cup of water slowly and continue to simmer for a few minutes longer.

It is cooked like you would cook risotto or couscous. Slowly as it absorbs all the water and the bulgur starts to puff up. I usually cook it until it starts to bubble like lava in a volcano and then turn it off. It will continue to cook and thicken off the stove.

Serve immediately or serve it like I do, lukewarm.

Aunt Rosie and Uncle Tony

Aunt Rose was my mother's younger sister and a wonderful lady whom we all loved dearly. She baked great Arabic bread and used to sell it every Friday. Everyone would get their "Marook" or flat bread and their Tillamee (pita) from her and when she baked you could smell it all over the neighborhood. She was also in the restaurant business. The story has it that when my mom and dad first got into the bar/restaurant business, Aunt Rose would run the register every Saturday night. After about a year of doing this she would go home and tell my Uncle Tonous (Tony) about all the money we were making and that they should build a restaurant next to their house on an empty lot. It was across the street from the knitting mill, which generated a lot of traffic.

So, they went into the restaurant business in direct competition with us and called their place Mody's Restaurant. Then the battles began. My dad was mad as hell and a year later (1951) he went into debt to the tune of $50,000, putting up a brand new facility with a bar and dining room, complete with new chrome chairs, Formica tables, booths, parquet floors, and recessed colored lighting to compliment the solid mahogany bar with huge beveled mirrors. He called it Lewis's Restaurant and Cocktail Lounge.

It was a showplace. We would have a 5 piece orchestra every Saturday night and people would get all dressed up, come and have a sizzling T-Bone steak for $2.75 with a chef salad and French fries or have a huge sizzling sirloin steak for $2.85. Then they would finish the night off drinking daiquiris, Bacardis or Pink Squirrels and dance the night away until the next Saturday night.

We also served Spaghetti and Meat Balls with a salad for $.85, Baked Lasagna and salad, $.95, Chicken-in-the-Basket with French Fries, $1.25. Mody's sold the same things but 10 cents cheaper. That really upset my Dad. They sold their coffee for a nickel a cup and no refills and we sold ours for 10 cents and a refill. Their pie was 15 cents a slice and ours was 25 cents. Of course ours was better. My mother's Banana Cream pie would be 3" high while Aunt Rosie's was about an inch high and had a soggy crust. On Fridays we sold our Fish Fry with French Fries and Cole Slaw for $.75, they sold their Fish Fry for - you guessed it - $.65. Their beer was 20 cents a bottle and ours was $.25, and so it went. Strangely enough there was enough business to go around and both of us had different clientele. Although the competition was fierce, they remained good friends, continuing to visit each other, go places, do things together and remain loyal within. And if bad words were ever spoken against either you never heard a word of it because what was or might have been said never left either house to become public knowledge. After all they were family and still are. Of course that doesn't dismiss the fact that my mother was a far better cook and the food we served was far superior to what they put out, but then I think with everything a nickel and dime cheaper even if it wasn't that good, how could you miss?

Mody's Restaurant

They closed their restaurant on Sundays. That would generally prompt a family dinner either at their house or ours or at my Aunt Helen's. Because Aunt Helen's place was small we would usually gather at Aunt Rosie's. The good news was it always fun to go there. The bad news was she wasn't a good cook. But she did have one good dish and that was her fried potatoes, and they were good.

Let me reiterate here. It wasn't I who said she wasn't a good cook, but my mother. She would always complain about Aunt Rose's food, claiming she never seasoned her food enough and that it was too bland for her tastes. They were very close. My mother was the older sister, and I guess she could get away with it.

Rose and Tony Mody wedding picture

Aunt Rosie's Fried Potatoes

2 lbs. russet potatoes, peeled and cut into thirds
2 cups of olive or canola oil
Salt and pepper to taste

Put potatoes in a large kettle and cover with cold water
Bring water to a boil, lower flame and cook over low heat until potatoes are tender
Drain and set aside

Add oil to a medium sized saucepan and heat until the oil starts to boil
Add 1/3 of the potatoes to the oil and cook until they turn a nice golden brown
Remove with slotted spoon onto a plate lined with paper towels
Repeat the process with another third of the potatoes
Continue to do so until all the potatoes are cooked
Sprinkle salt and pepper and serve hot.

Pan Fried Chicken Breasts

6 boneless chicken breasts
2 cups of seasoned bread crumbs (preferably Italian), mixed with 1 teaspoon cornstarch
3 tablespoons butter
3 tablespoons olive oil
1 teaspoon granulated garlic powder
1 teaspoon cumin
1 teaspoon paprika
1 teaspoon each of salt and pepper

In a large frying pan bring the butter and oil to a slow boil and the butter begins to brown
Mix together bread crumbs, garlic powder, cumin, paprika, salt and pepper.
Bread the chicken with the bread crumb mixture.

Add the chicken pieces, one at a time, and cook for 4 to 5 minutes
Turn chicken over and continue to cook another 3 to 4 minutes
Remove from pan and transfer to ovenproof plate
Pour pan juices over chicken and put into pre-heated 300° oven for 10 minutes
Remove and serve or let sit and serve at room temperature.

You can do this with bone-in chicken breasts too. Just increase the oil and butter to 5 tablespoons each and cook each breast about 10 to 12 minutes on each side.

Equally good either way.

More on Uncle Tony Mody

Rose Meelan Mody and Tony Mody

Our Uncle Tony was quite the character. He came to this country in 1910 and settled in Utica where he met my Aunt Rose. They were married in 1925, a union that lasted some 55 years. He wore long underwear, a flannel shirt and a wool sweater over the shirt and always a hat. He was always cold. Even in the summer when the weather was sweltering he was dressed that way. Tony had a way with the ladies. Not that he was adulterous or unfaithful but gregarious and fun loving. If the men went to a ballgame, Tony stayed behind with the woman. If they went fishing, the same thing. If the women were sitting around talking, he was with them. He had a green thumb and a productive garden. He grew beautiful peonies and poppies. I don't think he realized that they were of the opiate variety as were all the rest of the poppies growing in the neighborhood.

One day he came over to see my father and he was forlorn and close to tears. In his hand was a letter from Lebanon written in Arabic and my Dad, who was two years older than him, sensed impending bad news with the hysterical state Tony was in. He asked him in Arabic, "shoo ghal taan" (what's wrong) and Tony showed him the letter, moaning "read it." My Dad couldn't read Arabic and swore at Tony, asking him 'what did it say?' Tony looked up and, wiping tears from his eyes, said, "They sent me my baptismal records from the church and I'm two years older than I thought I was. Ya harhroum (poor me). What am I going to do?" My dad said "nothing" and laughed like hell.

Quite the showman, he was usually the center of attention with his funny stories and old country ways. He loved to dance Arabic with his hand behind his back as was the custom, keeping in step with the music and the clapping rhythm of the guests. Tony was thrifty with a dollar. That's probably why he made and saved a lot of money in the restaurant business. Tony knew zilch about the business. For starters he couldn't read or write English. He wasn't illiterate, he could read Arabic, but that didn't count. He would take your order and tell Aunt Rose and she would write the ticket up. One day he was alone in the restaurant when a group came in and wanted ham and eggs. Tony, not a cook but not wanting to lose the business, obliged them. He fried the ham, made the toast, cooked the eggs and served them to the customers. When they got their order one person said they wanted their eggs sunny side up and another wanted theirs over easy. Tony said you wanted eggs and this is the way you get them. They ate and paid and didn't argue. Neither did the guy who came in for two tuna sandwiches to go. He should have checked the sandwiches before he left, because Tony had made the sandwiches with cocktail sauce (ketchup and horseradish) instead of mayonnaise, and so it went. He never wrote an order down and to everyone's knowledge was pretty accurate. He called everyone "Boss." "Hello Boss," "How are you Boss?" "How's the boss today?" etc., etc. Needless to say everyone called him "Boss." Only fitting.

One day, a couple of years before he died, he was sunning himself at the side of his house on an 80° day, still wearing long underwear, a flannel shirt, a sweater and a cap and reminiscing on his life, saying he felt so alone. "All my friends are gone. Your father, Saba, Fuad, Uncle Buddy, Ummee Naceem, Domit, and Mr. Abraham. They're all up on the hill and I'm all alone, me and the women." "Layish intee, Ya Allah" (Why me God?) He lived to nearly 90.

Dinner at The Mody's, late 1940's. N. Main St., Sherburne
Pictured far left: Aunt Leona, Bobby Meelan, Carlo Marano.
Standing in back: Lila Marano, Carlo Marano Jr., Don Newman, Jeanette Newman, Tony Mody, Rose Mody, Sito Ruffo.
Seated Front: Eddie Meelan Jr., Eddie Meelan, Irmin Mody

Shahneenah-Shahneenah

Easter! Easter! Along with the leg of lamb and the Virginia ham, another great tradition in our family was the cracking of the eggs. After second mass the Saba family and the Lewis family would square off with their Easter eggs to see who had the strongest egg. You would take your colored dyed egg and wrap your left hand around the bottom half and the other person would wrap their hand over their egg the same way, then perch his hand above yours and hit it. Whoever's egg cracked lost, and the winner would go on to challenge someone else. The person whose egg didn't crack was the winner and had bragging rights till the next Easter. The secret was to lightly tap the other egg rather than hit it hard. The old timers claimed the forces of gravity controlled the hit and the lighter the touch, the more deadly the blow, comparing it to David and Goliath and the slingshot with the stone. The harder you hit the more likely your egg would get smashed. The consolation prize was that you got to eat your beautifully decorated smashed egg. For some reason the Sabas generally had the edge. They would cook their eggs in onion skins which in turn would turn them brown, and although it was never substantiated it was an old wives' tale that the onion skins made the egg shells tougher. We haven't done that in a long time. Both sets of parents are gone, the families are spread apart and getting everyone together is much more difficult today.

Onion Skinned Easter Eggs

2 dozen uncooked eggs
8 large onions
6 quarts of cold water

Peel the onions, saving everything that you have peeled off, the brown outer layers too.
Add onion skins and eggs to water in saucepan and bring to a boil
Lower flame and simmer another 10 minutes.
Remove eggs from water and let air dry until they are cooled.
They will be a deep golden brown
They can sit out all day but should be refrigerated after 3 or 4 hours.
Good Luck!!

Beet Eggs

Cook the eggs the same as above but instead of using the onion skins add 3 or 4 beets to the kettle. They will turn a beautiful burgundy color once they have cooked.
The beet eggs were never as strong as the onion eggs, but they were prettier.

Easter Ham

1 10 lb boneless ham
1 cup honey
3 tablespoons prepared mustard
1 tablespoon each of ground cinnamon, cloves, allspice, and cumin
2 16 oz. canned pineapple rings, reserving juice
2 tablespoons sugar

1 tablespoon black pepper
2 large oranges cut in half and then cut into 1/4" slices
2 cups ginger ale

Pre-heat oven to 400° .
Put ham in large baking dish
Pour ginger ale and pineapple juice over ham
Smother honey and mustard all over ham
Equally sprinkle spices and black pepper all over ham
Place as many pineapple slices as you can get all over ham
Sprinkle them evenly with sugar
Bake for 1 hour at 400°
Reduce oven temperature to 350° and bake for another 2 hours, basting occasionally
Insert thermometer to check for desired doneness

I usually cook the ham until the spices and skin turn a dark crackly brown
Remove from pan and let sit for 1/2 hour before serving
Do not discard pineapple rings but arrange on a dish around ham
Pour pan juices in a gravy boat and serve along side the ham

Scalloped Potatoes

5 lb bag of potatoes
1/2 lb melted butter
3 tablespoons olive oil
1 half gallon of milk
2 tablespoons of granulated garlic powder
2 tablespoons granulated onion powder
2 cups shredded cheddar cheese
1 cup grated parmesan cheese
1 tablespoons salt
2 tablespoons black pepper

Slice potatoes across about 1/8" thick with skins on
Put potatoes in large kettle and cover with cold water
Bring to a boil, turn off stove and let potatoes sit in water for 10 minutes
Drain potatoes of water and add them to a large bowl
Add butter and olive oil and stir together
Add remaining ingredients and stir together thoroughly
Transfer to baking dish, cover with foil and bake at 350° for 1 1/2 hours
Remove foil and bake another 1/2 hour
Remove from oven and serve. Also good at room temperature.

Fuad and Fanny and The Farm

Fuad (Foo-add) was a farmer. He grew and sold beans, peas and cabbage. Every summer he would bring in migrant workers to pick the fields of produce, load the trucks ship them to the canneries in Pennsylvania where they were sold. A lot of people in the neighborhood would also pick beans for extra income. The old school bus would come in the morning, pick everyone up, and off to the fields you would go. You earned 50 cents a bushel and the older women would pick up to 20 bushels a day. When you had a bushel picked you would call one of the field hands to come and get your bushel. I can still hear old Mrs. Marano yelling out, "Donny, um a gotta booshel." He would give her a green ticket and she would continue to pick another bushel of beans. Fuad was the overseer and when he was in the fields you didn't fool around. Either you picked your share or he kicked you out of the fields. With him it was work, work, work.

He and Fanny had four daughter and two sons and like all ethnic families at the time if you misbehaved you got punished and usually with the dreaded strap that hung on the wall. And every family had one hanging. It was as much a fixture as a picture of the last supper and a crucifix. Fuad would add insult to injury. If you were going to get a licking, he would make you go get the strap. He also was old country, where the male was the superior who ruled the roost and women knew where their place was, especially in his household. I must say it is nothing different than the role woman play in the Catholic Church today. If you think I'm crazy for saying that ask any Nun you run into and see what they have to say. Especially those not in habit.

But by keeping an upper hand on the ladies it must be said that they were tremendously good cooks and when they cooked at the farm it was always a feast. One story has it that some relatives of ours had come to visit on a Sunday afternoon and Fuad asked them to stay and have dinner. He asked them if they wanted chicken and they said yes. Grape leaves? Kibbee? Rice, Tabouleh, Stuffed Squash? They said yes to all of them. Fuad told Fanny to get dinner and she would oblige. The daughters weren't too happy because they had to do all the work. Off to the hen house to grab a chicken, cut off its head, plunge it into boiling water, pluck the feathers, clean and cut up the chicken and then fry it. In the meantime they would have to go and pick the grape leaves and gather the squash and stuff them. After that they would have to trim the fat from a leg of lamb, grind it up and add the spices to make Kibbee, then cut up the tomatoes, cucumbers, radishes, green onions, parsley and mint into bite sized pieces for the Tabouleh and put the rice on the stove. Luckily the bread was already made and a watermelon was cooling in the creek for dessert. Fuad and the men would sit in the shade under the grape arbor drinking his homemade brand of Arak, a home brew prized by the Lebanese. The women worked in the hot kitchen, set the table and put the food on the table and told the men to come and eat. Fuad would say grace, thanking God and not the ladies, then he and the men would sit down to eat while the women waited on them. After the men had finished they would head back out to the grape arbor where the woman would serve Turkish coffee and Arabic sweets. With that accomplished and their male counterparts happy they sat down to a dirty table of what was left and ate their dinner. It's a good thing the men aren't around today because they wouldn't be happy about the way customs have changed.

Aunt Fanny's Grape Leaves

There are countless arguments as to who makes the best Warek Arriesh, Wara Enib, or Dolma, better known as Grape Leaves. The usual and most sanctimonious statement is generally "my mother!" Or every once in a while, "my grandmothers." Either way, many a heated argument or a righteous punch in the nose would try and settle the dispute. I remember teasing a cousin that his hometown had the dubious distinction of being the grape leaf capitol of the world, which got a blasphemous reply directed towards me, my family and anyone else he could berate. So it wasn't a discussion that could be dealt with lightly. At a family wedding that I had catered one of the guests said to me that I had a lot of courage and I asked what did he mean and he said "take a look over there - there are nine Lebanese women who are experts at making grape leaves and they're eating yours. Each lady had a different comment and I left the jury out on that one... But of all the grape leaves I have eaten and devoured over the years, Aunt Fanny made the best. Undisputedly! Hers were long and thin with just the right seasonings and taste that subtly melted in your mouth. And if you ever tasted one you would agree.

Grape Leaves

5 dozen fresh wild grape leaves or 1 jar of them in brine (available in Middle Eastern specialty stores)
2 cups of diced raw or ground lamb meat
2 cups of uncooked long grain rice
1 bunch of fresh parsley chopped fine (3 cups) or 2 cups dried
1 bunch fresh mint chopped fine (3 cups) or 2 cups dried
Juice of 1 lemon
1 tablespoon each of salt and pepper
1/2 teaspoon of cinnamon
1 cup of tomato sauce (optional)

3 cloves of garlic sliced thin and 1 lemon cut into 1/8" slices. Set aside and do not mix in with the other ingredients.

In a large bowl add the meat, rice, the rest of the ingredients and mix together
Take one leaf at a time and lay the rough side down with the stem part facing you.

Take a teaspoon full of the stuffing and place in the center

Fold the bottom of the leaf over the stuffing, rolling tight

Then fold it in from each side to the middle and roll tightly forming a roll about 3 to 4 inches long and about 3/4 to 1" thick.

Line the bottom of a large saucepan with grape leaves
Place the grape leave rolls in the pan side by side in a neat rows tightly
Repeat the process. You should have 3 to 4 layers.
Take 6 or 7 grape leaves and cover the top layer.
Sprinkle garlic and lemon slices on them
Place a heavy plate upside down on the leaves and press down lightly and add enough cold water to reach the top of the dish.

Cover the pan securely and bring water to a boil. Turn down the heat and simmer slowly for an hour. Remove plate and leave cover and take out grape leave rolls one or two at a time and transfer to a serving dish and serve with lemon wedges.

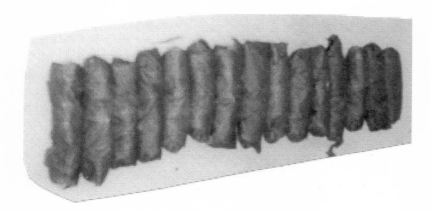

Would You Like To Try Some Kibbee?

One evening way back in 1963 I was dining in the Cedars of Lebanon restaurant in New York City with my good friend States Coyle, along with his first of a couple of wives and a bloke from London and his girlfriend. None of them had ever experienced Lebanese food so I took it upon myself to do the ordering for them. Let me note that there really isn't a main course in our cuisine with everything being referred to as "Mezze" (mezz-eeh). I ordered a number of things and we began to sup on hommous, feta cheese, marinated olives, tabouleh, and liffit (pickled turnips). So far so good. Then came the grape leaves, stuffed eggplant, shish kebab and rice. Everyone was devouring up a storm, enjoying as they munched. Then came the kibbee, a platter of ground lamb meat molded in the middle of the plate, garnished with onion wedges, parsley, pita bread, and a cruet of olive oil.

"What's this?" they asked, and I retorted, making the sign of the cross over it, "Kibbee, the national dish of Lebanon."

"Why does it have a cross imprinted in the middle of it?" they asked. Well, every Lebanese Christian knows that if you don't have a cross in the middle of your kibbee it may not be tasty. "Ya Allah, Ya Allah." (My God, my God).

As they ate their way into the kibbee, enjoying every morsel, they asked two questions: how is it made and why wasn't I eating any of it? I proceeded to tell them that it was raw ground lamb with spices and that "I wouldn't eat that crap, but if I told you how it was made you wouldn't have eaten it and I wanted you to have the full kibbee experience."

States along with George

Actually, I was polite because one day my niece brought a young beau to dinner and we were eating kibbee. After his second bite he inquired "This is good, what is it?" I replied "goat's testicles." He never came to dinner again.

By the way, my buddy States is doing just fine. States as in United – he was named after his grandmother (States was her maiden name). Financially secure, no longer married, and at 66 years old still sinfully good-looking and throbbing the heart of any female who crosses his path (last count about 5000). He is a good cook in his own right, yet his greatest asset other than breaking all the ladies hearts he comes in contact with is the knack he has for picking the right bottle of wine to go with every meal. And if you would like his phone number just give me a call, but if he promises you roast duck with blackberry sauce, beware! You could be victim 5001. Oh Lord, a scoundrel he may be – but the duck is to die for!

Kibbee

Kibbee is to Lebanon what the hamburger is to America. It is the national dish, made with lamb meat that is ground up and mixed with bulgur wheat, onion, herbs and spices and patted between the hands to resemble a hamburger. It is fried in olive oil or baked or as a real delicacy, eaten raw. Sounds gross eaten raw I'm sure, but oh, the subtle perfume that permeates from its Mediterranean spices combines so that it's the foods of the Gods. It was also one of the main staples served during biblical times.

There are different variations. In addition to lamb, during Lent, it was made with fish, Kibbee Samak, or potatoes, Kibbee Bydote, and in the fall with pumpkin, Kibbee Yaqtin. Little round meat pies, some made round like a meatball, and some made oval with a stuffing in the middle, some made to look like little footballs and some made flat to look like a hamburger. I like the flat ones, patting them out in your hands like little mud pies. They are good for snacking, eaten as a side dish or as a main course.

To make Kibbee you need 2 lbs of lean ground lamb meat, devoid of fat. Usually a boneless leg of lamb ground three times in a meat grinder is the norm. But today with lamb not as available, good lean ground top round of beef or sirloin will suffice.

Recipe

2 to 3 lbs of lamb meat or ground sirloin or beef
1 large onion
1 medium sweet red pepper
1 bunch of parsley
1 bunch of fresh mint or 2 cups dried
1 tablespoon of cinnamon
1 tablespoon of allspice
2 tablespoons of cumin
1 tablespoon salt
1 tablespoon black pepper
3 cups of bulgur wheat (the finer the grade the better)

Add meat to a large bowl and add bulgur
In a food processor puree onion, pepper, parsley, and mint and add to the meat
Add spices, salt and pepper and mix everything all together thoroughly, forming into an oval mound.
Make a cross in the middle using the side of the palms of your hands
This is an old superstition that if you don't make the cross the Kibbee won't be any good. That can be disputed because many people I know made the perfect cross but lousy Kibbee.

At this point the Kibbee is ready to be eaten raw and is called Kibbee Nayeh. Olive oil is drizzled over it and wedges of raw onion and pieces of pita bread are served with it. Most of us scoop up a little piece with the bread and eat it that way. I was never fond of the onion wedges but if you had good fresh tender green onions that was always a refreshing taste to go along with the Kibbee. Such was the way it was served in our house, redolent with the flavors of parsley, onion, mint and meat.

At one function I served the Kibbee Nayeh. When the guests asked what it was and were told raw lamb it was given a thumbs down and left untouched. Not to be out done I tricked my guests the next time. I took the Kibbee Nayeh and made a ball about an inch round. I chopped up some parsley, mint and green onions real fine and mixed them together. Then I brushed the ball with olive oil and rolled it around the green mixture until it was completely covered and put them side by side on a serving tray, stuck a toothpick in each one and served them as a fancy canapé. The tray was devoured and not until everyone had eaten their fair share did I reveal to them what they had eaten. Oh the power of the foods of the Gods.....

Raw Kibbee. Note cross in middle.

Cooked Kibbee

This can be either fried or baked. I prefer it fried although baking it in a hot oven can achieve the same results. Whatever type of pan you are using fill it 1/3 full with Olive or Canola Oil. (I prefer a medium to large sized frying pan)

Take about an ice cream scoop size of the Kibbee and pat it out with your hands into a hamburger shape, about three to four inches in diameter and 3/4" thick. Sometimes it is a good idea to have a little bowl of cold water to dip your hands in so as not to let the meat stick to your hands. Another way to do them is to take the same amount like the ice cream scoop and make a ball. Pat your hands with the cold water and stick your thumb in the middle of the ball. Then proceed to shape a small football around your thumb. Then remove your thumb and seal the end. Again a pat of cold water on the hands will make it easier to shape. Continue to make patties or footballs and lay them out side by side on a plate.

Meanwhile, slowly bring the heat up to about 370° or until the oil starts to looks like it has underground currents swirling around. Drop the Kibbee one by one into the hot oil, spacing them about an inch apart in the pan. Cook for about 4 minutes and then turn them over and cook for another three minutes. They will turn a nice golden brown on each side. Remove from pan with a slotted spoon and lay on a plate lined with paper towels to absorb the excess oil. Keep in warm oven until ready to serve, or they can be served at room temperature.

To bake you would want to oil lightly a baking pan and place the Kibbee an inch apart side by side and brush lightly with olive oil. Bake in a 400° oven for about 20 minutes or until they turn a nice brown. Remove from oven and serve.

I make little hors d'oeuvres using an ounce of the Kibbee to make half dollar size, patting them out the same as above and frying them.

Stuffed Kibbee

To stuff a kibbee you need to make a hushwee, which in Arabic means "stuffing." There are different variations of hushwees. Some with meat filling, some with rice and some just plain vegetables and spices.

Hushwee meat filling:

1/2 cup of olive oil,
1 lb. of raw ground lamb
1 cup of pignolia nuts
1/2 cup of fresh chopped parsley
1/2 cup of fresh mint or 2 tablespoons dried and crumbled
1/2 teaspoon each of cinnamon, allspice, cumin, salt and black pepper

Sauté lamb in olive oil until lightly browned. Add pignolia nuts and the rest of ingredients and sauté until the pignolia nuts are lightly browned. Remove from stove and set aside.

Hushwee

Take raw kibbee (see recipe above) and put about 1 ½ ounces of meat (about the size of a small egg) in your hand and flatten it out between your hand, as if you were making a hamburger patty or a mud pie, to about ¼" thickness. It is essential that you have a small bowl of ice water to moisten your hands when patting out the kibbees. This makes the whole process easier and makes them easier to form. Your patty will be about 3 to 3 ½" in diameter. Mound a teaspoon of the hushwee in the middle of it and make another patty like the first one.

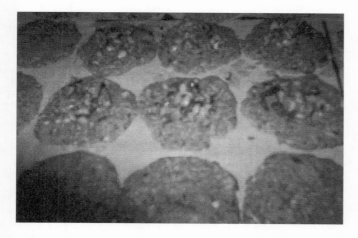

Moisten the edges with ice water lightly and put the patty on top, molding it together with both hands as if you were making a snowball. Seal the edges and make sure there are no holes in the patty, moistening your hands as necessary to form a smooth oval ball. Repeat the process until you run out of meat and hushwee.

There are two ways to cook these. I prefer to deep fry them in olive or canola oil until they are golden brown (usually for about 3 to 4 minutes) and then remove from oil with a slotted spoon onto paper towels to drain. Your oil should be at 365 degrees. The other way is to brush a cookie tray with the oil like you would bake cookies, brushing a little oil on the kibbees and baking at 400° for 20 minutes or so until they reach a golden brown.

Serve with a salad, pita bread and a sauce of yogurt laced with chopped cucumber, diced tomatoes and chopped green onions

Alice Doyle and her chicken

My good friend Patti Doyle Caprio (referred to as Mrs. Colgate in the book) serves this God awful dish every time she hosts a social function, whether it be a bridal shower, funeral reception, office party or a gossipy white wine luncheon for her close intimate girlfriends affectionately known as "the ladies." I truly think it is the worst concoction I have yet to come across and to this day believe this recipe could be found on the back page of an old Protestant church cookbook. I also think if you served this dish the Catholic Church would charge you with a mortal sin, sending you straight into the pitfalls of hell without turning a corner, where you and this chicken mixture both should burn forever.

Yet everyone would ooh, aah, rant and simply wail about the delicateness of the dish. Patti's father was a chicken farmer amongst other things and probably had excess chicken to spare. Alice, Pat's mother, who grew up during the Depression with a 'waste not, want not' sensibility put the chicken to good use. They ran a very successful deli in downtown Sherburne, serving the best apple turnovers and poppy seed rolls you ever tasted. And John Q. Public lined up every day and paid $1.49 for her chicken salad, mounded on a lettuce leaf, with a fresh baked croissant without butter. I might add that if you asked for butter she probably would have charged you a nickel more. I think the damn thing was as plain as her steamed green beans – but then I would not dare tell Alice, not while she was alive.

I really preferred her jell-o salad mold that she served our 6th grade class when President Eisenhower was inaugurated in 1953. Her daughter Elaine was in our class and went to her house to watch it on one of the rare televisions to be had back then. The ginger snap cookies were good too.

By the way, if you are ever down around Hamilton, New York on a fall Saturday afternoon, Patti hosts a tailgate party before each Colgate home football game. She serves up mounds of her famous chicken supreme and can be spotted by this huge maroon flag with a large "C" in the middle, flying high above the tent. There's always plenty for everyone as her guests come running for seconds and she is fully prepared to load up your plate. Yum-Yum.

One word of caution: don't let her husband Joe induce you to try a bowl of his not so famous venison stew. Just stick to his roasted red peppers. A word of advice – sprinkle a little salt and give the peppers a good squeeze of lemon and tell Joe next year, serve a piece of pita bread with them. Toasted! He'll love your suggestion…

Patti Doyle Caprio, her son Drew, and her husband Joe

Alice Doyle's Chicken Delight

6 boneless chicken breasts, cooked, cut into 1" pieces
1 cup mayonnaise
½ cup chopped red onion
1 cup fresh chopped parsley
2 cups green grapes, cut in half
1 cup chopped walnuts, almonds or pecans (optional)
3 tablespoons fresh chopped tarragon (optional)
1 teaspoon Worcestershire sauce
1 teaspoon Dijon mustard or 1 teaspoon dried mustard
2 tablespoons of apple cider or red wine vinegar
¾ teaspoon each sugar, salt and pepper
1 teaspoon curry powder

Mix all ingredients together in a bowl and refrigerate one hour before serving. Can be made the day before. Serves 6 – 8 people.

Don't forget the croissants and lettuce leaves or your chicken delight won't be supreme!

Alice's Molded Jell-O Salad

2 packages strawberry flavored gelatin
2 cups hot water
½ cup granulated sugar
1 pint frozen strawberries
1 pint frozen raspberries
Pinch of salt and squeeze of lemon juice
1 pint heavy cream whipped or 2 cups cool whip

Dissolve gelatin in hot water
Add remaining ingredients except for the whipped cream
Mix together thoroughly
Fold in whipped cream until all is mixed.
Pour in a glass bowl and refrigerate until firm
Serve with extra whipped cream and garnish with fresh strawberries

An absolute delight!

Margaret's Split Pea Soup

This recipe was given to me by my friend Vince Quinn. It was from his mother Margaret Seehan.

1 ham bone or 1 lb., of salt pork
1 pint green split peas (2 cups)
2 1/2 quarts cold water
2 stalks of celery chopped fine
2 medium sized carrots chopped fine
1 large onion chopped fine
¼ teaspoon dried thyme
¼ teaspoon dried marjoram
Dash of cayenne pepper
1 clove garlic, chopped fine
1 bay leaf
Salt and pepper to taste

Place ham bone in 2 1/2 cups of water and simmer for 1 1/2 hours

Remove bone from water and set aside

Mix all ingredients together, add to water, bring to a boil and then cover the pot and simmer slowly for about an hour or more or until the peas are mushy.

Re-adjust seasonings and serve piping hot.

When the soup is cold, refrigerate it. The soup becomes very thick. Do not dilute with water to thin it. As it heats the soup will become thin again. Add water if it too thick for you, but only if necessary.

Cut up some ham and add it to the soup for extra flavor.

This is a meal in itself and will serve 6 to 8 people.

Author with friend Vince Quinn

Lehman, Lewicki, and Lewis

We were all born in 1942, Ed, Carolyn and myself. From day one, thanks to alphabetical order we were always together. Kindergarten class, First Communion, grade school, Confirmation and high school. Regardless, we were there together and still are today. Two dumb Pollocks and a smart-ass Syrian. Carolyn is married to my first cousin Rick and hasn't really assimilated. She's still Polish. Ed married Chris, she's Swedish Methodist and he left the Catholic Church to get married in hers. That was in the 1960's. Damn near got him ex-communicated back then but they're back in the Catholic fold, more fanatical than when they left. When we get together Carolyn always warns me not to mention the abortion issue and women in the priesthood. I always oblige her, keeping peace until Ed starts spouting at the mouth about unborn kids and Arab terrorists. Then the fun begins. Ed starts to rave. Cousin Rick starts to laugh, Carolyn throws her hands in the air trying her utmost to shut us up. I usually have had enough of his ranting and politely tell him in my finest, most eloquent tone that he is "starting to urinate me off." I then leave the room for a few minutes until we all calm down. Carolyn usually becomes the great peacemaker with her famous "Now George, now Ed," and we call each other an ethnic slur and go back to being friends. But every once in a while Carolyn has to interject a "Now Ed!"

A couple of years back Carolyn, Rick and I went to visit Ed and Chris, who lived in Boston, for the weekend. After an eventful Saturday we were up having coffee at 9 am the next morning, discussing what we were

Ed Lehman, Carolyn Lewicki Merhib and George Lewis

going to do for the day. One thing was certain, they were going to 11 o'clock mass at St. Someone's. I thought, "Great! I'll lounge around, have more coffee and read The Boston Globe." "Hell, no!" was their reply – you're going to church with us. I replied with a "bull blank. Just pick me up after mass." No way – church was on the way to where we were going and it would be out of their way and inconvenient to come back to the house. I retorted with a few blasphemies and dumb Pollock slurs but ended up going to St. So and So's for an hour of plenary bliss. I put on my Arab scarf (a hajiib), grabbed a book I had with me on how to learn Arabic and was off, not too happy but much to Ed and Carolyn's delight. You would have thought they had witnessed the second coming of Christ getting me to church.

I was right for it wasn't the best idea in the world marching into that church with an Arabian scarf and book in hand, especially in light of the fact that Islamic terrorists were blowing up people around the world. I looked at my book, ignoring the stares of the religious faithful, thinking why didn't they pay attention to the mass and quit worrying about me. I didn't have a bomb on me and where the hell was their Catholic charity.

Carolyn and Ed kept their heads bowed low, fervently praying and realizing it was a real blunder bringing me along. Cousin Rick just looked straight ahead and smiled.

The climax to the day came when they started to take up the collection. I had twenty dollar bills on me and nothing else. The guy passed the basket and I ignored it. Not so fast. It was a double collection day. Here we go again. But God does work in mysterious ways for I had a bank deposit envelope in my book that I used for a bookmark. The guy came around again and this time was ignoring me with his basket when I said "Wait a minute." I took the bank envelope and put it in the basket, getting an approval rating from all that were still watching. I would have loved to have seen the expression on all their faces, along with the priests. The envelope was empty … Amen, amen. Carolyn is still praying for me.

Later that night, we were sitting around having after dinner drinks and eating the delicious cookies Carolyn had made at home and brought with her. I up and confessed about the envelope, had another of her cookies and laughed like hell.

Carolyn's Polish Cookies

Pizzelles

Beat together:
6 eggs
2 sticks soft butter or margarine
1 ½ cups sugar
2 teaspoons vanilla

Sift together:
3 ½ cups flour
4 teaspoons baking powder
Pinch salt

Add flour mixture to wet ingredients a little at a time and mix well
Put one rounded teaspoon onto a hot griddle for approximately 30 – 45 seconds

Chocolate pizzelles:
Add:
½ cup cocoa
½ cup extra sugar
4 teaspoons extra baking powder

Lemon Cookies

Preheat the oven for 350°

Mix together:
2/3 cup oil
4 eggs
2/3 cup sugar

Add to above mixture:
3 cups flour
3 teaspoons baking powder
5 teaspoons lemon juice

Mix well. Roll and shape in balls or drop from teaspoon. Place about 2" apart.
Bake on greased cookie sheet for 8 – 10 minutes or until light brown on bottom

Frost with confectionary sugar mixed with juice of one fresh lemon (and lemon zest, if desired)

The Hunch Is A Brunch

A while back I did a brunch for a priest and his parish flock. The priest, being a finicky health conscious eater who abhorred the likes of bacon, sausage and ham with its wondrous amounts of calories and high-end cholesterol, wanted me to do something with salmon along with other brunchie things I had on the menu. Little did I know, thanks to his secretary he had struck gold at the local supermarket, finding plain labeled salmon at 99 cents a can, and had bought a whole case. Well, he didn't care for the bacon and I didn't like the thought of canned salmon. A bit of an impolite discussion ensued, and I told him that I would use the canned salmon when the church admitted women into the priesthood. But in the meantime until that issue was resolved we were serving the real McCoy, just like the church and its male dominance. No substitutes! Resolving that issue wasn't so difficult. The problem was how to make a piece of salmon into a brunch dish. I looked through a couple of cookbooks but no luck. James Beard was dead, Julia Childs was no help. Could I cream it with a little dill? Too much cholesterol in the sauce. Smoke it? No, it would be too expensive. I decided to call my good friend Patti "Colgate" down at the university, hoping to reach her at home. She was always throwing brunches and I was positive she would have a good idea or two. Unfortunately she wasn't home (never is) but down in New York City hosting a brunch and getting ready to fleece the alumni for untold contributions and probably serving her famous chicken salad with sweet green grapes on Bibb lettuce, which by the way is pretty good especially with her tasty croissants. I had the salmon – now what in God's blankety-blank name was I going to do?

Perhaps the blankety-blank got God's attention. About an hour before the brunch and the 75 unsuspecting guests divine intervention set in, as I threw some olive oil and butter in a pan and started to melt it. Then I took some fresh green onions, chopped them up along with a couple of thin sliced garlic cloves and added them to the pan. While that was sautéing I diced up a sweet red pepper, sliced up a pound of fresh mushrooms and added them. While that was slowly cooking I took the filet of Salmon, cut it into 1" chunks, added it to the pan and stirred it a couple of times. Then came a little sherry wine, a squeeze of fresh lemon, 3 tablespoons of tomato sauce, a handful of chopped parsley, a dash of fresh thyme, salt and pepper, cooked it another minute or two and added 3 cups of 2% milk. I simmered the dumb thing for about 1/2 hour, then asked one of the girls working with me to taste it. They did and gave me the thumbs up, whence I tossed a handful of parmesan cheese in it, gave it a final stir and took it off the stove. We toasted some English muffins, buttered them, laid them in a chafing dish and ladled a couple of tablespoons of Fr. Finicky's concoction over the muffins and sent it to the buffet line. Needless to say they love it. One woman (Aunt Flunsy, who also is an authority on food) asked if there was any left over because she wanted to take it home and serve it over linguini for supper. So much for divine intervention…

The brunch was a success. Along with the salmon we served a baked cheese omelet, blintzes with fresh berry glaze, assorted Danish, cranberry/orange muffins, blueberry coffee cakes, pumpkin bread, chilled melon balls and hulled strawberries. The only thing missing were the Bloody Marys and Mimosas, but then it was a Sunday morning church affair. But we did have chilled fruit juices. As for the finicky priest, well, he didn't know what he missed. He got tied up at an interdenominational coffee and donut social, showing up just as we were locking up the kitchen an hour later. He asked about the salmon and I told him it was good and too bad that he had to miss it, but if he were hungry he could call Aunt Flunsy and invite himself for dinner and savor a plate of linguini. Don't know if he ever did – a shame if he didn't but then he could open a can of salmon. And if he was inventive he could add it to a can of mushroom soup and consider it a heavenly delight. So much for high calories...

Divine Sherried Salmon

1 3 to 4 lb filet of fresh Salmon cut into 1" chunks
3 tablespoons olive oil
3 tablespoons butter
2 bunches green onions chopped fine
3 garlic cloves sliced thin
1 sweet red bell pepper diced fine
1 lb fresh mushrooms sliced thin
1 bunch of parsley chopped fine
1 teaspoon fresh chopped thyme or 2 teaspoons dried
1/2 teaspoon each of salt and pepper
3 tablespoons of tomato sauce
2 tablespoon of dry sherry
3 cups of 2% milk
2 tablespoons of fresh grated parmesan cheese

Melt olive oil and butter in a large sauce pan over low flame
Add onions and garlic and cook for two minutes
Add red peppers and mushrooms and cook another two minutes stirring as you go
Add salmon and cook for two more minutes continuing to stir
Add sherry, parsley, thyme, tomato sauce, milk, salt and pepper
Continue to cook slowly (simmering) for 20 minutes to a half hour
Remove from stove and stir in the grated cheese

Serve over English Muffins or toast tips.

Other Brunch Suggestions

Eggs Newport

2 lbs bacon
2 cans of Cream of Mushroom Soup
1 32 oz. jar of mayonnaise
2 dozen hardboiled eggs, peeled
1 teaspoon freshly ground pepper
No salt (bacon adds enough)

Fry bacon crisp, drain grease and crumble
Mix mayonnaise and mushroom soup together and simmer 5 to 10 minutes
Add bacon and simmer 5 to 10 minutes more
Skim off excessive fat as some will accumulate
Slice eggs and put one layer in a casserole dish
Add a layer of mushroom soup mixture over eggs
Continue to repeat the layering leaving room for a last layer of soup mixture on top
Bake uncovered at 350° 20 to 25 minutes or until bubbly
Sprinkle top with paprika and let stand 5 min before serving

Note: For best results fry bacon and cook hard boil eggs the day before. Bacon crumbles better and the eggs are easier to slice.

A great brunch dish.

Gas House Eggs

6 slices of bread
6 raw eggs
3 tablespoons Butter

Cut a hole in the center of the bread about the size of a half dollar
Melt butter in a large frying pan over medium heat
Add bread slices, side by side
Crack an egg over each hole
Let cook for about a minute or two
Flip bread over and cook another minute or two to desired doneness of eggs
The bread will toast on both sides.
Serve immediately

This dish was apparently served along roadhouses and gas stations for people looking for a quick bite and easy breakfast. I saw them done on an old high society movie on television years ago. Can't remember the movie though.

O Solo Mio

There was a man named Old Dominick who lived alone just down the street from us. People said he had no family but thought he had a wife in Italy who died, which caused him to immigrate to America where he had a cousin who brought him here. He was a colorful man who spoke with a heavy Italian accent and very little English. But he got along well with everyone. His one fault and criticism was that he didn't go to church and always blamed God for the death of his wife. Back then that was a sure ticket to hell without turning a corner. Everyone prayed for his salvation. Lucky man if he only knew how many prayer and rosaries were recited on his behalf; even St. Peter couldn't turn him down at the pearly gates, especially with that repertoire. He drank wine but that was OK because he made his own and would jokingly offer you a glass of his "Deigo Red."

He was a gifted musician who would sit on his front porch on hot summer nights and play his banjo to the delight of everyone in the neighborhood. People would gather and sit on his lawn and he would strum the banjo strings, singing and playing old Italian songs. It was said that he couldn't read music but would play by ear and what an ear he had. It was almost like having a concert in the park after dinner. If you knew the songs you would sing and dance along to the melodies. Every once in a while he would strum out a "Tarantella" and the old Italian ladies would work their feet to the peasant Italian folk dance. And when it got dark Dominick would play an Italian version of "Good night ladies," which signaled the end of the music and everyone would go home or we would play a game of "kick the can" (where you would put a can in the middle of the street count to 25 and then see who could kick the can without getting caught). By 10 o'clock everyone had to be home and the game would end. If you were lucky your family had a radio and you had some form of entertainment. You didn't have to take a bath because bath night was on Saturday so you would be nice and clean for mass the next morning. Plus if you went swimming down at the river someone brought a bar of soap and you bathed there.

But Dominick had another talent. He was a good cook and back then quite innovating. No one could understand why he would go to grocery store and buy those shanks of veal that no one had any use for and the butcher would usually throw out. But not Dominick. He had come from the "famed Arthur Avenue" in the Bronx where each Italian eatery and grocery store was better than the next. That became our first experience with Osso Buco or better yet, Dominick's version.

Osso Bucco

6 to 8 veal shanks
Flour to coat veal shanks (2 cups)
4 tablespoons olive oil
1 tablespoon butter
1cup chopped onion
1 cup carrots finely diced
1 cup celery finely diced
1 16 oz can Italian plum tomatoes
1 cup dry white wine
1cup parsley chopped fine
2 cloves of garlic minced
Salt and pepper to taste

Coat veal shanks with flour and set aside
In a large skillet heat olive oil and butter until it starts to foam
Add veal shanks and brown on all sides (about 10 minutes)
Remove veal shanks and set aside on warm plate
Add onions, carrots, and celery and sauté until vegetables are limp
Re-add veal and stir
Add white wine and cook until wine is reduced by half
Stir in plum tomatoes, salt and pepper
Cover the skillet and simmer the veal for 1 1/2 hours or until meat falls from bones
Add garlic and parsley and simmer 10 minutes more
Remove from stove
Add veal shanks to a plate and cover with remaining sauce and serve

Note: most people serve it with risotto but like Dominick I prefer serving it over spinach fettuccine noodles and a green salad.

Hot Spinach Salad

2 bags of fresh spinach
1 pint cherry tomatoes
1 lb fresh mushrooms, sliced
1 lb fresh asparagus spears cut in 2" pieces
2 bunches green onions coarsely chopped
3 cloves of garlic sliced thin
1/4 cup olive oil
1/2 teaspoon each of salt and pepper
1/4 teaspoon hot pepper flakes
1 tablespoon Balsamic vinegar

In a large fry pan cook onions for 2 minutes over medium flame
Add garlic and continue to cook until it turns a very light brown
Add tomatoes, mushrooms, salt, pepper, pepper flakes, and stir fry for 2 minutes
Add spinach, toss in pan as you would when mixing a salad, stirring for 2 minutes more

Drizzle Balsamic vinegar over spinach and mix lightly
Remove from stove and transfer to a bowl and serve.

It is important to continue stir the spinach lightly while still cooking
You want the spinach to be just wilted and not thoroughly cooked

Avocado With Vinaigrette

3 ripe Avocados
Cut Avocados in half and remove the large pit
With a tablespoon scoop out Avocado (trying it keep it whole) from its skin

4 or 5 leaf lettuce leaves washed and pat dried
2 tablespoons of prepared vinaigrette
Squeeze of fresh lemon
Salt and pepper to taste

Arrange lettuce leaves on plate
Slice Avocado halves lengthwise about an inch wide (like peach slices)
Arrange slices on lettuce leaves and drizzle Vinaigrette over them
Squeeze lemon over avocado
Salt and pepper and serve

Note: This should be prepared at the last minute because the avocado slices will turn dark if exposed to air. You can also toss the avocado slices with lemon juice to stop discoloring. If you do this refrigerate until ready to serve.

Sno-Ball

That's what Leo the Irish called Helena the Lebanese. Helena Ibrahim had a very dark complexion and Leo in one of his inebriated stages (which could be often) nicknamed her Sno-ball and the name stuck. Helena, who was never for a loss of words, called him a "Teeza Kullub" which in Arabic is the derriere of a dog, which translates into one of the higher forms of profanity in the Arab world and a term never used in polite society. That name stuck.

Helena had a high school education and Leo was a magna cum laude Fordham University graduate. Helena worked in the lab at the hospital which was menial labor but to her it was important being around and hobnobbing with all the doctors. It was kind of like my job of cooking and interacting with priests and bishops. But the interesting thing about both jobs is that after you see enough of us and we do the hard labor, you have to listen to us too. Kind of a blending of philosophies! She also moonlighted as a waitress for us at Lewis' restaurant two nights a week. Leo worked for the post office, was married, had four children, and drank Utica Club Beer, frequenting our bar every night. And that's where the meeting of the minds began. Helena would ask Leo for a bit of his knowledge and Leo would retort with his usual arrogant Irish rhetoric and then the name calling and battle of the wits would begin. Back and forth they would go. The educated versus the not-so-educated. "Dumb Lebanese" to "Street trash Irish." But despite the dog fighting and ethnic name calling, they were the best of friends.

Helena was another one of those ethnics who still knew where the first nickel she earned was. She never married until her middle 60's and lived with her mother and sister. All the money came home and it never left. If you went to their house they would offer you a drink of a sort, but only one! They would come to your house for dinner if you invited them but would rarely reciprocate. I think I was one of the few people who ever ate at their table. I always joked that I was going to marry her sister just to get a piece of the family fortune or the beautiful signed Tiffany lamp that sat in their living room. The lamp was one of the rarer ones and was rumored to be valued in the high thousands. Apparently the mother went to a rummage sale in the early 1940's and bought it for 25 cents. Everyone laughed at her for buying someone else's junk. Even her daughters admonished her for spending so much money.

But if you bought Helena a drink at the bar, she would buy you one back because that was the proper thing to do. If you invited her to a wedding or party she would bring a gift. But it would end there. I remember that when I went away to school in the 1960's a letter came from her. In it was a five dollar bill. For Helena that was a lot of money. I was grateful but could never understand her parting with it, but that was her way. When my sister first started out in business she needed $1,000. Helena heard about it and immediately gave it to her and told her to pay her when she could. They ate a lot of greens and a lot of pasta and rarely meat but on Christmas they splurged and did a magnificent Roast Leg of Lamb accompanied by linguini in tomato sauce and oh was it good. Her tomato sauce was simple but redolent with black pepper that gave it one hell of a bite and strangely enough complimented the leg of lamb with fresh greens.

Roast Leg of Lamb

6 to 7 lb boneless leg of lamb
(you can also use a leg of lamb with the bone in and cook the same way)
2 tablespoons olive oil
3 garlic cloves crushed to a paste
6 garlic cloves cut in half
2 tablespoons fresh mint chopped fine or 3 tablespoons of dried
2 tablespoons fresh thyme chopped fine or 3 tablespoons of dried
1 cup fresh chopped parsley or 3 tablespoons dried
2 tablespoons of Dijon mustard
2 tablespoons of Worcestershire sauce
1 tablespoon fresh ground pepper
1 teaspoon salt
2 cups dry white wine
3 carrots chopped fine
3 celery stalks chopped fine
1 large onion cut in wedges

Pre-heat oven to 400°

Take a knife and cut 12 incisions into leg of lamb and insert garlic halves
Rub with olive oil and sprinkle Worcestershire sauce all over it
Make a paste with the mustard, garlic salt, pepper thyme and mint
Rub it all over the leg of lamb
Put leg of lamb into a large roasting pan and add celery, onion, carrot and wine
Put in oven and bake for 1/2 hour and then reduce oven temp to 350°

Bake for 1 hour or more, allowing about 20 minutes per pound
(a food thermometer can guide you to desired doneness of rare, medium or well done)
Remove roast from pan, set on a warm platter and reserve juices*
I like to take the vegetables and mash them through a sieve for added flavor to the sauce.

Let sit for 20 minutes before carving slices
Put pan juices in a saucepan and whisk in 1 tablespoon of cornstarch and bring to a boil
Simmer slowly for 15 minutes and serve with lamb

Sauce for Linguine

2 large cans of tomato paste
2 tablespoon olive oil
6 cloves garlic sliced thin
1 1/2 tablespoons black pepper
1/2 teaspoon crushed red pepper
1 teaspoon salt

Sauté garlic in olive oil until lightly browned
Add tomato paste and 2 cups of water, salt and peppers
Bring to a boil and simmer for 45 minutes
If sauce gets too thick slowly add water to thin it out

Every Dog Gets His Day

That was one of Aunt Dolly's favorite sayings. Whenever she or anyone else were wronged by someone those were the words she would repeat and how true they were on many an occasion. Once a relative had died and at the funeral Aunt Dolly asked where this cousin of ours was. Someone said "You know her- she wouldn't come because she thinks the Lebanese people and their custom of doing things are beneath her." Aunt Dolly muttered her famous SOB's and said "every dog gets their day". A few months later the relative's husband died and no one came. The widow was aghast that very few people came. Aunt Dolly was one of the mourners and if she said it once she said it twenty times. They do get their day... And she was outspoken too. But then only when it was morally right to do so. When my uncle died in January of '82 she never forgave my two aunts, who spent their winters in Florida, for not coming to the funeral. Words were spoken and it took a bit of smoothing over and peacemaking to make it all right again. Yet she had her say, and they knew it.

Aunt Dolly had a hard life. Her husband had a rare blood disease and was always sick and unable to work. But she always was able to get by. When her husband, Uncle Buddy, was in the hospital in Utica before he died she managed to get there every day for six months even though the hospital was 45 miles away and she didn't drive. She outlived all of her siblings, never understanding why she was able to outlast the others. She was regarded as the grand matriarch of the family, ever present at all of our functions right up until she died. I once saw her bridal picture and I must say that she made a beautiful bride, wearing a lace veil over her head and a bouquet of white lilies. To this day I've never seen one that duplicated the beauty of it. I would have loved to have seen the photograph in color, but way back when they were just black and white.

One day my sister had driven her to Sunday mass. My sister, who was having trouble with her leg and was walking with a cane, got behind Aunt Dolly and told her to go up the steps first. Aunt Dolly, who was 80 at the time, told her to go first because if she fell she could catch her.

But after Sunday mass, Aunt Dolly was famous for her brunches with family and friends coming from near and far to attend. Like clockwork every Sunday morning after first mass there was homemade pita bread, mile high coconut cream pie, her famous fah'toy'ees (herbed spinach triangles encased in bread dough), and fresh brewed percolated coffee. My mothers fah'toy'ees were better and so was her coconut pie. But that debate could go on forever with no one side conceding as to whose were better and it's best to stick to your own opinion and leave that one for the books. If you missed a brunch all I can say is you missed it! I never made one. Working late on Saturdays made 9:30 AM Sunday just too difficult for me to be up and at it. I kept saying I would make one but unfortunately I never got to it.

Anyhow I wouldn't dare to recreate the coconut cream pie because my mother and Aunt Dolly took those recipes to the cemetery with them. What I will do is recreate the spinach pie recipe that I have modified for the sake of convenience and time, yet not omitting any of the original flavors. The only thing I can't give it is the love that they put into it - though with a dash of this and a dash of that, a pinch here and a pinch there, a mix and a stir, and Voila! Almost as good as theirs...

I don't know if any of Aunt Dolly's children picked up any of her culinary skills but I would venture to say that her daughter Angela came the closest. When she worked with me in the catering business, it took a few tries but she finally learned how to cook the pasta properly. After that I knew she had the knack But as for her cooking skills I know she can cook pulled pork with bottled BBQ sauce. She starts that in a crock pot, which pulls it until she gets home (I don't think Aunt Dolly would agree). Anyhow I'm not going to give you the recipe, because you can get the pork at your local rib joint. That makes sense because she is never home.

There isn't a person she doesn't know, and she's so friendly, pretty and outgoing that you can't help but love her on first sight. Whenever I introduce her socially, she always tells the person that she is my favorite cousin. Perhaps she thinks I'm important. She's also religious as hell. Every Wednesday morning she goes mass to St. Bartholomew's with a bunch of old Italian ladies and is a fixture at their Sunday 9AM services too. She claims half her prayers are for me. I think she had better quit praying for me and start praying for St. Bart's because they just lost their priest and chances are they'll close it down. I hope they keep it open long enough for her to help make the sauce and meatballs for their annual spaghetti dinner. And from what I understand she uses Aunt Helen's recipe for the sauce. I can hear Aunt Helen now, "Those damn Merhib kids, They have no respect."

Fah'toy'ees (Spinach Pies)

Filling:
4 cups of spinach, cooked and finely chopped
1 bunch fresh parsley, chopped fine
2 bunches green onions, finely chopped
1/2 cup of fresh mint finely chopped or 1 tablespoon dried
1 tablespoon fresh thyme, chopped fine or 1 teaspoon dried
1 teaspoon each of cinnamon, allspice, and cumin
Juice of 2 lemons
1 1/2 teaspoons of salt
1 teaspoon of black pepper

Mix together.

Dough:
2 lbs fresh commercial bread or pizza dough, thawed
Flour for dusting the work area or cutting board (about 2 cups)
1 cup of cold water and a small basting brush
1/3 cup olive oil

Method:
Put bread dough in a large bowl, cover with wrap and let it sit out at room temperature 3 – 5 hours or until the bread has risen (it will double or triple in size)
Remove wrap and poke a couple of holes in the dough
Using a knife cut off a piece of the dough about ½ the size of your fist
Dust your work surface with flour and put the piece of dough down to work it
With your finger tips pay out dough like you were making a pizza (It should be 5 to 6" round)
Take a tablespoon of the spinach mix and put it in the middle of the patted out dough
Lightly brush the edges of the dough with water (lightly!)

You are now going to make a triangle by taking the edge of the dough and bringing it to cover the spinach mix in the center. This will cover 1/3 of it. Repeat with other 1/3 and then the last 1/3. This will resemble a triangle. Pinch all the edges together tightly so the mixture won't ooze out and make a smoky mess.

Brush lightly with olive oil and bake on lightly floured cookie tray at 350° for 10 to 15 minutes until they lightly brown. Remove from baking pan and serve at room temperature.

Moo Shoo Shoo (Lebanese Greens and beans)

1 lb. black eyed peas soaked in 3 quarts of cold water overnight
Drain water and add 2 cups freshwater to the beans
Bring to a boil, add 1 large onion chopped fine and 1 cup chopped celery
Simmer till beans are tender
Drain reserving 2 cups of water

1 lb. of chopped endive or kale
3 tablespoons olive oil
2 cloves chopped garlic
1 teaspoon salt

In a fry pan add olive oil and chopped endive or kale
Sauté 2 minutes. Add garlic and salt and stir.
Add drained black eyed peas, onion and celery and stir.
Add 1/2 tsp of black pepper and 1/3 tsp. red pepper flakes
Add 1 1/2 cups bulgher wheat, water and continue to simmer until all the water is absorbed and the wheat is tender. About 30 to 40 minutes.

Serve immediately, lukewarm or cold. It's good either of the ways.

Coconut Cream Pie

Pie Crust

This works best in a food processor with the chopper blade

1 1/4 cups flour
1/8 teaspoon salt
1/4 lb of chilled butter cut in 1/2" cubes
5 to 6 tablespoons of ice water

Add flour to food processor bowl
Add butter and salt and process for 10 seconds
(mixture will be mealy)

Add water slowly while machine is running until the mixture forms a ball
Turn off machine, remove dough and refrigerate until ready to use

For the Filling

1 cup of sugar
1/4 teaspoon salt
1 1/2 tablespoon flour
2 tablespoons cornstarch
3 cups of milk
3 egg yokes, slightly beaten (reserve egg whites for meringue)
2 tablespoons butter
2 teaspoons vanilla
3/4 cup shredded coconut

In a saucepan mix in first four ingredients
Add milk slowly, cook over low heat, stirring constantly until mixture thickens and boils
Remove from heat
Stir a little of the mix into the egg yokes, then add eggs to pan stirring constantly
Blend in butter and vanilla, stirring as you go and set aside for 5 minutes
Add to pie shell and top with meringue
Bake in 350° oven until meringue starts to brown lightly
Remove from oven and let cool thoroughly before serving.

Blessing Of The River

When I was a kid we would go behind the mill and across the railroad tracks to the Chenango River, where we would swim, fish and generally hang out. It was quite the hub of activity and really special on Sundays. People coming home from church would change out of their church clothes (and everyone would dress up in those days) and head to the river, especially if it was a hot sunny day. Upwards of a hundred or so people would bring their bathing suits, fishing poles, and picnic baskets laden with their Sunday lunch, which never consisted of hot dogs and potato or macaroni salads. That's what the Americans and Irish who lived downtown would eat. And they would never come to the river where all the "quarter" people would go. That was one of the politer names they called us, "Quarter Ducks." Our part of the town was labeled the quarter (a part of the town that encompassed about 4 city blocks). The quarter got its nickname not because we lived there but rather because when the town was chartered in the 1870's, a quarter of the town lived there. But anyway you looked at it, the section was considered different from the rest of the community and stayed that way for many decades. I don't think they liked the smell of garlic, which was grown in every garden and permeated the air. Their potato and macaroni salads didn't contain garlic, and we didn't start eating those dishes until the 1960s, when we finally realized we weren't going to be lynched for putting garlic in them. I also suspect that the reason we all had to sit in the back of the church was we all smelled of the bulb, which didn't sit well while trying to recite the "Our Father."

The entire "quarter" would gather on Sundays, bringing their dinners along with them, either to cook or already prepared, so they could feed their families and any others they would share with. None of the old folks spoke good English but with nods and hand signals, sights and smells, everyone was able to communicate and bond, together sharing their old country foods. The Pollock's would eat their Kielbasa and cabbage, the Italians their ravioli's with meatballs and the Lebanese their grape leaves and shish kabobs. The women all wore aprons, had their hair tied in buns and did most of the cooking. The men would build the fires for them to cook on, then go and fish or play cards till dinner was ready. Blankets were spread to sit on and folding tables were set with tablecloths to put the food on and we would go swim while dinner was being prepared.

But before we could go into the river, usually around Memorial Day when the water would warm up, the river had to be blessed. That was the tradition. And what a blessed event that was, with old Father Kissane trudging up the dirt road in his long black cassock with a white lace surplice over it, prayer book in one hand, rosary in the other, flanked by two altar boys, one carrying the holy water and the other carrying the incense. Thus the ceremony would begin, with him muttering some Latin phrases no one ever understood, plus a few Hail Marys. He would empty the container of holy water into the river. Everyone would make the sign of the cross, he would tip the miter from his head, which gave the okay, and we would all jump in. Everyone would make the sign of the cross, the men would go back to fishing and playing cards, some of the younger women would cook, and those not quick enough to find something to do were stuck with father and the old ladies as he recited the rosary. The season had begun, the water was safe and we were too. We had made the sign of the cross so God was on our side.

Kielbasa and Cabbage

5 lbs of uncooked Kielbasa
6 cups cold water
2 bay leaves
2 cloves garlic
1 large onion
1 teaspoon black peppercorns
1 head cabbage
6 carrots cut in 2" pieces
6 large potatoes cut in quarters

In a large kettle add water, Kielbasa, onions, garlic, bay leaves and peppercorns
Bring to a boil and lower flame and cook slowly for an hour
Add cabbage, carrots, and potatoes and cook for another half hour or so until the vegetables are tender.
Remove vegetables and arrange on a large plate
Remove Kielbasa, cut into 2 to 3 inch pieces and arrange around vegetables

Serve with white vinegar, a good spicy mustard and a loaf of rye bread.

Red Cabbage and Apples

1 head of red cabbage shredded
2 Granny Smith or Golden Delicious Apples, cored, peeled, and diced
1/2 cup of sugar
1 cup of red wine or apple cider vinegar
1 tablespoon olive oil
Salt and pepper to taste
1 cup water

Heat oil lightly in a large skillet
Add red cabbage and stir
Add sugar and stir
Add water, vinegar, salt and pepper and sauté for 10 minutes
Add apples and continue to cook over low flame for an hour or until cabbage is tender
Stir occasionally while cooking
Water or white wine can be added if mixture starts to dry out.
Adjust seasonings and serve warm.

Our Aunt Helen

Aunt Helen was my favorite aunt. She was the youngest of my mother's sisters and probably the most modern. She was a pretty woman, a hairdresser by trade who was always impeccably dressed with never a strand of hair out of place. She was a very creative person who was hellishly fussy and properly smart. She was a good criticizer, especially of some of her nieces and nephews, who had no choice but to tolerate her behavior because she was their mother's sister and that's the way it was. We have a great picture of her on her wedding day. In her bouquet she carried 24 calla lilies. How they got them all into the bouquet without overpowering her I'll never know. She lived downtown, across from the school and away from the rest of us. She was also the first one to marry outside of the race. She did the unpardonable thing by marrying Uncle Onofrio, an Italian.

Aunt Helen and Uncle Nofe

My grandfather Saleem wasn't a happy camper. Nor were Nofe's people. The good thing was we were all dark skinned and had that one common trait. I guess it didn't matter; they had a happy union of some 40 years before he died. Nofe was kind of a maverick. After all, his brother-in-laws were all Lebanese, and if there was a big family gathering, Arabic was the preferred language, which kind of left him out in left field. But he got along. He didn't have a choice.

He did hold his ground in one area and that was Sunday dinner, which was always at his mother's house. And that was sheer heaven if you were fortunate enough to be invited. Old Mrs. Biviano spoke no English and made meatballs that were 4 inches round. Her homemade pasta was the talk of the town and her tomato sauce had such a subtle sweetness you never got "angina" from it. But it didn't stop there; her cannellonis, fried calamari, eggplant parmesan, antipasti, and cannolis told you her repertoire was more than spaghetti and meatballs. And her fresh baked crusty Italian bread to dip in the sauce was what every Italian lived for on Sunday. Unfortunately she neither could read nor write and none of her recipes were ever recorded. But Aunt Helen did teach me to make her Eggplant Parmesan. She also taught me how to make her meatballs and after a thousand tries with each batch being better than the other I still haven't got the taste that I remember from her kitchen. I guess maybe that "when the book is called up yonder" I'll be there to collect those recipes that went six feet under...

Aunt Helen had a good heart and never missed a graduation, birthday, First Communion, etc. without a card and a monetary supplement in it. In her later years she started to become quite forgetful and that got a bit scary because at 80 years old she was still driving. We all worried, considering that when she got to her destination she couldn't remember driving there. She must have driven to where she had to go out of habit.

At a family wedding the band started playing an Arabic tune and Aunt Helen, against her sisters' objections, was out there on the floor doing a traditional dance, gracefully displaying her skills, doing all the fancy footwork, shaking her hips in belly dancing fashion, showing all the younger folks how it was done. When it was over everyone stood up and gave her a standing ovation, including her sisters. Aunt Dolly's kids, who weren't too fond of her, made a few disparaging remarks. She would always complain about them, saying they had bad manners, never sent her a birthday card and generally would ignore her. She would always say "Those damn Merhib kids." They had to tolerate her because their mother didn't drive and was at the mercy of Aunt Helen. And both being retired they were always on the go. That kept Aunt Helen around to voice her opinions and concerns to them, which most likely were never welcomed. That would cause them to hold their tongues while muttering a few profanities under their breath. She would always say they were bad kids and were going straight to hell. I tended to agree with her.

Aunt Helen would spend her winters in Florida every year. She and Uncle Nofe lived in a retirement village, did all the things that people in those kinds of places did and were really quite content. Nofe would go fishing every day and she would do all the ladies hair at a fraction of the price they would pay in a beauty shop, which was good with all of them retired and on fixed incomes. Anyhow I was living in Ft. Lauderdale one winter, unemployed and holding on to my last few bucks. It was Christmas and she invited me over for dinner. I picked some flowers at a public park, made a bouquet and gave them to her. She loved flowers. Somewhere during the course of the day she pulled me aside and slipped a twenty dollar bill in my hand, wished me a Merry Christmas and told me twice not to mention it to Uncle Nofe. Somehow she knew I was broke, but that didn't stop her from giving. She was like that. In spite of her continuous nagging, telling you your skirt was too short, or your sweater was too tight, or you needed a haircut, or you should stand when someone entered the room, or your makeup was all wrong, or NEVER criticize her own kids, she had a good heart, always caring and there for you when you needed her to be. I loved her, regardless of what Aunt Dolly's kids would say, as she would nit pick them for walking on this earth...

Aunt Helen's Eggplant Parmesan

6 firm eggplants
1/2 cup olive oil
3 cups Italian seasoned breadcrumbs
2 lbs ricotta cheese
2 lbs shredded mozzarella cheese
1 cup grated parmesan
3 eggs
1 bunch fresh parsley chopped fine
3 cups of marinara or spaghetti sauce
Salt and pepper to taste

Cut eggplant diagonally in 1/4" slices
Sprinkle lightly with salt and set aside for 15 minutes and drain excess water
Brush lightly with olive oil and sprinkle breadcrumbs on each side heavily
Lay eggplant slices side by side on a cookie sheet and bake 10 minutes at 350°
Remove from oven and repeat this until all eggplant slices are baked

In a large bowl mix cheese, parsley, eggs, salt and pepper thoroughly, set aside
In a large baking dish brush bottom lightly with olive oil
Lay individual eggplant slices side by side until bottom is covered
Spread a layer of cheese mixture over slices about 1/4" thick
Ladle 3 or 4 tablespoons of sauce over it
Repeat the process until all are used
Cover the mixture with sauce

Bake at 350° for 45 minutes
Remove from oven and let sit for 10 minutes then cut in wedges and serve
Top wedges with remaining sauce and sprinkle grated cheese over it.

Aunt Helen's Meatballs

1lb ground chuck, pork, and veal
2 cups breadcrumbs soaked in 1/2 cup milk
2 eggs lightly beaten
1 teaspoon granulated garlic powder
2 teaspoon granulated onion powder
2 cup Romano cheese
1/2 cup chopped parsley
1 teaspoon each of salt and pepper

Mix all ingredients together thoroughly
Form 2" balls, rolling between your hands
Lay balls side by side in an oiled baking dish

Bake at 400° for 15 minutes, reduce temperature to 350° and bake 30 minutes more
Remove from oven and cover with sauce and serve

Saba-Saba

Saba-Saba came to this country from Lebanon in 1920. When he got to the gate at Ellis Island they asked him what his name was. He said "Saba, ibn Saba." Ibn means 'son of.' In Arab culture a man goes by his first name followed by his father's first name. So he said Saba, son of Saba. Bewildered the clerk kind of scratched his head, stamped his papers and thus he became Saba-Saba. Somewhere along the line it became Saba J. Saba, but whether his name was James or Joseph, we'll never know. It was just Saba-Saba, as he was known by. He also picked up the title "the boss," and that stuck with him all his life.

Saba was a clever man, one of the few men who could read and write Arabic. That brought him a level of respect among his peers and the contents of every letter that arrived from Lebanon in Arabic script.

Saba was a barber by trade and everyone went to get their hair cut by him. It cost 25 cents and you got hair tonic and a splash of some smelly water called "Eau de France." That was one hell of a thrill. You got your hair cut and all the old ladies would pat you on the head, smell your hair and say "duh-la-eynick" which meant something like "aren't you a good child."

Saba married Jenny Abdullah somewhere in the early 1930s. The day of their wedding, all the old ladies gathered at the Abdullah house to sing to the bride before she went to the church and tied the knot. Back then it was a good thing women didn't wear a lot of make-up because the women always made the bride cry with their songs of the trials and tribulations of marriage: "Oh, you must be a good wife or your husband will beat you," or "Oh you are now his family and they come first," or "Oh it will be a sad day as your dead grandmother will cry from the heavens wishing she could be there," and so on. They would also tell her of the horrible things that would happen to her on her wedding night, so that when she was ready to leave for the church she was a nervous wreck. But one nice little custom was putting a piece of bread dough over the front door. If the bread stayed over the door the marriage would last. If it fell off then the marriage was doomed, so the local superstition went...

From the left: Rita Abbott, Dolly Merhib, Fanny Abbott, Flora Sherman, Jenny Lewicki, Jenny Abdullah Saba, Mary Lewis

Saba was quite meticulous. He was good with gadgets and always made the best crosses out of the palms on Palm Sunday. Every tool in his garage had its rightful place on the wall and if you didn't return what you borrowed he would come after you looking for it.

He also grew fruit. He had plum, apple, cherry, fig, and apricot trees in his back yard, along with grapes. For years I wouldn't eat any of the fruit because it didn't come from a grocery store and I didn't think it was any good. Oh, but to taste those sweet yellow sugar plums or those luscious purple apricots. He also grew blackberries and again I didn't think they were any good because they didn't grow in the woods. So much for my culinary knowledge.

Jenny was a good cook. Never did you go to their house without her setting something on the table for you to eat. There were olives, cheeses, pickles, dates, pistachios and home baked Pita bread. They always had a lot of company so the table was always set and no one ever went away hungry. There was a lot of gaiety in that house, with Arabic music ringing off the walls. Both of their families lived in Utica and were always visiting, so the food and music never stopped. One day after a weekend of guests and merriment I went over to say hello and Jenny and Saba were sitting at the their kitchen table and she was crying. I asked her what was wrong and she said nothing, but she was sad that the house was empty and so quiet after everyone had left. That's why she was crying. Loneliness had set in. Regardless, a fresh pot of coffee was brewed and edible Arabic delights were set upon the table, even though I was the only guest. But that was their way and what a nice way it was.

Jenny's sister worked in the kitchen of an upscale country club and did a lot of those plain but fancy "Mamie Eisenhower" canapés. They were simplistic, boring and meant to entice the appetite. Things like the watercress sandwich or the cucumber tidbit served on a triangle of bread with the crusts removed. I guess it was then that I learned that appetizers and hors d'oeuvres didn't have to taste good. All they had to do was look good. But with this new knowledge of what the "waspy set" were eating before cocktails, Jenny had an edge on the ladies of the neighborhood with her tray of "select" canapés to set before her guests. The irony is that none of our people were imbibers back then. It took a few generations later for us to hit the bottle. Just as well, her appetizers were always a hit and kind of made her the "belle of the ball."

Onion and Bacon Bread Rounds

1 loaf of white or whole wheat bread
1 large onion sliced and finely chopped
6 slices of cooked bacon crumbled
1 cup of mayonnaise
1 2" round cookie cutter

Take a slice of bread and cut out rounds, omitting crusts
Brush each round with mayonnaise
Sprinkle chopped onions to cover the entire top
Sprinkle bacon bits over onions
Arrange in rows on ungreased cookie sheet

Bake in 350° oven until onions lightly brown or mixture starts to bubble
Remove from oven, arrange on tray and serve. Makes about 25.

Hearts of Celery With Herbed Cream Cheese

2 bunches celery

1 16 oz. package of cream cheese
1 teaspoon of fresh summer savory or thyme chopped fine
(dried herbs may be used)
12 tablespoons of fresh chives chopped fine
2 tablespoon of Spanish olives with pimento chopped fine
Pinch of salt and pepper
Dash of Tabasco sauce

Wash celery and cut off 1/2 inch of bottom root
(the heart of the celery is the whiter part of the celery at the bottom of the stalk)
Cut the hearts about 1 1/2 inches wide from the bottom of the stalk

Mix up all the remaining ingredients in a bowl
With a teaspoon spread cream cheese mix onto the hearts of celery 1/2" thick
Arrange on tray and refrigerate until ready to use.

Makes about 20.

The Nylon Stocking Savings Bank

Mrs. Saber's first name was Emma, but everyone knew her and called her Mrs. Saber. She was a short, little woman of strong character, who wore her graying black hair in a bun with round spectacle glasses and always had an apron over her black dress. She and her husband Joe ran a grocery store. She wore black for many years in memory of her husband Joe who died very young of a heart attack. When Joe died she and her son Johnny ran the store, which was known for its fine quality meats. Saber's market was a hubbub of activity. They lived in an apartment above the store where they raised their family. It opened at 7AM and would close at 10PM, seven days a week, with Mrs. Saber tending the cash register daily. She didn't speak much English but oh, did she know the color and make of each dollar bill and piece of silver that came across her counter. She was a caring person too. She gave you credit and sometimes would throw an extra little something in your bag. Many would try to cheat her but she was too crafty for that and usually caught you in the act, with those eyes of hers protruding from the back of her head.

On one particular occasion an old Lebanese woman of questionable character would have gotten away with a theft had it not been for a five year old boy buying candy. The woman in question was buying eggs. Back then you would go to the egg crate and put your eggs in a bag and tell Mrs. Saber how many you had. She put her bag on the counter and told her she had 12 eggs. Being a trusting soul she took her word for it and charged her for a dozen eggs. But then a little boy buying candy said "but you've got 24 eggs in that bag." Upon opening the bag there were 24 eggs, a pound of butter and a package of cheese. She kicked the woman out of the store, gave the boy another candy bar and generally opened up all bags at the counter to check their contents.

Rumor has it that after they got into the grocery business they wanted to add a meat department so Old Joe Saber went to Utica to buy some cows that he could slaughter, butcher and sell in his store. Well, after a day's journey he came back to the store weary and dejected. Mrs. Saber asked him what was wrong and he told her had wanted to buy cows but didn't have the money needed to purchase them. She asked him how much he needed and he told her about $700.00. She lifted the skirt under her apron, reached down into her stockings, peeled off eight one hundred dollar bills and gave them to him. He was dumbfounded and then got mad as hell at her that unbeknownst to him she had that kind of money on her.

It wasn't long before all was forgiven, they were selling meats and Joe was driving a new 1946 Cadillac. So much for nylon stockings. The old timers really didn't trust the banks especially after the Great Depression, when a lot of them lost their savings when the banks went bust. Naturally their stockings or under their beds became the storage places for their nest eggs.

Everyone knew Mrs. Saber had a lot of money. One day someone asked her why she didn't retire and take life easy. She was in her seventies, lived alone and had worked every day in her life. Philosophically she said, "And what am I going to do? Go upstairs and sit by myself? I work because it keeps me busy and I see all my friends." I can still see her there, taking your money, asking how your mother was, selling you cigarettes and promising not to tell your mother. It was ironic that when her daughter got married she closed the store, threw her a big wedding, invited everyone in the neighborhood, spared no expense, wined and dined you, sang and danced Arabic, wore a dress other than black and in reality looked and played the part of a lady of means, which in all sincerity, she really was.

Mrs. Saber's Lentil Soup

2 tablespoons olive oil
1 medium onion sliced and chopped fine
1 cup of celery chopped fine
2 garlic cloves chopped fine
2 cups lentils
4 cups beef broth (water can be substituted for vegetarian diet)
Salt and pepper to taste
1/2 fresh chopped parsley
Juice of 1/2 lemon

In a large saucepan heat oil over medium heat
Add onions and celery and sauté until limp (4 minutes)
Add lentils and garlic and stir around
Add beef stock, salt and pepper and bring to a boil
Reduce heat to a slow boil and cook for 25-30 minutes or until lentils are soft
Add lemon juice and parsley, stir and serve.

Sitto Ruffo

Sitto Ruffo was my mother's mother. We would say "hello Sitto" and she would reply "hello Sitto." I never figured that one out. She was a short, stocky lady with good looking features, wore her graying hair pulled back in a bun and the same black pill box hat with a black veil as far back as I can remember. As pleasant a woman you would ever meet. She came from Lebanon around 1914 with my mother and Aunt Rose. My grandfather, Jiddo Saleem, had come in 1912, settling in Utica, New York, following his father Jiddo Anthony, or as we knew him, Jiddo Old Man, who emigrated in 1910.

Sitto Ruffo had five children, four girls and a boy. Her life was a hard one of poverty and hardships, coming here with two children and then three more born here. She spoke no English and stayed at home to raise her family and make do with her vegetable garden and whatever income my grandfather would generate, and that wasn't much. Upon learning of my grandfather's infidelities, that he was a gambler and womanizer, after twenty some odd years of his carousing she threw him out of the house, much to the dismay of her relatives and neighbors. But she got by. She worked in a factory and Jiddo old man would help with his pay check.

Meelan family. Standing: Mary, Jiddo Anthony, Jiddo Saleem, Rose. Seated: Dolly, Sitto Ruffo holding Eddie, and Helen.

When my mother and aunts were old enough they took to working in the knitting mills, with their paychecks coming home to support the family. She and my grandfather would patch things up and she would take him back and after a year or two he would go back to his wandering ways and she would kick him out again. She was a strong lady of pride and she wasn't going to tolerate it. They remained split for some forty years and finally reconciled when they were in their sixties. Either she felt sorry for him and still loved him or he was too old too carry on anymore. Who knows? In the old days justice was severe. If you did wrong then you were shunned by everyone and the sympathies went to the victim, in this case that being my grandmother.

One thing was for certain, Sitto was a good cook and she made a chili sauce that she would put up in jars and we were able to enjoy it all winter. She would always make dozens of jars for friends and relatives, who came calling every August for those light blue mason jars filled with her sauce. If she only knew the value of those jars today.

Sitto's Chili Sauce

20 large ripe homegrown or in season tomatoes, cut in quarters
3/4 cup olive oil
2 large sweet onions, sliced and diced
6 cloves of garlic, minced
3 large sweet red bell peppers
2 cups of celery diced fine
2 chili peppers diced fine with seeds included*
1 teaspoon hot pepper sauce
1 teaspoon sugar
1 teaspoon each of ground cinnamon, allspice, cloves, cumin, and paprika
1 teaspoon of oregano
1 teaspoon thyme
1/4 cup fresh chopped parsley
Salt and pepper to taste (1 teaspoon each)

In a large sauce pan sauté onions in oil for 2 minutes
Add celery and peppers and sauté five minutes longer, stirring as you go
Add tomatoes and cook until mixture starts to boil
Add remaining ingredients and bring to a boil again.
Lower flame and simmer mixture for 2 to 3 hours, stirring occasionally
Remove from stove and let cool for about an hour
This will enable it to thicken and be ready to serve or put into canning jars**

**Note: Back then they didn't have freezers and everything was put up in canning jars to be preserved throughout the winter months. I have found that this will last for a month in the refrigerator, but better yet can be put into containers and frozen. But there is no better colorful sight than to see jars of the sauce set on shelves and brought to the table to spoon over fish, chicken or meat. Yum, yum.

Sitto's Plum Sauce

1 /4 bushel (tomato basket) of ripe black or red plums
4 to six cups of sugar
Juice of 1 lemon
Dash of salt

Wash plums and remove the pits
Add plums to a large saucepan and bring heat to medium
Add sugar, salt, and lemon and stir thoroughly
Bring plum mixture to a boil and reduce to a simmer
Let mixture cook slowly for 1 1/2 to 2 hours until mixture thickens
Stir every 10 to 15 minutes to prevent sticking

Remove from stove and cool
Run mixture through a blender or food processor and puree the plums.
Put in jars and can or put into containers and freeze. They will hold about a week in the refrigerator.

(back then there were no blenders or processors so they strained the cooked plums through a fine sieve or also used a potato ricer)

Old Misses "Haroum"

Whenever anyone died in the Lebanese community Misses Haroum was always the first one there and the last one to leave. Clad in black from head to toe and with a cache of handkerchiefs you would have thought she was a professional mourner like the Italian people used to hire for their wakes. She usually sat in the second row behind the family and was a presence not to be ignored. She was a heavy set woman who was extremely homely with a mole on her chin and hair growing out of it, not to mention the moustache that seemed to be with her forever. All the kids in the neighborhood liked her and would always say hello and couldn't understand why all the ladies would not speak to her or would cross the street to avoid her. After all we would go to their house and were friendly with her kids. It was many years later that that the story finally came to light; we found out that she and some of the married men in the neighborhood were having or had had affairs. And to make matters worse some other men were related to her. That was a scandal that no one could bear and she became a marked woman. We also finally understood what the hushed word "Maa-kloo-tow" meant.

One story has it that a cousin had died and Misses Haroum had gone to the wake and sat in a chair near the casket, weeping and wailing in true Lebanese fashion when her cousin and a cousin of the deceased went into a rage and in front of everyone told her to leave and literally kicked her out. As she was walking down the stairs he called her a "maa-kloo-tow," picked up the chair she was sitting in, broke it into pieces and threw it down after her, yelling in Arabic that no one would ever sit in that chair again. Such was Lebanese justice.

I always felt sorry for her, for her husband, a young man, was killed in WW1 and had left her with six children to raise, which she did and managed to do a good job of it.

Misses Haroum could always tell you when winter was over. It wasn't by the Canadian Geese flying overhead honking their arrival or the sighting of a robin but the sight of a little old lady out in the fields digging dandelion greens. That was the first and surest sign of spring. And the neighborhood joke amongst us kids was that she should join the Olympics for she sure as hell would get the gold medal for being the first one out there every year to get the greens. How lucky the Haroum family was to have the first greens of the season. How unlucky they were to have to eat them daily for the next month and a half even after they had flowered and gotten bitter. But knowing the cost of food and 6 children to feed, it was self-satisfying to know you were eating for free.

The irony of it all was that when she died in the 1980's very few people were wearing black and not too many people showed up at the funeral. Anyhow we still buried the good women in true Lebanese fashion.

Misses Haroum's Lubbneh (yogurt dip)

1 quart Laban
Strain with cheese cloth for approximately 4 hours, or until all the whey is out and it has the consistency of cream cheese

To this add:
      Squeeze of lemon
      Pinch of salt
      ½ teaspoon zatar (thyme or summer savory)
      ½ teaspoon garlic paste
      ¼ teaspoon red pepper flakes

Mix and serve with pita wedges

The Best Cup Of Coffee In Town

If you wanted a good cup of coffee and the best conversation in town you went down School Street to the "Ethnic Ghetto" where Mary Naizek Acee lived. Long before Mr. Coffee and Starbucks, there was always a pot percolating on the kitchen counter of her home, with an aroma you could smell all the way up the street. Mary was always the first one up in her house and no matter how early you arrived there was always a warm greeting and a smile on her face. She would pour you a cup of her fresh brew and the rest of the actors would stumble in. First would be her husband, Theo, then one of her three boys, then Yaashoo the Pollock and Sno-Ball, along with fat Abboud, Sno-Ball's brother Abraham, Ella the Turk, my sister June, and anyone else who could fit at the table.

Conversation usually centered around the church and that awfully strict Father Basssney, who drove a Cadillac and went to the race track every night. You can bet your sweet "Blank-blank" that that topic went around the table once or twice. Then we got to politics as Theo was the only registered Republican in our whole part of town plus a politician, and that always generated another pot of coffee, a second cup for disagreement and Theo with his famous "you're full of you know what." From there it went to local sports, gossip, the good old days, whose wedding was the best, why women were being disrespectful and not wearing black to the wakes anymore, to what funeral was the biggest and why? By 9:15 AM, the table was cleared and everyone went their separate ways until the next day when the same scenario would take place give or take a few new people at the table. It's a good thing coffee was cheap back then for no one ever contributed a dime for the coffee, nor did Mary complain. Of course you knew it was time to leave when Mary would start to prepare dinner for that evening. Tonight's dinner was going to be special, not that most of hers weren't but her oldest boy, who was home from college, was bringing a girl for dinner and first impressions were important if Mary was finally going to have a daughter in the family. Even Theo was told to watch his language and keep his political, religious, and racial opinions to himself, even if the girl was Italian.

Mary was a beautiful, intelligent woman with strikingly dark features that stood out wherever she went. She was also the mother of three boys and had played and watched enough football, baseball, and basketball until she was tired of being the only woman in the "jock strap" crowd. So when it was announced that her son was interested in a girl of fine qualities she was ecstatic. Her other son was about to join a pack of Jesuit intellects and her youngest son was still in 7th grade. The table was set with fine china, the dinner was simmering on the stove and this bastion of male dominance was about to be penetrated by a timid but spirited Italian girl, who unbeknownst to Mary had already set her sights on her first born. Hot dogs and beans would have sufficed and there was no need to worry about Theo's foul mouth.

Tonight's dinner was an old Levantine favorite, probably repeated by every Lebanese family hosting a special event: Yukh'nee b' Riz b' Loub-ya (Chicken with Rice and Peas).

Yukh'nee b' Riz b' Loub-ya   (chicken and rice)

1 roasting chicken, cut up (legs, thighs, breasts, etc.)
1/4 cup of olive oil
1 1/2 large onions sliced and diced
3 cloves garlic sliced thin
6 fresh tomatoes cut in wedges or 1 16 oz. can of plum tomatoes
1 cup of fresh mint chopped up or 3 tablespoon dried
2 cups of water
1 cup of fresh chopped parsley
1 teaspoon of cinnamon
1 teaspoon of allspice
1 teaspoon of cumin
1 1/2 teaspoons of salt
1 teaspoon black pepper

Using a large sauce pan, heat olive oil
Add chicken pieces and onions and brown thoroughly on all sides
Add tomatoes, water, mint, spices, salt and pepper and bring to a boil and lower heat
Simmer for 45 minutes stirring occasionally. Remove from stove and set aside

Meanwhile cook your rice

To cook rice you will need

1 1/2 cups of Rosa Marina pasta, or orzo (Available in the pasta aisles or specialty food stores)
3 cups of uncooked long grain rice
3 tablespoons of butter
8 cups of boiling water
1/2 teaspoon salt

In a large kettle melt butter over low and add Rosa Marina
Sauté Rosa Marina, stirring, bringing it to a light brown color
(it is important to stir this and not let the Rosa Marina burn)
Add rice and stir in for 30 seconds
Add water, salt, cover tightly and bring to a boil
Lower flame and simmer for 1/2 hour or until the rice becomes fluffy
Remove from stove and let sit for 10 minutes
Fluff rice with a fork and spoon out onto a large platter

Spoon chicken pieces over rice
Pour remaining sauce into a bowl to ladle over the chicken and rice

Note: Yogurt is a nice balancing condiment to lightly drizzle over the chicken and rice for added flavor and contrast.

A green salad with oil and vinegar is a good compliment to the spices in this dish.

Lunch For A Priest

A couple of times a year we have an early evening dinner for all the retired priests in the diocese. They come from near and far: some in wheelchairs, others with the help of a cane, while most just walk right in. The walkers include Monsignor Bossy, who usually arrives after the tables are set and the cocktails are in place, armed with enough chutzpah to want to start changing everything around to satisfy himself, upsetting the entire apple cart. After a couple of nerve wracking experiences with this man, acquiescing to his demands, I'd decided that I'd had enough. When the next dinner came he waltzed in, surveyed the room, and was about to make some changes when I interjected that he had better check with the office staff upstairs because they and the bishop's secretary had been down earlier setting up the room to the Bishop's specifications. A bit chagrinned, he backed off and we've never had a problem with him since, other than one other dinner and I'll tell that story later.

It's a fun day, starting with a thirty minute cocktail hour that usually extends to another twenty minutes, followed by a dinner with wine, little gift bags of chocolate and an ever inspiring talk by the bishop that lasts long enough to let the flame go out in the Baked Alaska. On one particular evening we were serving dinner outdoors on the terrace. It was a warm night in the eighty degree range and we were celebrating a retired bishop's birthday. On the menu was a superb filet mignon, shrimp scampi, tortellini in a lemon garlic sauce, watercress and tomato salad, ending with an candle laden gooey, syrupy ice-cream cake. Dinner was served, quite the success, and after dinner drinks were poured when our old friend Monsignor Bossy, acting as master of ceremonies, motioned to me to light the candles and present the cake to the birthday recipient. With lit candles and Monsignor Bossy ready to bellow out a rendition of "happy birthday," the bishop got up and started one of his after dinner talks. Quietly I blew out the candles and stepped back into obscurity. Msgr. B quickly sat down, not wanting to upstage the boss and the bishop started his talk. Ten minutes later myself and my three member staff waited patiently for him to finish while the cake started to melt away rapidly. Three or four minutes, later dismayed by the sight of the cake, I told the staff that at the end of his next sentence where there was a pause to join me in clapping. They were reluctant at first but the sight of the cake convinced them to follow my lead. During the next pause, and rightfully so, we started clapping. So did all the retired priests. Msgr. Bossy stood up, thanked the bishop and we came marching out to the strains of happy birthday and served soft ice cream cake to all the guests. It was one hell of a mess and I guess forty years ago it would have been a mortal sin and a detour to heaven to interrupt the bishop's speech but when the roll gets called up yonder I'm sure the seated priests were secretly praying for the speech to end and the cake to be served. Otherwise to this day I'd probably be able to say, "I'll be there."

Msgr. Bossy and I have long ago become friends. He now trusts me to set the tables, arrange the bar and do the job I was hired to do. Nor do I suggest in my many conversations to God that He, in His all knowing wisdom, please find a place for him in His kingdom. From God's perspective, I think the tables are all set, the wine has been poured, and when He is ready He'll make room for the monsignor to come up there and put a monkey wrench into the works. Amen! Amen!

Tenderloin Of Beef

I like to grill this over a hot fire on the outdoor grill. I take the whole tenderloin and place it on a hot grill or wood fire with just enough of a flame to flicker at it and give it a flame broil, marinating as I go. I usually cook it about four to five minutes on each side to reach a nice medium rare. Cook it a few minutes longer if you want it a little more well done. You can cook this the same way you would cook steaks or chicken over your grill. Otherwise you could bake it in a 450° oven for 15 minutes. If you decide to bake it make sure your oven is very hot before you begin. Another method is to put it under the broiler and cook it that way. The only problem is that you have got to turn it over every other minute to prevent burning. This will take about 12 to 15 minutes for medium rare and a few more turns for well done.

The best way is to do it outdoors with a wood fire. The wood reaches a high heat and the flavors that permeate from the wood give it an added touch. I usually use apple wood and also throw in grape vines for smell and the high flames they bring. If you are using gas then just get the flames high enough to sear the meat. Any way you decide to do it works well and if you're familiar with outdoor grilling just follow your instincts.

A 5 to 6 lb tenderloin of beef

Trim off excess fat and silver skin from tenderloin (your butcher can do this)
Place tenderloin in a large pan and pour 2 cups of Worcestershire sauce over it
Sprinkle 3 tablespoons of granulated garlic all over it
Sprinkle 3 tablespoons of coarse ground black pepper over it
Cover with foil or plastic wrap and let marinate 4 to 5 hours or overnight

Follow the above instructions for grilling or baking.
Remove from grill and let the tenderloin rest for 15 minutes.
With a sharp knife slice the tenderloin, cutting crosswise, making 1/4 to 1/2 inch slices.
(you can cut the slices to the desired thickness you want, but when I have a crowd to feed the 1/4 to 1/2 inch slices work well for a crowd, enabling you to feed around 20 people with one tenderloin, and at $8 to $10 per pound this makes economical sense with a top grade of meat.)

I like to serve a horseradish sauce with this that combines:

3 tablespoons of horseradish
1 cup of mayonnaise
1/4 cup heavy cream
Squeeze of lemon and a pinch of salt
Mix all together, refrigerate and serve chilled

Shrimp Scampi

4 lbs of 16/20 per pound size shrimp, peeled and de-veined
4 cloves of garlic cloves crushed to a paste and mixed with 1/4 cup of olive oil
3 tablespoons butter
2 tablespoons of fresh oregano minced fine or 1 tablespoon dried
3 tablespoons of fresh basil minced fine or 2 tablespoon dried
1 tablespoon coarse black pepper
¾ teaspoon salt
1 cup dry white wine
1 lemon sliced thin
1/2 cup fresh chopped parsley
3 tablespoons of marinara sauce
2 tablespoons of fresh grated parmesan cheese

Mix shrimp with garlic and oil in a large bowl. Stir in basil, oregano and black pepper. Cover with wrap and refrigerate overnight, stirring occasionally.
In a large skillet heat butter to boiling point but don't burn
Add 1/2 of the shrimp, stirring 1 minute later (shrimp will start to turn pinkish)
Add wine and lemon and continue to cook 1 more minute, stirring
Add marinara sauce and cook another minute or two.
Taste and add salt as necessary
Sprinkle in grated cheese, stir in and remove from stove
With a slotted spoon transfer shrimp to a heated platter
Bring remaining sauce in pan to a boil and add remaining shrimp

Cook for 3 minutes, stirring as you go until they start to curl and turn pink
Add cooked shrimp and stir thoroughly
Remove from stove and pour shrimp and sauce onto large serving platter

Sprinkle parsley over shrimp and serve with extra lemon wedges.

Tortellini In Lemon Sauce

2 lbs of frozen tortellini
4 cloves of garlic mashed to a paste
1/2 cup olive oil
1/2 cup minced fresh basil
1/4 cup minced fresh oregano
1 cup chopped green onion
1/2 cup roasted red pepper diced
1/2 cup sliced black olives
1 1/2 teaspoons salt
1 teaspoon coarse ground black pepper
Juice of 2 lemons

Cook tortellini according to package directions and drain
In a large bowl mix garlic, oil, basil, oregano, green onion, red pepper and olives
Add tortellini, salt and pepper and mix thoroughly
Add lemon juice and parsley and mix again thoroughly

Serve at room temperature

Chicken Caesar Salad For The Boss

Four to five times a year "The Boss," our director, takes the staff out to lunch to celebrate Christmas, St. Patrick's Day, the advent of Summer, Secretaries day, someone's birthday, or whatever. Inevitably he orders the same thing, year in and year out. A bowl of French onion soup and a Chicken Caesar salad. The soup generally looks good but the salad always leaves something to be desired, and myself, who loves to criticize and justifiably so, never likes the looks of what I see on his plate. So one day for lunch for a group of about 30 people I made my own version, minus the anchovy. All 30 people loved it and gave me rave reviews. The boss ate and liked his but was a bit upset that there were no croutons. All the croutons on his salads in the different restaurants looked like commercially boxed or store bought ones and simply awful. I told him I would make some but he said "why don't you just buy some?" And I replied, with a sense of authority, "And ruin the salad!" Even Caesar would denounce and un-hail his salad.

4 boneless chicken breasts, uncooked
4 tablespoons of Worcestershire sauce
1 tablespoon of granulated garlic powder
1 teaspoon black pepper
1 dash of hot pepper sauce
Pinch of salt

Marinate the chicken in all the above ingredients for 5 hours or overnight

1 head of Romaine lettuce, washed, trimmed and cut up into bite size pieces
1 head of leaf lettuce or 1 lb of fancy field greens
1 red onion sliced thin
3 cloves of garlic
3 tablespoons of olive oil
1 cup of fresh grated parmesan
Juice of 2 fresh lemons
1 tablespoon of tarragon or apple cider vinegar
1 teaspoon salt
1 teaspoon black pepper

Cook chicken breasts on an outdoor grill over a hot fire on each side for 4 minutes
(or bake in oven for 20 minutes or broil for 12 minutes, turning them every 2 minutes)
Set aside, cool and cut crosswise, making 5 or 6 slices

In a large bowl pound garlic and salt to a fine paste
Add olive oil and mix or emulsify thoroughly
Add chicken slices and mix together
Add lettuce leaves, toss very lightly (once or twice, gingerly)
Add vinegar, lemon juice, cheese, and pepper and mix together lightly.
A pinch of salt may be needed
Serve immediately with extra shaved parmesan for garnish.

French Onion Soup

6 large Spanish onions, peeled and cut in thin slices
3 tablespoons olive or canola oil
6 cups water
1 cup sherry wine
1 teaspoon of black pepper 1 teaspoon salt
2 cups of shredded gruyere cheese
6 slices of Swiss cheese
1/2 cup of grated Romano
6 1/2 inch slices of dried crusty bread

Sauté onions in oil in a large sauce pan until they become transparent and browned
Add water, salt and pepper and bring to a boil
Add sherry wine, lower flame and continue to cook slowly for 1/2 to 1 hour
Turn on oven and set dial at broil and get oven hot
Remove pan from stove and ladle soup into 6 large cups or soup bowls with lots of onions
Cover each bowl with bread crusts and evenly sprinkle gruyere cheese over crusts
Top with a slice of Swiss cheese
Put soup bowls on broiler pan
Put under broiler, bake until the cheese turns brown and bubbles
Remove from broiler and put hot bowls on a liner plate
Sprinkle with a little grated Romano cheese and serve

Farfelle With Sage, Butter, and Cheese

1 lb of Farfelle (bowties)
1 cup of fresh sage
4 cloves of garlic sliced thin
1/2 cup olive oil
1 cup of fresh grated Parmesan cheese
1/2 cup chopped fresh parsley
1 teaspoon red pepper flakes
Salt and Pepper to taste

In a large skillet heat oil and add garlic and sauté 2 minutes
Add sage, pepper flakes, salt and pepper and simmer for fifteen minutes
Meanwhile cook pasta according to directions on package, and drain reserving 2 tablespoons of pasta water
Add pasta to a large bowl and pour sauce over it
Add reserved pasta water and mix lightly
Add cheese and parsley and mix together and serve

Note: Most pasta dishes of this sort require no more than 20 minutes cooking time. I like to start my pasta water and cook it while I am preparing the sauce. The sauce can be made ahead of time. I prefer it the latter way.

Broiled Scallops

1 lb of fresh large scallops
3 cloves of garlic sliced thin
1/4 lb of butter melted
2 tablespoon of olive oil
1 tablespoon of fresh chopped oregano or 1 teaspoon dried
2 tablespoon of fresh minced basil or 2 tablespoon dried
1 cup of Italian bread crumbs, tossed with 1 teaspoon of olive oil
1 lemon sliced thin
1 cup of fresh chopped parsley or 3 tablespoon dried
1/2 teaspoon salt
1 teaspoon fresh black pepper

Set oven dial to broil and pre-heat 10 minutes
In a large bowl mix scallops, garlic, butter and olive oil together
Add oregano and basil and mix together
(you can mix scallops with the above and let marinate overnight)
Lay scallops side by side on a broiler pan
Sprinkle oiled bread crumbs over scallops
Sprinkle salt and pepper over them
Put scallops under broiler and broil for 8 to 10 minutes or until the breadcrumbs brown
Remove from oven and carefully transfer scallops to a warm platter
Sprinkle parsley lightly over scallops and garnish with lemon slices.

Mussels in White Wine

2 lbs of Mussels, rinsed, scrubbed clean and beards removed
2 cups dry white wine
6 cloves of garlic, minced
1 bunch green onions chopped fine
1 tablespoon fresh basil, minced
1/2 cup flat leaf parsley chopped fine
1 lemon sliced thin
1/2 teaspoon salt
1 teaspoon fresh black pepper
1 teaspoon red pepper flakes
1 fresh tomato diced fine (optional)

In a large pan or skillet add white wine and mussels
Add garlic, onion, basil, parsley, salt and pepper and red pepper flakes
Cover with tight fitting lid and bring to a boil
Lower flame and let simmer until all the mussels open their shells
Discard any mussels that don't open
Transfer opened mussels to a warm serving platter
Add lemon slices and bring juice in pan to a boil
Pour pan juices over mussels and sprinkle tomatoes over it.

Serve with a loaf of good crusty bread to sop up the juices.

Irish By Assimilation

Back in the late 1920s and 30s our people started to settle in Sherburne, population 1000, give or take a few and it was starting to get a diverse ethnic population. There were approximately 400 Irish, 200 European-American mix, 50 Italians, 100 Poles, and about 150 Lebanese. The Euro mix was mostly Protestant but the rest of us adhered to Catholicism. There was only one Roman church in town, St. Malachy of Armagh. Needless to say it was named, populated and controlled by the 400 from Ireland and their own Irish priest, the beloved Fr. Kissane.

All the ethnic people in Sherburne needed a place to worship but unfortunately were not able to travel forty miles to Utica every Sunday to hear the mass in their native tongue. The Poles were used to going to the Polish church, St. Stanislaus, and the Italians had their mass at St. Anthony's, and the Lebanese at St. Louis where theirs was in Arabic. Our God was Allah, the Poles' God was Borja, and the Italians' God was Bobo and in the Irish church it was God, and by God there would be no substitutions. The one common denominator was they all knew how to make the sign of the cross and they all understood that because that was in sign language. As for the mass it was all in Latin and nobody understood that including the priest who always looked a little hung over from a tip of the bottle the night before. Probably it was from hearing all those confessions on Saturday from four to five o'clock. And after a heady earful of listening to the faithful pour out their sins it was time to get out the Old Crow and have a Manhattan.

So given that bond, they got in the front door and that was fine, but where were they going to sit? All the pews were rented and each family (Irish of course) had their names on the pews, and God forbid you tried to sit in one. It was like going to a major stadium where the rented pews were like box seats on the fifty yard line. The more you paid the better your seating was. Seventy-five percent of the pews were rented and the only available seating was in the far right and left pews in the back where you couldn't hear the priest, nor see the choir. The only good thing was if you were late the priest couldn't see you and if you wanted to sneak out after communion, nobody missed you.

So we sat in the far right hand corner of the church dubbed "The Syrian Ghetto." The Pollock's were allowed to sit a few pews ahead of us because their pigmentation was quite a few shades lighter than ours and because of the standard belief in their slower mentality. I guess you could call it a gift from heaven. The Italians were on the left back side and they sat alone because of the common belief that they smelled of onions. They should have waited until after Sunday mass to start their sauce rather than Saturday night.

But we were a force to be reckoned with, especially when there is strength in numbers. When someone died the Lebanese community from miles around would show up, thus filling every seat in the church. That was to be reckoned with. When someone got married, invitations weren't sent out but it was a word of mouth deal and tons of people would arrive. Given that scenario it wasn't odd that old E. H. O'Connor, Esq., approached my dad after mass one day and told him he was running for district attorney for the county and could he help him get out the vote with "his people?" My dad, feeling quite important being befriended by this man of means, readily agreed to do what he could. My day went house to house and told everyone to vote "Row B", for old E. H." even though most of them couldn't read English let alone understand what was going on, but between the Poles, Italians, and Lebanese, we were able to carry the county for him and he was elected.

E. H. was district attorney and a political favor was in store for my dad. Well, it wasn't quite political but more religious, for the following Sunday, E. H. invited my mom and dad to sit with him in his pew during mass and thus ended the so-called segregation of the Catholics. After that major feat the Lebanese were allowed to sit anywhere they blank-blanked pleased to in the church. Such was Irish charity. It took the Poles and Italians a few years to move out of their pews, but they finally succeeded. One little irony to this twist of fate was that before the election, with all of us still relegated to the back of the bus, i.e. church, a local

Lebanese man known as Mahmoud died. As his family entered the church behind his casket, they veered off to the right and went to their pews in the far right back of the church. A bit chagrinned, the local undertaker and priest had all they could do to convince them that it was all right to sit up front near the casket. It took a bit of coaxing for the family to take those seats but I'm sure it wasn't the fear of death that made them uncomfortable in those rented pews but the curses that only the Irish seat holders could bestow. . .

Another little irony was that the owner of a major dog food company was from our town and went to church there. He had two pews in the middle of the church (prime seating) for himself and his family. What was hysterical was that no one but them sat in those pews, even when they were out of town. No one dared sit in them even on Christmas Eve when the family was in Florida and the church was packed. I guess even the Irish understood the phrase, "No Irish apply here!" And the pews remained empty.

My good friend Ed Lehman's father Leo also rented a pew. It was in the last row in the church. How he managed to get the last pew is a mystery. They were Polish and I don't imagine back in 1950 they wanted any of them up front and the further back you were the cheaper the rent. But one Sunday the church was rather full (something unheard of these days) when Leo and family walked into the church and found people sitting in their pew. Needless to say Leo told them who he was and kicked them out of there. My friend Ed was totally embarrassed, but after all, Leo was a deeply religious man and like the affluent members of the parish had paid his dues to have a seat in the church, even if it was in the last row.

One of my unfondest memories of Leo was on a beautiful Saturday spring morning in April 1949. I was 7 years old and playing hooky from my first communion classes. I had told my mother that Father had cancelled our class for the day and was about to embark over to the river with some Protestant friends when all of a sudden like the angel Gabriel up drove Leo. He jumped out of his car, yelled at me in Polish, put me in his car, and drove me to St. Malachy's, where I joined my communion class (next to Lehman and Lewicki, of course). Then he went and told my mother what happened. I don't remember the consequences but made my first holy communion three weeks later and collected more than $20.00 from friends and relatives for my accomplishment. After that I wished I could make my holy communion every year.

E. H. O'Connor's Boiled Dinner

1 5 lb ham, bone in
2 heads of cabbage
6 large potatoes quartered
5 lbs carrots, peeled and cut in 2" pieces
1 large onion cut in half
2 bay leaves
8 cups water

In a large pot add ham and cold water and bring to a boil
Lower heat and continue to cook for an hour at a very light boil
Add cabbage, potatoes, carrots and bay leaves
Cook for another 1 1/2 hours or until the vegetables are tender
Remove vegetables to a warm platter
Continue to let the ham simmer for another hour or until the meat falls off the bone
(you don't want the meat to fall off entirely, but to be tender enough to do so)
Add ham to vegetables and pour a little of the juice over them and serve.

Mrs. Spinella

Old Mrs. Spinella was the one exception to the rule about where the Italians sat. Her husband had died many years ago, leaving her with five daughters to raise and a wardrobe of black dresses, because that's all she ever wore. She had a special in with God and that was because one of her daughters became a nun, which kind of put them atop the rosary bead chain. Well, one Sunday the nun came to church and sat in the front pew. That was okay because you weren't going to put her back with the Italians in the onion section. But when the rest of the family followed that set a precedent for squatter's rights. Every Sunday and holy day that followed, Mrs. Spinella and her daughters marched up to that front pew and occupied it rent free until she died in the 1970's. Such was divine intervention.

Another interesting aspect of Mrs. Spinella was that she had a vegetable stand in the middle of town and sold fresh produce from her garden. Her garden wasn't just any garden. It comprised about three quarters of an acre of land and had every kind of vegetable imaginable, along with gladiolas and zinnias that she sold by the bouquet. They also picked beans for the usual fifty cents a bushel and she would take her girls to the fields to pick and would keep them close by to keep an eye on them. One person commented that she watched the girls closely to keep the young men away from them but the real truth was that time was money, and if she saw any of them fooling around or lollygagging she threw a stone at them, which meant to get back to work. When she died they had her laid out in a white casket in a white dress. I guess that was the only day in her ninety some odd years that she wasn't in black. Lily white to meet her Lord, may her soul rest in peace.

Mrs. Spinella's Broccoli Rabe and Ziti

Note: Mrs. Spinella made her own ziti. Different from the short tubular ones that come in one pound boxes, she never cut hers and they were about a foot long. You can still find this kind of ziti in most good Italian food stores. Also, broccoli rabe is the younger form of broccoli, leafy with little yellow flowers and all edible. Regular broccoli flowerets can be substituted if you can't find the other.

2 bunches of broccoli rabe cut across in 1" pieces
1/3 cup olive oil
6 cloves of garlic minced
1 cup of flat leaf Italian parsley chopped fine
1 teaspoon hot red pepper flakes
1 teaspoon black pepper
1 teaspoon salt
1 cup of fresh grated Romano cheese
1 box of ziti or penne (ziti preferred)

In a large skillet sauté garlic in olive oil until it slightly starts to turn color
Add broccoli, salt, and pepper and stir. Continue to stir fry for 3 to 4 minutes
Add parsley and red pepper flakes, stir and cook one more minute. Set aside

Cook ziti according to directions on the package. Drain and reserve 2 tablespoons of cooking water
Put ziti in a large bowl, add reserved water and broccoli rabe and mix together
Sprinkle generously with grated cheese and serve

More grated cheese can be served on the side.

Altar Boy

My mother was determined that I would become an altar boy. If I had a choice in the matter you could forget that. It was a done deal. One of the big problems about being an altar boy was how not to laugh when you were on the altar. Everyone was watching you and your friends in the pews would make faces with an occasional obscene gesture, especially when Father's back was turned to the altar. Remember back then their back was to you, so it was easy for your friends to raise hell in the congregation. And once you started to giggle it would always lead to laughter, with a stern look from the priest that meant to "cut it out, or else."

Other than stumbling over your cassock or sermons beyond boredom and getting caught yawning the job did have its perks. You got a dollar for every wedding you served and seventy-five cents for funerals, plus everyone thought you were a good boy because you served on the altar. The downside of it was that once every four months you had to serve the 6:30 AM mass for a week. It was just my luck that my turn fell in the middle of January during a very cold spell. The church was a mile away from home and no one in our family was going to get out of bed and drive me there. So every morning at 5:45 AM I would throw on a heavy coat, put on my goulashes, earmuffs, gloves and scarf and head out in the cold and snow to church. About the third day of doing this and being wet and frozen to the bone I got mad. And the madder I got the more blasphemies I uttered. First I cursed the world, then the church, then the priest and with no lightning strike from above I took on God and some of the things a twelve year old boy might say just weren't pleasant. I don't think God minded at all. He knew I was talking to him and it just got colder and snowed more. But what really brought out another curse or two was that when mass started I would look out into the congregation and the place was empty other than the man who owned the dog food company and old Mrs. Spinella, with three of her daughters, clad in mourning black and in the front pew. I wouldn't have questioned God on the wisdom of all this except that during Father's sermon last Sunday he berated the parishioners for not being as generous as they could with their dollars for the annual fuel collection and that it cost a fortune to heat the church and he would have to cut back on the fuel. Before he started giving them hell for their lack of generosity he gave them a lecture on how to conserve and not to waste. In one of my few friendlier conversations with God I asked him to please show Father the wisdom of his words and instead of heating the church every morning for six people that it would be wiser to combine all those masses and do them just once a week, which would bring a considerable amount of savings.

God didn't listen and I continued to trudge to mass the remainder of the week. If there was any justice in this it was that I had liked the smell of the wine that Father would drink every morning before communion. Well, one day a friend and myself got into the liquor cabinet of my dad's restaurant and stole a bottle of Muscatel, which was the same color as the nice Christian Brothers Wine Father was drinking. My dad kept that Muscatel rot gut for a few winos who would sap it up at 25 cents a glass. So with the stolen bottle we exchanged the wines. When Father took a swallow the next morning at mass, he made an awful face, cursed under his breath and darn near spit it out. I'm sure he knew who had done it - but God was on my side – and he could never prove it. . .

More On St. Malachy's

I must say it was fascinating sitting in our places in church, seeing the same scenario unfold in the "Syrian Ghetto" Sunday after Sunday, holy day after holy day. In would walk the Lawrence Family – they were two pews strong, sometimes three. They sat behind the dog food moguls. Then came the Cunninghams and they were three pews strong. They were followed by Mr. Dineen, his son the doctor and his three unmarried daughters. Then came the Kehoes who ran a furniture store and undertaking parlor.

After that it was the Dromogooles, Morans, Rileys, Mulligans, McDaniels, Daniels and the O'Connors. Mr. and Mrs. and their daughters, with the sons straggling in, with the last one arriving at their pew just before communion. Then came the Newmans, Cahills, Mettlers and Doyles, with Harold always late. And then there was Ward Quinn with his family. He sat across the aisle with his family, never joining the conclave. I could never figure that one out. And there was Connie Coyle. He always said hello to everyone but sat in the back, unshaven in his wrinkled Sunday suit, always reeking of the ale that he drank at my father's gin mill the night before.

We didn't really know them. We knew who they were by the little card holders that had their names on them in their pews. But to say "Hi Joe, Harry, Bernie, Frank or Bill" – forget it. We didn't know them like that. And that's the way it was, year after year, until we all started to move away or die off and our numbers started to dwindle on all sides. In fact, in the mid 1980's St. Malachy's got their first non-Irish priest. An Italian. Talk about a major blockbuster. Eventually we all started dancing and playing bingo together and the barriers were lifting.

I recall attending a funeral in 1990. After the services I went downstairs to the church parlor for the mercy dinner that followed. I loved going to them because the Alter Rosary society always served a fine meal and the pies were homemade and sinfully delicious. Being a cook in my own right each lady was eager to bestow a piece of her pie on me and not only did I not object but was able to have 3 or 4 pieces. Anyhow after the dinner and everyone was leaving the society members were sitting at a table and eating. It was ironic. There were 3 Lebanese, 2 Polish, 1 Lithuanian, 2 Italian, 3 Irish and 2 American ladies all at the same table. After thanking them for a fine job and their delicious pies I said, "Lo and behold, Lord have mercy, I never thought I would live to see the day with you all sitting at the same table." A couple of them, a bit chagrinned, told me to shut up and mind my business which I did in good stride. All the ladies were long standing members of the parish and with all the newcomers moving into the church they themselves were becoming a minority. After all these years it was great to see ecumenism at its beat. As for the pew cards, well if you can find one they've become collectors items. Amen, Amen.

Two ever present dishes always standout at these funeral receptions; both are as common as they are delicious. I don't know who makes them as all the food is donated but it wouldn't be a true funeral dinner if they weren't there. One is the famous "Green Bean Casserole" that you see advertised on television around Christmas time with the mushroom soup and Durkees can of fried onion sticks. Mm, mm. The other is always present at graduation parties, an Ambrosia or fruit salad of sorts, thus labeled graduation surprise. They were mainstays, to my knowledge, when Aunt Florence Marano and my sister June were running the show, which dates back some 40 years or so. Aunt Flunsy (Florence), who just turned 80 years young still has a hand in it and you can always count on her famous Baked Ziti, though her family wishes she would slow down a bit. God bless her.

Green Bean Casserole

2 lbs frozen or canned green beans, preferably French cut
2 cans cream of mushroom soup
! can of Durkees Fried Onion Sticks
Lay green beans in a casserole dish
Add mushroom soup
Top with fried onion sticks
Bake at 350° for 20 minutes, remove from oven and serve.

Such a delight.

Ambrosia Salad

2 16 oz.cans of chunk pineapple
2 8 oz cans of mandarin oranges
1/2 cup marachino cherries cut in half
1 16 oz. can of sliced peaches cut up fine
1 lb. bag of minature marshmallows
2 cups of shredded coconut
1 16 oz. container of sour cream

Drain all fruits in collander and let stand for 5 minutes
In a large bowl add all ingredients together, mixing thoroughly
Chill for two hours before serving.
Chopped nuts can be added if desired.

Please be aware that you will find this at the next graduation party you go to. I doubt it will be as good as the Rosary Society's. If you want to savor that taste then I suggest you attend someone's funeral. The girls won't turn you away, and who knows? If you look important enough they may offer you a second piece of their homemade pie or a slice of my cousin Jeanette's cheesecake. Good luck.

Sheiks Of The Desert

I was catering a graduation party when I saw them get out of their car. Three stalwart men walking tall and proud, carrying themselves with the dignified atmosphere that only a Saudi Arabian Sheikh could command. Following behind them, in true Arabic fashion, were their wives. The moment they entered the room they commanded your respect and attention and got it. Such were my good Lebanese friends, the Fuleihans. Gracious, warm and hospitable. Their homes were always open to you and you never walked out without being fed great food and sensible conversation (sometimes one sided – their way – which was easier to accept than to argue the point.) Tradition abounded along with their culture, which was instilled in them by their mother, whom they referred to as "Sitto." She was also affectionately known by relatives and friends as "Aunt Alice." Alice is now deceased but her culinary wisdom and recipes still carry on.

Sitto Alice was a phenomenal cook. Gifted in her skills, her Lebanese cooking was one of a kind. As she would constantly remind her daughter-in-law Karen, "You haven't got enough salt." And she was generally right. One key to the success of Lebanese cooking is adding enough salt. Otherwise it's difficult to bring out the flavors of the herbs and spices used. Her cooking was quite different from ours. The same dishes but different seasonings, stuffings, and presentations, with a lot of it being regional depending upon the area you came from.   Her salads were legendary and I was quite flattered one night when I sent a salad to her son's home. I knew it wasn't going to compare to his mother's, yet he did make the comment that it was as close to Sitto's as you were going to get. I was okay with the compliment, bearing in mind that one time I had brought over grape leaves and her other son told me that his mother's were better as he continue to eat mine (of course).

Again I love to vent off: There are two ways to do things: Dr. Dan's way or Dr. David's way! Oh how I love my Lebanese friends – especially doctors.

One of their family favorites is an old Bedouin dish called Fett-Teeh. A mixture of rice, lamb and yogurt. In the desert it was done in an earthenware clay pot over a wood fire and then unfolded onto a flat ribbed round basket. Everyone would sit around it and scoop it up with their hands or with pieces of pita. As civilization emerged forks were introduced. The dish became more sanitary and everyone kept their hands clean.

Fett – Teeh

2 lbs. raw lamb or beef
4 loaves pita bread lightly toasted and cut into 1" pieces
6 cups Lebanese style cooked rice (recipe below)
1 ½ cups pignolia nuts sautéed until light brown
4 cups yogurt
Salt and pepper to taste
½ cup melted butter

Add meat to 3 quarts of water and bring to a boil
Reduce flame and simmer until meat becomes tender
Remove from water and cut into ½" pieces and set aside
In a 9 X 13" glass dish or Dutch oven cover the bottom with a layer of rice
Add a layer of meat atop the rice
Spoon a cup of yogurt and spread all over the meat
Add a layer of the toasted pita pieces
Repeat the process until you have 4 layers
Sprinkle pignolia nuts over it evenly
Poke a hole in the layers every 2" apart
Drizzle melted butter in the holes

Bake at 350° for 45 minutes to an hour
Remove and let rest 10 minutes before serving

Keep a bowl of yogurt on hand to spoon over the dish

Lebanese Rice

1 cup Rosa Maria or Orzo Pasta
¼ stick of butter melted (2 tablespoons)
3 cups long grained rice
9 cups hot water
1 teaspoon salt

Sauté Rosa Maria or Orzo in butter until they lightly brown
Add rice and stir around a minute or two
Add water and salt and bring mixture to a boil
Cook over a light flame for ½ hour or until the rice is tender
Let rest 10 minutes, fluff with a fork and its ready to serve

A Lesson In Fine Dining

My brother Bob was the first person in our family to go to college. He went to a State University about an hour away from our home and on occasional weekends our house was filled with fraternity brothers, co-eds and Long Island accents. Being congenial hosts a big family dinner would usually take place for the guests before their departure, with friends and relatives mixed in for the festivities. Traditional Lebanese food was always served, along with a few familiar items such as chicken and pork chops for the guests who were unfamiliar with our food, since my mother had a fear of them going away hungry. A taboo in the Lebanese culture. There was also another catch; Arabic was spoken alongside English, much to the horrors of my brothers who didn't want our guests, especially some of the pretty college girls, to think we were old-fashioned, old country peasants, especially considering that they addressed my mother and father as Mr. and Mrs. in all conversations and good manners were in place.

The downside of all this was my grandparents, who spoke no English and fervently chatted back and forth in Arabic, and also ate with their hands and scooped up their food with pita bread. Horrors oh horrors. Our guests didn't know if they were being discussed, which in most instances they were, although everyone tried to assure them they weren't. But it was hard as hell convincing them that they weren't being talked about with the elders conversing in Arabic and looking at the dinner guests. Further perplexing was whether to use their forks or do what the old people were doing and scoop it up. Prior to one of these dinners my dad was forewarned by my brothers to PLEASE abandon the old ways and use a fork and knife in front of our educated guests. My dad agreed and explained to my grandparents the circumstances. All was set for a flawless Sunday dinner. Then a platter of fried chicken came out, accompanied by a wooden bowl filled with crushed garlic and olive oil. My dad took a piece, passed the dish to the next person and proceeded to pull some meat from the bone and dip it in the bowl of garlic and eat it. My grandparents did the same and my brothers started to cringe, being mortified out of their wits, especially after pleading with my father to abandon the old country ways.

Dinner at the Retreat House: Seated: Jim Lewis. Standing: Bob Lewis, wife Jean Lewis, George Lewis, Jim's wife Vickie Lewis

Suddenly one of the pretty sophisticated young co-eds at the table picked up a piece of chicken and dipped it into the bowl and inquisitively asked my father, "Is this how you do it, Mr. Lewis?" My dad, with a mouthful of food, said yes, and everyone at the table followed suit and the day was saved and we weren't so uncivilized...

For years forks were very rarely used, with most of the food easy to eat with your fingers and flat bread to scoop it up with. Another common practice was dipping your food into the same bowl and repeating the procedure. We still do it in my house and if you don't like to double dip and find the practice abominable then "hudda" to you![2] You don't know what you're missing.

---

[2] For an explanation of 'hudda', ask someone of Arabic descent

Lebanese Fried Chicken With Garlic Sauce

2 chicken fryers cut up
6 cups of olive or canola oil
No breading is required. Just wash the chicken pieces in cold water and pat dry before frying them.

In a large saucepan bring oil to a medium heat (360° using a heat thermometer)
Add chicken pieces, a few at a time, starting with the breasts, then the legs, thighs and wings, backs and necks, doing no more than 5 or 6 pieces at a time.
Cook each piece about 9 minutes on each side with a little less time for the wings and necks. When the chicken starts to float to the top and takes on a nice brown hue you know the chicken is done.

Remove from oil with a slotted spoon and drain on paper towels.
Repeat the process until all are cooked.
Set on a warm plate and serve accompanied by a bowl of garlic sauce for dipping.

Garlic Sauce:
6 cloves of garlic, peeled and sliced thin
1/2 teaspoon salt
1 cup olive oil

Using a mortar and pestle, add garlic and salt and pound into a paste
Drizzle in olive oil slowly and stir thoroughly as you go

Fahtoush (bread salad)

This is a simple bread salad and for best results you want your tomatoes and cucumbers to be in season, so it is usually served in the summer.

4 loaves of pita bread
Lettuce (about 2 or 3 cups)
6 tomatoes sliced thin and cut in half
6 cucumbers sliced thin and cut in half
1 bunch of fresh mint chopped (1 cup)
1 bunch green onions chopped fine
1/2 cup fresh parsley chopped fine

Olive oil and vinegar to dress

3 tablespoons of garlic sauce mixed with juice of 1 fresh lemon
1/2 teaspoon of fresh ground pepper

Cut open the pita bread, using a knife to cut all around and opening the pocket
Bake the pita, smooth side down for a few minutes or until it turns light brown
Drizzle garlic sauce lightly over each pita and sprinkle with black pepper

Now, there are two methods for preparing this salad, depending on how you want to present it.

1. All mixed up.
Toss all the vegetables and herbs together. Just before serving, break the pita into pieces and add to the salad.
Then drizzle with olive oil and vinegar, toss, and taste to adjust the dressing.

2. Layered.
On a plate, arrange the pita pieces around the edges
Next, add a bed of lettuce
Then, arrange tomatoes evenly
Do the same with the cucumbers atop the tomatoes
Repeat the process with the onions, parsley and mint
Drizzle on olive oil and vinegar

Also, either salad can be prepared without the pita added. Then you can serve it with the pita for people to use to scoop up the salad.

The pita does get soggy quickly, so either serve it as soon as the pita is added or with the pita on the side.

Uncle Jack and the Dandelion Greens

Usually around the third or fourth week in March my phone would ring and before I could say "hello" the voice on the other end would say "Are the greens out yet?" That was my brother Jack, calling from Pittsburgh. I would reply that they would be out in another week or two and that we needed another few days of sunshiny 55° weather or better, then a good rain and they would be ready to go.

You only have about a three week period to dig. Like age they are superb when they are young and tender but as the season progresses and they begin to bud and flower they become old, tough and bitter. After they have flowered they are perfect for the infamous dandelion wine. If it was an early spring they would be popping out of the ground around St. Patty's day and everything would be green. But if it was a later spring you almost had to wait until April.

Uncle Jack was a very generous man. He had a lot of money and spread his wealth. At Christmas time there was always a check in the mail. At first it would be three figures. Then as he grew richer the check got bigger and increased from four figures then to five. And like his annual phone call inquiring upon the greens the check was always in the mail the second week in December. And if it was a day or two late my sister June would call and say "do you think maybe he isn't sending a check this year?" I always told her not to worry, it would be there, and it always was. So everyone kind of kowtowed to Uncle Jack. He commanded the performance and you were expected to applaud. He also used his money as a weapon, constantly reminding you that he could forget you at Christmas – though he never did. But it was a warning shot.

Jack Lewis, with his great niece Victoria Jackson and his wife Sissy Lewis, October 2003

Well, one cold spring day, with the temperatures hovering in the high 30's, the greens were out along with the crocuses, robins and pussy willows. I was out on the Retreat House grounds digging away in the cold and wet soil, freezing my 'you know what' off but doing what you have to do. After filling two grocery size bags I went into the kitchen and started to clean them, which is also a messy and meticulous job. Members of the staff would come into the kitchen and ask me what I was doing. I would tell them and continue on, repeating myself half a dozen times. They all thought I was a bit crazy. I kind of agree with them, but then retorted, "If your brother sent you a check every Christmas for five figures you would have your butt out there in this cold miserable weather digging the whole field up." Then I would wrap them in a towel, put them in a paper bag, put the bag in a cardboard box and ship them off to Pittsburgh. When Jack and Sis got them two days later they would soak them in cold water for an hour to refresh them to their original state. Thus I would insure myself of getting another check next Christmas. Not being satisfied Jack would call my brother Rich and ask him the same questions about the greens that he would ask me. Even before he received my greens he would tell him I had already sent them. That would set off a mad scramble to appease Uncle Jack.

The greens season always coincided with the Lenten season. I don't know if God planned it that way but it sure as hell helped a lot of families out who were looking for a meatless substitute on Fridays. You also have to figure in that most Catholics used to give up meat for the whole 40 days of Lent. Today that's past history. Like everyone used to get dressed up for church in their Sunday finest – thus came the term "Sunday suits" – nobody does it anymore and only observes meatless Fridays until Lent is over.

One interesting aspect of digging greens is that it is a lost art. One day I was digging in the heart of the city and an old Italian woman was walking up the street, spotted me, and shouted "Chicory, Chicory." (Italian for dandelion greens). Whenever I was digging greens, if you were over the age of 60 you knew exactly what I was doing. If you were under 60 and saw me in the field with a knife and a bag in my hand you would be a bit puzzled, think I was loony, and be ready to call 911.

Another story worth noting was that the Italian and Lebanese population was burgeoning in New York City, infiltrating long held Irish and Jewish neighborhoods, disrupting the culture. Someone came up with the idea of planting dandelions along the NYS Thruway, which subsequently rid the city of the problem…

Dandelion Green Salad

1 lb. fresh young dandelion greens*
3 tablespoons of olive oil
2 tablespoons red wine vinegar
½ teaspoon salt

Put greens in a salad bowl
Add olive oil, then vinegar, then salt
Toss together and serve

* Dandelion greens are commonly available in the spring at most farmers markets and big chain supermarkets. Today it is quite difficult to know where to dig because most fields and lawns have been sprayed with chemicals and toxic materials. Finding a spray free field is difficult and you really have to know what you are doing. In the older days such practices were never a problem.

I am not going into detail as to how to dig and clean them because it is too lengthy a process and perhaps in a few years I will have it on CD or on a television show – that is if I cave in to the networks. Otherwise as I said before it's a lost art, but who knows which one of you readers might see me out in the middle of a field wielding a knife with a 15" blade.

Cooked Dandelion Greens

1 lb. fresh dandelion greens
1 large onion chopped fine
¼ cup olive oil
Salt and pepper to taste

Heat olive oil in a large fry pan or wok
Add onion and sauté until golden brown
Stir in greens, salt and pepper and cook on low heat five to ten minutes and serve

My Mother and Her Sisters

Meelan family, 1940's. Helen Biviano, Mary Lewis, Eddie Meelan, Rose Mody, Dolly Merhib.

When this picture was taken in 1943, Uncle Eddie was home on leave. The girls wanted a family picture and they all went out and bought new dresses. Aunt Rose asked Aunt Dolly what she paid for hers: $10. Then Aunt Rose asked Aunt Helen what she hers cost: $12. My mother (Mary) asked Aunt Rose what hers cost: $15. Then when Aunt Rose asked my mother what she spent, she said $75. Aunt Rose got madder than hell.

Helen Biviano, Rose Mody, Mary Lewis and Dolly Merhib

Another rather interesting story took place back in the 1920s. Both my mother and Aunt Rose were in their teens. Rose was dating Uncle Tony and my mom was dating my dad. They went to the picture show at the now defunct Stanley Theater in downtown Utica, N.Y. After the movie was over and the girls went home, Aunt Rose asked my mother if my dad had put his arm around her. My mom said yes. She then asked Rose if Tony had done the same. Aunt Rose said yes and that he had tried to kiss her. My mom asked her if she let him and Aunt Rose said no. My mom asked her why she didn't let him because she and my dad had kissed, and Aunt Rose was mortified. She said, "Don't you know you can get pregnant!" Poor Uncle Tony!

They're All Gone

Recently I went to a relative's funeral in Utica, N. Y., at St. Louis of Gonzaga, the Lebanese church where it all started with our people. It was a bittersweet reunion of sorts. I hadn't been back there for a service in more than twenty years and I must admit I was a bit amazed at the changes that had taken place. I guess the title of Thomas Wolfe's novel, "You can't go home again," really hit the nail on the head here. The building, altar, stained glass windows, interior, and pews were all the same, with bouquets of flowers and candles all where they should be, but the structuring culture that had dominated before and gave the parish an exclusiveness was morally and disappointingly absent. Everything had been Americanized. The "Our Father" and "Hail Mary" were in English. The 'Sign Of The Cross' was also Anglicized. The mass no longer had that Aramaic flavor. The chanters and the chanting were gone. The icons were nowhere to be seen. The music was in English and half the parish didn't look Lebanese. Even the holy water looked fake. It made you want to cry that what you had remembered, known and made fun of was no longer there. Gone were the smells and aromas of the mercy dinner being prepared in the church basement, only to be replaced with a boring roast beef dinner at some nondescript restaurant. Gone were all the old women draped in black with their hair in buns. Gone were the men with black ties who used to sneak out for coffee as the mass started and be back in their seats right after communion. Gone were the uncontrollable grieving widows who would bring tears to everyone's eyes with their wailing lamentations. Gone were the dark haired altar boys who really looked Lebanese and like they had just got off the boat from Beirut. Gone were the throngs of people who filled the pews for every funeral whether they knew you or not. Gone! It was all gone and replaced by "Amazing Grace" and people with mass cards in their hands, which would ensure the deceased easy access to heaven and help the church restoration fund. It makes you want to wonder whether St. Peter, too, has become contemporary and traded in his white robes and staff for a business suit and briefcase.

Looking around this old religious bastion of ethnicity I realized that the old ways were memories left to stories that had been handed down through the generations. Any preservation was what we could and would care to hold on to. There were a few people I recognized; they were old when I was a kid and now they are just a few years older than me. That old generation is me. The second generation. I thought, "Christ, when they're gone, who will be left? Will my second and third cousins or the children of my first cousins know who they are and where we came from? Will we know each other or will that be a passing memory?"

After our generation the next to come will never know the pleasures of homemade Pita bread, hommous, grape leaves, or tabouleh. They'll think they reached culinary heaven with the versions that are now available in most deli sections of the supermarket. None of the first generation of Lebanese Americans are left and I guess that is what is sad, for it was they who laid the foundations, set the standards, cooked the foods and danced the songs. It was they who waked the dead for three days, threw a traditional LeyLee-ah (party celebration) the night before their daughters wedding, sang to the bride as she left her house for the church, and danced the "Dabkee" (traditional Lebanese Line Dance) at her wedding. It was they who would dress themselves in black for a year in honor of their deceased family member. Also gone were the ones who criticized the mourners in black saying that that wouldn't bring them back.

It's also too bad they thought it was proper for us to all speak English and let the native tongue go out the door. Especially since they preserved all of our culture except the language. They so wanted to be accepted and a part of the American culture that they kind of bribed their way in with their foods, dance and customs and shunned the language for that was what made them foreign. I always made comments to school friends that when their relatives came to visit they could understand them, but when ours came we couldn't understand a thing they were saying because their conversations were all in Arabic and they wouldn't encourage us to learn it.

I decided, as I reminisced, that I'm a bit nostalgic, like my friend Helen Dubiel. We hated to see and let go of the past. There are just so many things you can't replace or go back to. Everything they did had a purpose. Who today cooks with a pinch of this and a handful of that? Who percolates a cup of coffee? Who doesn't use a bottle of store bought spaghetti sauce? Who today cooks with love? Sure as hell it ain't Betty Crocker and her boxed chocolate cake soufflé mix. Like Helen and her husband's Ballantine Beer, the old ways are gone, and they are never coming back and I guess that's why I have written about them. To preserve recipes, share old stories and take our forbearers ways into the future as a way of holding onto the past. For it's easier to embrace the years to come, tell the stories, cook the dishes and make sense of it all, having had the privilege of living it.

The woman who had died at this funeral I attended in Utica was cousin Alice. She was married to my second cousin Mike. They had a blessed union of sixty-two years. I was at another cousin's wake and ran into her sister and asked her if she was up to having visitors. She said yes, so I went to see her and had planned to spend about twenty minutes visiting. Well, the visit and her conversation were so exhilarating that I ended up spending three and a half hours with her. We had a wonderful visit and her wit and wisdom paid tribute to her eighty two years on this earth. We talked about the cousin who had died, and I mentioned that there weren't as many people at the calling hours as I thought there would be. She matter-of-factly said, "There aren't many wake-goers any more," and how true her words were. Either people don't know or they have other priorities was what she was saying. She passed away two months later and I'm so glad I had taken the time for that visit, for her words and company will stay with me forever.

It is worth noting that Alice's Irish son-in-law gave a wonderfully moving eulogy, recalling her gracious Lebanese hospitality, delicious grape leaves, kibbee, shish kabobs and baklava. She also told him to marry her daughter. He took her advice and during the text of his farewell speech to her acknowledged that she was right, for he has never been sorry.

Nor am I, for having the privilege of knowing all these people and eating their foods. The days of the wake-goers are over but the traditions and culture live on, especially at dinner in my home on my mother's dining room table, and there the legacy continues. As the guests are sitting down to another meal I can hear my mother in the background saying "Sut-tan" which translates into "Welcome and Enjoy!"

Food Index: Lebanese Food And Its Descriptions

Arak: A traditional Lebanese liquor made from grapes and anise with a bit of potency and served with Turkish coffees and Arabic desserts.

B'Laaywaa (baklava): A traditionally rich pastry of walnuts, sugar and rosewater, topped with phyllo dough and cut into diamond shapes

Chicken and Rice (Jagh el Riz): Tender pieces of chicken, pulled from the bone and cooked in its own broth of rice, pignolia nuts, herbs and spices

Cousa: a light green summer squash, like a zucchini, hollowed out and stuffed with a mixture of rice, lamb, spearmint, tomatoes, parsley, garlic, Middle Eastern spices, and topped with a light fresh tomato sauce

Grape Leaves (Wariq-Ar-Eesh): Tender vine leaves stuffed with rice, lamb, spearmint, parsley, and Middle East spices

Hommous: A dip made of ground chick peas (garbanzo beans), tahina (sesame seed sauce), garlic, olive oil, and lemon juice

Kibbee Nayeh: A blend of ground lamb, infused with bulgur wheat, onion, sweet pepper, parsley, spearmint and a blend of cinnamon, allspice and cumin

Kibbee Suniah: A Lebanese meat pie (a flat meatball) made of ground lamb, bulgur wheat, onion, pepper, herbs and spices, shaped into a small meat patty and baked in the oven

Laban: Homemade yogurt, generally used as an accompaniment or sauce for most of the Lebanese dishes

Mishee Malfoof (stuffed cabbage leaves): rolled cabbage leaves, stuffed with rice, lamb, and tomatoes and Middle Eastern spices in a sauce of fresh tomatoes

Mock-room-toom (homemade macaroni): A homemade macaroni similar to a gnocchi and sauced with a delicate balance of garlic, olive oil, and lemon juice

Pickled vegetables: turnips, cauliflower, celery, carrots, hot peppers, and onions

Shish Kabob: Tender pieces of seasoned lamb, char-broiled over an open flame and served with grilled onions, tomatoes, and peppers.

Sheik El Mishee: Eggplant stuffed with lamb, herbed spices, sautéed pignolia nuts and bathed in a light garlic tomato sauce

Tabouleh: A fresh spring salad of finely chopped tomatoes, cucumbers, green onions, spearmint, parsley and bulgur wheat, seasoned with olive oil and lemon juice

Midfudlack – Eat and Enjoy!

About the author:

George Lewis, Jr. is the 5th of 6 children born to Lebanese immigrants George and Mary Lewis in Sherburne,

New York. He dropped the "Jr." from his name in 1968 upon father's death. He never did like it anyway. According to him he never finished a college course, having been kicked out of high school a month before graduation. After that disgraceful episode he left his small town, headed downstate to the bright lights of New York City and landed a job in "bunny land", at the now defunct but infamous Playboy Club. After 8 1/2 months of working there, according to George, "it only took 3 days to get my high school diploma, and in one month I had enough knowledge to qualify for a PhD!"

From there he spent much of his twenties and thirties traveling and playing hard, which is why he is still working at the age of 67.

During his travels he worked in a couple of top notch restaurants waiting tables and bartending, gaining a greater knowledge of the food industry trade, especially in Los Angeles, then New York City. Of course his initial training came from his familial restaurant in Sherburne, where he started at the age of 12, bussing tables for his sister June, who was the sole waitress at the time.

In 1976, while living on the west coast, he came east for a Labor Day family reunion. A couple days later he got a call from a frantic hostess to cater a party in three days. He did, serving champagne, fancy hors d'oeuvres and delicate pastries to some 500 odd people at approximately 75 cents per head. By weeks end he had six bookings. He never returned to the West Coast, eventually settling in Syracuse, New York. As his business card reads, "Serving the needs of Upstate New York since 1976."

In 2000, he saw an ad in the paper for the position of chef/kitchen manager at Christ the King Retreat House and Conference Center in Syracuse. He went to apply, took a look, decided it too religious a place and drove away. On second thought he went back, walked in and was handed a four page job application. He looked it over, decided it was to much work to fill out, and wrote on it "I can cook anything from A - Z: artichokes to zabaglione." "I'm sorry Sister but I haven't filled out an application in 30 years," he said, handed it back to her, and walked out the door. An hour later he was called back, interviewed and hired. Unbeknownst to him the head priest at the retreat house had made a phone call to the priest in Sherburne. The priest in Sherburne said "Don't let him get away! But I must warn you, he's a character." The rest is history. There he was amongst the multitudes, rubbing elbows with priests, bishops, nuns, and thousands of lay people, feeding them great food, ambiance and good conversation, offering his opinion when need be. Sometimes unsolicited. To quote one member of the staff, "The Retreat House is not responsible for any of the words that come out of his mouth."

On his second day on the job a rather harrowing experience occurred. Edward Cardinal Egan, Archbishop of the Archdiocese of New York, came to the Retreat House. George was hellishly nervous. Never having met a Cardinal he asked the hierarchy "how do you address a Cardinal?" No one had an answer. He called St. Patrick's Cathedral in New York and asked that same question. They told him he could address the Cardinal as Your Eminence, Excellency, or just plain Cardinal. In morning, when George was making breakfast he was late with the bacon and eggs. The Cardinal was pacing and George apologized, saying breakfast would be out in a few minutes. The Cardinal told him to "take your time; we have plenty of it today." From that point on George knew everything was going to be okay. At least he knew how to address a Cardinal.

The rest of his adventures at The Monastery are detailed in this book.

Acknowledgements:

From the author:

Special thanks to Katy, Maureen, and Beth for those kitchen morning round table talks and to Charlene for eating up all those burnt chocolate chip cookies. Ann's 'pain-in-the-butt' persistance was instrumental in getting the book out of the drawer. Many thanks to Doc and Kathy Elliot for their wonderful friendship. And a special "thank-you" to Maryanne, who must be happy as hell that I have retired and she doesn't have to send me any more little reminder notes. Now that I'm gone, everyone at the Retreat House plays by the rules, and the Retreat House Handbook can go back in the drawer and everything is topsy-turvy. Of course she had better keep a watchful eye on Todd – he bends the rules a bit.

An additional thank you to Monsignor Heagerty, for the absolution he served up for all those momentous spiritual, political and sporting confessions. I do hope to see him in full "Monsignor Regalia", mitre included, before I pass this world.

Lastly, a special thank you to Father Carmola, who has been a wonderful friend, boss and mentor. Even though he doesn't know "hudda" about food it doesn't matter. Although HE wouldn't let them make him a bishop, I have it on good authority that they'll make him a saint. Enshallah! - Arabic for 'God willing'. In fact, if Benedict in Rome will listen to me, I'm sure they will.
- George Lewis

From the editor:

I want to thank a number of people who helped me get this cookbook/memoir together and out the door. First, thank you to George's friend Vince Quinn, who came up to me when I was originally at my uncle's house, looking through the file. Vince said something to the effect of, "can you please get this published!" Thanks also to my cousin Tom Mody and my uncle and aunt Rich and Cindy Lewis, who supplemented the pictures George already had, helping to make the book richer and more interesting. During my trips to Syracuse I needed a place to stay, so a special thank you to the staff of the Retreat House, who put me up on my first visit north, and to Karen and Dan Fuleihan, who graciously opened their home to me during an editing trip. Lastly, there are never enough words to thank my wonderful husband Steve and my children Marc, Tori, and Montana, who endlessly put up with my immersion in this project, my trips north to work on it, and the stops we made in Syracuse to move the project along when we were on our way somewhere else. I hope I didn't ignore all of you too much, and that you'll appreciate this legacy that Uncle George and I are leaving for you and future generations of Lewis descendents.

-Karen Lewis Jackson

Made in the USA
Charleston, SC
13 August 2012